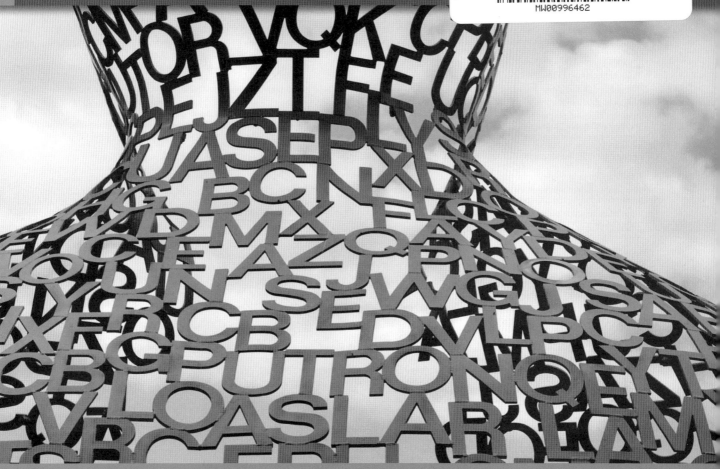

English B

FOR THE IB DIPLOMA

Kawther Saa'd AlDin

Jeehan Abu Awad

Tiia Tempakka

Kevin Morley

OXFORD
UNIVERSITY PRESS

OXFORD

UNIVERSITY PRESS

Great Clarendon Street, Oxford, OX2 6DP, United Kingdom

Oxford University Press is a department of the University of Oxford. It furthers the University's objective of excellence in research, scholarship, and education by publishing worldwide. Oxford is a registered trade mark of Oxford University Press in the UK and in certain other countries

© Oxford University Press 2014

The moral rights of the authors have been asserted

First published in 2014

British Library Cataloguing in Publication Data
Data available

978-0-19-839284-2

10 9 8 7 6 5 4

Paper used in the production of this book is a natural, recyclable product made from wood grown in sustainable forests.
The manufacturing process conforms to the environmental regulations of the country of origin.

Printed in India by Manipal Technologies Ltd

Acknowledgements

The publishers would like to thank the following for permissions to use their photographs:

Cover: Steve Barnett / Alamy; **p44:** zmkstudio/shutterstock; **p81:** RTimages/shutterstock; **p86:** Shahid Ali Khan/shutterstock; **p91:** AF archive / Alamy; **p100:** Tayside Nutrition; **p101:** 2012 Kidsafe NSW Inc.; **p102-103:** source: http://www.scotland.gov.uk/Publications/2009/09/16093124/3; **p106:** The Advertising Archive; **p107:** Dan Breckwoldt/shutterstock; **p109:** Office of Road Safety, Western Australia; **p110:** 5+ A Day; **p110:** Ionia/shutterstock; **p113:** Shi Yali/shutterstock; **p114:** Crime Museum, Washington DC; **p114:** sutsaiy/shutterstock; **p155:** Dave Carpenter/www.cartoonstock.com; **p167:** Ron Morgan/www.cartoonstock.com; **p168:** diane39/istock; **p169:** Jim West/Alamy; **p170:** Helder Almeida/shutterstock; **p171:** Monkey Business Images/shutterstock; **p171:** Rex May Baloo/www.cartoonstock.com; **p173:** Deklofenak/shutterstock; **p174:** Paul Carstairs/Alamy; **p175:** Phil Judd/www.cartoonstock.com; **p177:** Hemis/Alamy; **p180:** AF archive/Alamy; **p189:** Moviestore collection Ltd/Alamy

The author and publisher are grateful for permission to reprint extracts from the following copyright material:

Nasseem Ackbarally: 'Green-fingered Mauritian farmers go green', www.ipsnews.net, reprinted by permission.

Sonal Agarwal: 'Mind your e-language', 14 October 2012, from www.livemint.com, reprinted by permission.

AllAfrica.com: 'South Africa: Social Media 'Breaking Barriers' in SA', 4 October 2012, reprinted by permission.

Jamie Berke: 'Growing Up Deaf - Discovering Sign Language', © 2013 Jamie Berke (http://deafness.about.com/), reprinted by permission of About Inc., which can be found online at www.about.com, all rights reserved.

David Cameron & Jeffrey Sachs: 'Educated women hold the key to ending poverty', *The Independent*, 18 April 2010, www.independent.co.uk, reprinted by permission.

Vince Chadwick: 'More than two million living in poverty', 15 October 2012, *The Age*, reprinted by permission of Copyright Agency Limited (CAL), except as permitted by the Copyright Act, you must not re-use this work without the permission of the copyright owner or CAL.

Juliet Clark: 'Floods', a blog entry dated 11 October 2010 from www.juliet-in-cambodia.blogspot.co.uk, reprinted by permission.

Daralyn Danns: 'Destination Manchester', from All About Hair UK, (http://allabouthairuk.blogspot.co.uk), reprinted by permission.

Daniel DiClerico: 'Five questions to ask before buying a toaster', copyright 2012 by Consumers Union of U.S., Inc. Yonkers, NY 10703-1057, a non-profit organization. , reprinted by permission from the August 2012 posting on ConsumerReports.org for educational purposes only, www.ConsumerReports.org.

Ben Doherty: 'India's tribal people fast becoming lost for words', 29 April 2012, *The Age*, reprinted by permission of Copyright Agency Limited (CAL), except as permitted by the Copyright Act, you must not re-use this work without the permission of the copyright owner or CAL.

Berlie Doherty: *Dear Nobody* (285 words), (Hamish Hamilton, 1991), copyright © Berlie Doherty, 1991, reprinted by permission of Penguin UK Ltd and David Higham Associates.

Steve Doughty: 'The rise of the stay-at-home dad: One in seven families now have father as primary carer for children', *The Daily Mail*, 25 October 2011, reprinted by permission.

David Edelstein: 'Freshman Disorientation: The Perks of Being a Wallflower Nails Teenage Alienation', *New York Magazine*, 16 September 2012, www.nymag.com, reprinted by permission.

BJ Gallagher: 'The problem with political correctness', *Huffington Post*, 25 February 2013, reprinted with permission of the author at www.peacockproductions.com.

Tiffany Gilbert: 'A Review: Pigeon English by Stephen Kelman', www.booksmatter.tumblr.com, 17 October 2011, reprinted by permission.

John Hennessey: *A Stalker's Game*, reprinted by kind permission of the author.

Aldous Huxley: *Crome Yellow*, copyright © 1921 by Aldous Huxley, reprinted by permission of Georges Borchardt, Inc., for the Estate of Aldous Huxley.

Lee Jackson: 'The story behind the legend of Sweeney Todd', TimeOut.com, reprinted by permission of Time Out.

Malcolm Jones: 'The History and Lost Art of Letter Writing', 17 January 2009, © 2009 Newsweek, all rights reserved, used by permission and protected by the copyright laws of the United States, the printing, copying, redistribution or retransmission of the content without express written permission is prohibited.

Stephen Khalek: 'Stuck in the mud', a blog entry dated 9 August 2010, from Summer in Ladakh at www.threeidiots.livejournal.com, reprinted by permission.

Craig and Marc Kielburger: '7 tips for eco-friendly transportation', excerpt from *Living Me to We: The Guide for Socially Conscious Canadians* © 2012 by Craig Kielburger and Marc Kielburger, published by Me to We, reprinted by permission.

Ariel Leve: 'Angela Lansbury interview: "I'm never left behind. I'm the bionic woman"', 21 May 2012, *The Telegraph*, © Telegraph Media Group Ltd 2012, reprinted by permission.

The Lowdown: 'Row Zambezi', from www.lowdownzambia.com, reprinted by permission.

Jonathan Margolis: 'Growing food in the desert: is this the solution to the world's food crisis?', *The Observer*, 24 November 2012, © Guardian News & Media Ltd 2012, reprinted by permission.

Julian Matthews: 'Can ecotourism save tigers in India?', from EcoTour www.ecotourdirectory.com, reprinted by kind permission of the author.

MediaSmarts: 'The good things about television', MediaSmarts.ca, reprinted by permission.

Eric Paul Monroe: 'Evaluating online programs for studying foreign languages', 6 June 2007, from Education Space 360, www.educationspace360.com, reprinted by permission.

Sarah Na Li: 'Testimonial' – studying online for a Doctor of Education – Higher Education (EdD) from the University of Liverpool, from www.university-liverpool-online.com, reprinted by permission.

Lawrence Norfolk: 'Africa on the doorstep', *The Guardian*, 9 August 2008, © Guardian News & Media Ltd 2008, reprinted by permission.

Northwestern University School of Communication, Theater and Interpretation Center: 'How to End Poverty in 90 Minutes', www.communication.northwestern.edu, reprinted by kind permission of the director, Michael Rohd.

Karen Olsson: 'I Pledge Allegiance', *The New York Times*, 22 April 2007, © 2007 The New York Times, all rights reserved, used by permission and protected by the copyright laws of the United States, the printing, copying, redistribution or retransmission of the content without express written permission is prohibited.

Jay Patel: 'To Assimilate or to Acculturate?', reprinted by permission of the author and the Academic Writing Program at the University of Maryland. Published online in the spring 2012 edition of 'Interpolations', located on the English Department's webpage.

Bo Paul: 'Is it fair to blame todays negativity in society on musical influence', 29 April 2008, from Entertainment Scene 360, www.entertainmentscene360.com, reprinted by permission.

Jennifer Quigley-Jones: 'Think Harvard's too hard to get into? Think again', *The Independent*, 21 October 2013, www.independent.co.uk, reprinted by permission.

Dustin Rowles: 'Hugely entertaining! A masterwork! A total triumph!', 26 October 2010, from www.pajiba.com, reprinted by kind permission of the author.

Shropshire Newspapers Ltd: 'Dog rescued from five-foot deep rabbit warren', reprinted by permission.

Carol Tator: 'Taking a stand against racism in the media', October 1995, presented at Racism in the Media, a conference sponsored by the Toronto Community Reference Group on Ethno-Racial and Aboriginal Access to Metropolitan Services, reprinted by permission.

Amanda Thambounaris: 'Interview with award-winning ventriloquist comedian Jeff Dunham', 23 November 2011, TheCelebrityCafe.com, reprinted by permission.

Alexandra Topping: 'Human trafficking: 'I never thought it could happen in this country'', 18 October 2012, *The Guardian*, © Guardian News & Media Ltd, reprinted by permission.

Enda Tuomey: 'Animal testing has many advantages' from http://writefix.com/?page_id=1541, reprinted by permission of Enda Tuomey at writefix.com.

The Valleys: 'The Valleys of South Wales' from www.thevalleys.co.uk, reprinted by permission.

Warwick Castle tourist information reprinted by permission of Warwick Castle.

Any third party use of this material, outside of this publication, is prohibited. Interested parties should apply to the copyright holders indicated in each case.

Although we have made every effort to trace and contact all copyright holders before publication this has not been possible in all cases. If notified, the publisher will rectify any errors or omissions at the earliest opportunity.

Links to third party websites are provided by Oxford in good faith and for information only. Oxford disclaims any responsibility for the materials contained in any third party website referenced in this work.

Contents

Introduction

English B Skills and Practice has been designed to complement the *English B Course Companion* and to give you the latest, up-to-date information, advice and practice with the skills you will need to complete each of the four assessment components required for Standard and Higher Level English B (first examinations May 2015).

The chapters are designed to provide specific advice and guidance regarding each assessment component. In some components, such as the written assignment and Paper 2: *Written productive skills*, there are major differences between SL and HL. To simplify matters for you, we have provided individual SL and HL chapters to cover those differences.

In *English B Skills and Practice*, we have provided essential information to help you succeed in each assessment component. In each chapter, you will find advice about the best ways to tackle questions and/or tasks. For instance, in Chapter 1, there is expert guidance on tackling the different reading tasks in Paper 1. In Chapters 2 and 3, the authors have provided insights into improving your writing skills in English. There is also a unique and detailed analysis of all the individual text types and writing tasks. In Chapters 5 and 6, you can read detailed examiners' comments on the nature of the written assignment. You will also see how examiners assess student work and learn how to maximise your chances of scoring well. Chapter 6 tells you all you need to know about the oral examinations and gives expert advice on oral activities, and approaches to stimulus material for the individual oral.

Within each chapter of *English B Skills and Practice*, you will also find many opportunities to practice the specific receptive, productive, and interactive skills you need for each assessment component in English B. To round off your revision, you can turn to Chapter 7 and find practice papers to help you to prepare for the final examinations.

It has been our intention to make *English B Skills and Practice* as practical and accessible as the *English B Course Companion*. We sincerely hope that the book now in your hands helps you to develop the essential communicative skills in English B for the final examinations and for the wider world beyond.

Deconstructing Paper 1

When learning a new language, you will often hear a number of skills mentioned: reading, writing, listening, and speaking. Reading is a primary receptive skill, and becoming proficient at reading is one of the aims of English B.

We read for a variety of purposes like enjoyment and learning. In English B, the main purpose of developing reading skills is to enhance your communicative and critical thinking abilities. When reading any written text, you are to digest it in its entirety by understanding its main purpose and its finer details, such as use of vocabulary, grammar, and sentence structure. Consequently, you will become a better communicator in English because you will learn how to recognise written features and interpret them.

In this chapter, we will concern ourselves with developing the reading skills that are required for Paper 1, in which you are asked to respond to questions that test your understanding of written texts. In other words, Paper 1 measures your engagement with, and understanding of, a written text.

Skimming

When you skim a text, you read it quickly to understand the overall message it advocates. This overall message does not only appear in the content of the text, but it is also clarified in the tone, context, and communicative purpose the writer uses. When skimming a text, ask yourself the following questions:

- What is the main idea in the text?
- What is the aim or purpose of the text?
- How does the writer achieve this aim or purpose?

Read the following paragraph, paying special attention to the highlighted words.

In this chapter, you will find the following examples of Paper 1 text-handling exercises:

- Choosing which of a number of sentences are true according to the text
- Gap-filling exercises based on comprehension of the text
- Identifying clear inference from concepts (HL only)
- Identifying precise references of key phrases or structures
- Identifying related ideas that are in different parts of the text
- Identifying specific content items
- Identifying whether an explanation or definition is true or false, and finding the evidence for this in the text
- Identifying who says what in a text or a series of short texts
- Justifying an interpretation by locating evidence or key phrases (HL only)
- Matching summary sentences with different paragraphs of the text
- Matching words or phrases from the text with definitions
- Multiple-choice questions
- Short-answer questions

"A private equity client asked us to reference a candidate who had been recommended to run a portfolio company. The candidate's credentials stacked up reasonably well, as did his references.
5 Then, one of our researchers trawled his public social media profiles. Like most of us, he had opinions on Indian politics, corruption, football teams, the US elections, et al. Like many of us, he had chosen to air his views on social media platforms. Unfortunately,
10 he had not been particularly circumspect about the language or tone he used."

Sonal Agarwal, *Mind Your e-Language*, 2012

From the highlighted words, we construe that the main idea in the paragraph is to discuss the negative impact associated with expressing one's views vociferously on social network platforms:

Reference a candidate → credentials good → public social media profiles → airing views → UNFORTUNATELY → not circumspect → language or tone

The use of the word 'unfortunately' in line 9 implies that the candidate has not got the job he applied for. Why? Because the writer chose to use the word 'unfortunately' in relation to the views the candidate shared on public social media platforms. It is also the same word that shows the reader what the focus of the whole article will be.

Activity

Skim the following extracts and determine:
- the main idea in the text
- the aim of the text
- how the aim/purpose was achieved.

Extract 1

Why is it that non-native English speakers can speak the worst – or most creative – English imaginable, and we, native speakers, understand them, but although you've studied French or Thai for fifty years, only people who really love you understand what you are saying?

Linguists define dominant languages as: a set of very unforgiving languages, which demand that learners speak perfectly. With dominant languages, it's my way or the highway.

In this sense, French and Thai are dominant languages. English and Italian are not. You are free to speak English as badly as you desire. And as for Italian, if you speak any at all, Italians are happy to chat with you.

Antonio Graceffo, *Asian Tribune*, 2008

Extract 2

Gone are the days when women used to play the second fiddle to men, with their rights being trampled upon quietly without the possibility of claiming their due or their rights. The society has evolved much to their benefit, allowing them to play a more participative and active role at the highest levels. Much credit can be given in Mauritius to the Labour Party for bringing long awaited changes especially for instance by increasing representation of women in their party (through for instance at least one woman per constituency) and by assigning the role of vice president to a woman in the name of Mrs Monique Ohshan Bellepeau. This is clear evidence that the voice of women in our society is being heard and that gender discrimination is bound to crumble. Women had been contributing actively in the economy of the country as householders, to which no economic value has been assigned and which remains unaccounted for. This is part of the hidden economy. With enhanced rights and liberties, women are more and more moving out of the house to be a main player at all levels of society.

BouzerMaurice Online Directory, 2011

Scanning

Scanning a text involves reading selectively to find specific information. When answering comprehension questions, more often than not, you are asked to produce specific answers such as who said what, which words have similar meanings, or what happened at a specific point.

Example

I don't read for pleasure – I read to get information. I did have a novel about Brian Boru in 1993, but I lent it to a fellow Commando in Norway and he never returned it. I think it took me two weeks to notice.

5 Yet when my first son came along, I started to read to him – a lot. Everything about my own upbringing told me it was the right thing to do: my parents had read to me, and my three brothers, every night. I even remember some of the stories: *Mrs Pepperpot and*
10 *Mr Pink-Whistle*. At primary school, every day ended with a story. One of my favourite programmes on TV was *Jackanory*. Adults read to young troopers – that was the order of the Universe.

To be honest, I wasn't really aware of all the positive
15 benefits that reading out loud would give my troopers. I was helping them learn the language of course, but also helping them develop their own clear speech patterns (and believe me, I have three eloquent troopers here who can demonstrate how successful that was).

Neil Sinclair, 'Diary of a stay-at-home dad: reading to them', 2012

Q: Which phrase shows that reading is not one of Sinclair's hobbies?

✓ don't read for pleasure

> *Understanding the question is as important as understanding the text. A hobby is an activity one enjoys; therefore, not reading for pleasure indicates that reading is not one of Sinclair's hobbies.*

Q: Why did Sinclair read to his child?

✓ It was the right thing to do/ that was the order of the Universe/ his parents had read to him every night

> *The operative word in the question is why. This means that we are looking for a reason. When we read the text, we notice that Sinclair, to whom reading was not a hobby, started reading to his child because he thought it was the right thing to do for his parents had read to him every night – 'that was the order of the Universe' is also correct because it shows why Sinclair thought reading to his child was a good idea. His parents read to him, adults read to young troopers, so it is just the right thing to do.*

Q: To what does the word 'that' in 'that was the order of the Universe' refer?

✓ adults reading to young troopers

> *It is very important to grasp how certain words are used in a text. In non-physical referents (i.e. when we are not using 'this' or 'that', 'here' or 'there'- to express 'distance'), the pronoun 'that' is used to express something that had already been explained. Therefore, 'that' refers to something which had already been explained, and which is considered 'the order of the Universe': not reading in general, but 'adults reading to young troopers'.*

Q: Which word shows that Sinclair's children are articulate?

 ✓ eloquent

> *Questions are very specific. When asked for a word, you are expected to provide one word, not a phrase or a sentence. The word we are looking for means 'speak coherently and well'. Therefore, the only one word in the text that carries the same meaning is 'eloquent'.*

Q: Give **two** advantages to reading aloud to children.

 ✓ a. learning the language

 b. developing clear speech patterns.

> *Even when the question looks general, your answer must come from the text itself. In the question above, you are asked to provide 'two advantages' but it is not a general knowledge question. You should scan the text and identify the advantages mentioned before you answer. In addition, one might wonder why 'eloquence' is not accepted as an answer. Re-read that specific part in the text. What do you recognize? Eloquence is not an advantage; it results from learning the language and developing clear speech patterns.*

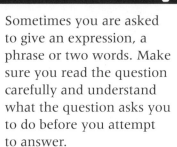

Exam tip ✓

Sometimes you are asked to give an expression, a phrase or two words. Make sure you read the question carefully and understand what the question asks you to do before you attempt to answer.

Activity

Scan the texts below to answer the questions that follow.

Extract 1

You must go back with me to the autumn of 1827.

My father, as you know, was a sort of gentleman farmer in-shire; and I, by his express desire,
5 succeeded him in the same quiet occupation, not very willingly, for ambition urged me to higher aims, and self-conceit assured me that, in disregarding its voice, I was burying my talent in the earth, and hiding my light under a bushel.
10 My mother had done her utmost to persuade me that I was capable of great achievements; but my father, who thought ambition was the surest road to ruin, and change but another word for destruction, would listen to no scheme
15 for bettering either my own condition, or that of my fellow mortals. He assured me it was all rubbish, and exhorted me, with his dying breath, to continue in the good old way, to follow his steps, and those of his father before
20 him, and let my highest ambition be to walk honestly through the world, looking neither to the right hand nor to the left, and to transmit the paternal acres to my children in, at least, as flourishing a condition as he left them to me.
25 In ascending to my room I was met upon the stairs by a smart, pretty girl of nineteen, with a tidy, dumpy figure, a round face, bright, blooming cheeks, glossy, clustering curls, and little merry brown eyes. I need not tell
30 you this was my sister Rose. She is, I know, a comely matron still, and, doubtless, no less lovely – in your eyes – than on the happy day you first beheld her.

  Anne Brontë, *The Tenant of Wildfell Hall*

1. What is 'the same quiet occupation' mentioned in line 5?

2. To what does 'its' in 'disregarding its voice' (line 8) refer?

3. Which phrase in the first paragraph indicates that the speaker was not very keen on following in his father's footsteps?

4. How did the father of the speaker regard ambition and change?

5. Which word in the first paragraph is closest in meaning to 'improving'?

6. To what does 'that' in 'or that of my fellow mortals' (lines 15 and 16) refer?

7. Which phrase in the first paragraph indicates that the son was expected to maintain the prosperity of the lands for his descendants?

8. Which phrase in the second paragraph tells us that the speaker's sister was on the plump side?

9. Who is the 'comely matron' referred to in line 31?

10. Which word in the second paragraph indicates that the speaker does not expect readers to change their opinion of his sister?

Extract 2

English continues to serve as the language of prestige in India. Efforts to switch to Hindi or other regional tongues encounter stiff opposition both from those who know English
5 well and whose privileged position requires proficiency in that tongue and from those who see it as a means of upward mobility. Partisans of English also maintain it is useful and indeed necessary as a link to the rest of
10 the world, that India is lucky that the colonial period left a language that is now the world's predominant international language in the fields of culture, science, technology, and commerce. They hold, too, that widespread
15 knowledge of English is necessary for technological and economic progress and that reducing its role would leave India a backwater in world affairs.

Linguistic diversity is apparent on a variety of
20 levels. Major regional languages have stylized literary forms, often with an extensive body of literature, which may date back from a few centuries to two millennia ago. These literary languages differ markedly from the spoken
25 forms and village dialects that coexist with a plethora of caste idioms and regional lingua franca. Part of the reason for such linguistic diversity lies in the complex social realities of South Asia. India's languages reflect the
30 intricate levels of social hierarchy and caste. Individuals have in their speech repertoire a variety of styles and dialects appropriate to various social situations. In general, the higher the speaker's status, the more speech
35 forms there are at his or her disposal. Speech is adapted in countless ways to reflect the specific social context and the relative standing of the speakers.

http://countrystudies.us, 2013

1. Why have efforts to make Hindi the Indian official language failed?

2. To what does 'it' in 'see it as a means of upward mobility' (line 7) refer?

3. Which word between lines 1 and 14 is closest in meaning to 'supporters'?

4. What, according to the article, will happen if India minimized its use of English?

5. How have major languages in India affected literature?

6. Which word between lines 19 and 30 is closest in meaning to 'excess'?

7. Why, according to the article, is India so linguistically diverse?

8. The text claims that social status affects a person's speech positively. Which sentence between lines 30 and 38 supports this claim?

Text-handling exercises
Word, words, everywhere!

When dealing with gap-filling questions, you need to understand both the gist of the text and its specific features.

Example

Challenging racism in the media requires **[-1-]** effort, resilience and tenacious resistance. We need to continue to vigilantly **[-2-]**, protest, demonstrate, document and oppose every form of racism in the
5 media. We need to raise our voices every time we read racist views expressed in the print media; every time we hear **[-3-]** bias communicated across airwaves; and every time we see it **[-4-]** in the images on billboards and flyers. We need to demand employment equity
10 within media organizations. We need to vigorously challenge those who attempt to silence resistance, with allegations of political correctness and **[-5-]**. We need to respond to those who speak in code words such as freedom of expression, artistic license, national
15 identity, unity, common values, special interest groups, special privilege, and quotas. **[-6-]** fairness, equity and justice in the media and in other social systems is not

deviant behaviour – it is called democracy! **[-7-]** our colleagues, allies and friends are attacked, we need to
20 quickly and publicly come to their defense. We need to demand equity in the hiring and selection practices of media organizations, **[-8-]** in twenty more years, but now! We need to develop networks and alliances between communities that are regularly subjected
25 to racism by the media. We **[-9-]** need a monitoring agency that regularly oversees and responds to bias and discriminatory practices in the media. We must press for more effective press councils and other self-regulating bodies. Most of all we need to continue to
30 demand responsibility, accountability and meaningful change in the decision-making processes and **[-10-]** practices of media organizations in Canada.

Carol Tator, 1995

Some of the words have been removed from the text, but before you embark on filling the gaps, ask yourself this question: What is the writer trying to communicate to her audience?

By skimming the text, we understand that the author insists that strong effort be made to fight racism in the Canadian media. Bearing that in mind, try to make the text more meaningful by filling the gaps using some of the words below.

before	*cautious*	*censored*	*censorship*	*daily*
perhaps	*demanding*	*depicted*	*freedom*	*foregoing*
hardly	*hidden*	*judge*	*monitor*	*not*
painstaking	*racial*	*regularly*	*still*	*when*

Parts of speech

Noun	Pronoun
Verb	Preposition
Adjective	Conjunction
Adverb	Interjection

For more information on parts of speech, visit http://www. writingcentre.uottawa.ca/ hypergrammar/partsp.html

When filling the gaps, take into consideration the appropriate part of speech required. Additionally, make sure that the word you have chosen makes sense in context. The words have been assigned to the appropriate gap in the table that follows. Fill in a justification for the placement of each word. The first two have been done for you.

	Word	Why
1.	painstaking	The part of speech needed is an adjective, and the only adjective that completes the sentence meaningfully is 'painstaking' because of the use of the word 'tenacious', which means persistent. Therefore, the word required must be something that complements 'tenacious'.
2.	monitor	We need a verb in the infinitive here (note the 'to' before vigilantly). The only words that fit are 'monitor' and 'judge'. 'Judge' is incorrect because it denotes subjective opinion rather than a concrete action that complements 'protest', 'demonstrate', 'document' and 'oppose'.
3.	racial	....
4.	depicted	....
5.	censorship	....
6.	demanding	....
7.	when	....
8.	not	....
9.	still	....
10.	daily	....

Activity

Read the following text.

Extract 1

I believe that tourism is a good thing for tiger conservation. It gives them extraordinary protection **[-1-]** the passive viewing and monitoring of these creatures. Tourism has a **[-2-]** impact on the perceived status of a park and its ability to attract local, governmental or **[-3-]** funding and tourism enhances the motivation and quality of its rangers and management, whilst the **[-4-]** vigil and
5 attention from conservationists, naturalist guides, visitors and hotel owners concerned over 'their' invaluable wildlife resource ensures park staff and management are kept on their toes. **[-5-]** parks fail is when communication, integration and cooperation collapse between any of the parties in this conservation equation.

[-6-] the Indian Forests Service (IFS), under **[-7-]** auspices all Indian parks and sanctuaries are
10 managed, has seen tourism as a necessary **[-8-]**, a harbinger of doom to be boxed up and contained within specific areas, whatever the crush; whatever the consequences. Last Christmas, tourism was even **[-9-]** of being the reason for the collapse in tiger numbers in Ranthambhore in Rajasthan. Woodcutters cut forests, poachers poach tigers, but tourism cannot be accused of **[-10-]** tiger populations!

Julian Matthews, 'Can ecotourism save tigers in India?' 2007

Which words go in the gaps (1–10) in the text? Choose the words from the box on the right.
Be prepared to justify your answer.

1. ....
2. ....
3. ....
4. ....
5. ....
6. ....
7. ....
8. ....
9. ....
10. ....

accused	concerned
confirmed	constant
decimating	do
evil	historically
increasing	individual
international	past
rarely	significant
small	sporadic
through	where
which	whose

Extract 2

The decline in letter writing constitutes a cultural shift so vast that in the future, historians may divide time not between B.C. and A.D. but between the eras when people wrote letters and **[-1-]**. Historians depend on the written record. Perhaps a better way of saying that is that they are **[-2-]** that record. Land transactions, birth and death records, weather reports, government documents—
5 to the historian, **[-3-]**, because it all contributes to the picture we have of the past. In the last century or so, as historians have turned away from their fixation on **[-4-]** and included the lives of average people in their study, the letters those people left behind are invaluable evidence of how life was once lived. We know what our ancestors ate, how they dressed, what they dreamed about love and what they thought about warfare, **[-5-]**. Without that correspondence, the guesswork mounts.

Malcolm Jones, 'The good word', *Newsweek*, **2009**

Which phrases go in the gaps (1–5)? Choose the phrases from the list below. Be prepared to justify your answer.

1. ....
2. ....
3. ....
4. ....
5. ....

a. all from their letters

b. at the mercy of

c. everything written is trivial

d. little from their letter

e. modern trivia

f. nothing written is trivial

g. quite liberated by

h. the doings of the great

i. when they communicated face-to-face

j. when they did not

Phrases, instead of words, may be taken out from the text at times. If you are asked to fill the gaps with the appropriate phrases, apply the same techniques you use when filling the gaps with words.

The whole truth, and nothing but the truth

When asked to provide a number of true statements based on the information given in a text, you have to remember a number of things:

1. Only fully true statements are required; half-truths do not count.

2. Do not jump to conclusions simply because you are familiar with the subject matter; you base your choice only on the information given in the text.

3. Handwriting is of utmost importance. You will be asked to write the appropriate letters in boxes; therefore, you will need to make sure that your letters are legible to someone who does not know you (the examiner). You will not be given the benefit of the doubt if the examiner cannot tell whether the answer given in the box is a C or an E, for example.

Example

So why do people think music should be blamed for negativity in a society? One reason is that it's fairly easy to do so as many parents, no matter how well meaning, tend to fall for blaming what they don't understand rather than exploring some of the problems in their own back yard. In addition, many proponents of blaming music tend to look nostalgically at the era they grew up in through a filtered view. They tend to think their generation was much better behaved than today's youth and forget that their parents' generation was likely making the same complaints that they're making now. In the process, those who blame music for a society's negative turn fail to see that the music may mirror of the parts of society we're having problems with (and unfortunately sometimes choose to ignore) and might in fact be shooting the messenger while the real causes of a society's problems go unaddressed.

So is it fair to blame music for the negativity in a society? Of course it's not fair to do so. However, it has become a convenient scapegoat which is one reason why people in every generation seem to do it. It is much easier to blame certain songs one may dislike and disapprove of rather than address the real issues of a society at large. Because of this fact, it is likely that the popular music of an era will continue to get blamed for the negative impact of a society (this goes back to Plato, unfortunately) rather than fixing the actual problems and making the society a better place to live.

Bo Paul, 'Is it fair to blame today's negativity in society on musical influence?', 2008

From statements A to F, select the three that are true according to the text above. Write the appropriate letters in the answer boxes provided.

A. Parents prefer to blame factors other than familial problems for their children's negativity.

B. People have objective views of their teenage years.

C. Parents across generations tend to make similar complaints about their children.

D. The author believes that music definitely reflects societal problems.

E. The author believes that one day people will quit blaming music for the failures of a society.

F. The author asserts that blaming music for the negativity in a society is a very old practice.

A

C

F

Justifications

A. The text says that parents '…tend to fall for blaming what they don't understand rather than exploring some of the problems in their own back yard', which means that it is easier for parents to blame factors other than their own internal problems as a family for their children's behavior. Therefore, **A is true**.

B. In the text, the author claims that people have 'filtered views' of their teenage years. When you filter something, you get rid of the impurities; therefore, those people do not have an objective (impartial, unbiased) view of their teenage years. Therefore, **B is untrue**.

C. The author claims that today's parents tend to forget that 'their parents' generation was likely making the same complaints that they're making now'. Therefore, **C is true**.

D. D is what we mean by a half-truth; the author uses the word 'may'. He does not assert his opinion by using words like 'always', or even stick to using the simple present. Therefore, **D is untrue**.

E. The author states that 'the popular music of an era will continue to get blamed for the negative impact of a society', which is the exact opposite of 'quit blaming'. Although the author says 'likely', he links it to a fact. Therefore, **E is untrue**.

F. The text states, 'this goes back to Plato', with 'this' referring to 'blaming music for the negative impact of a society'. The use of the simple present shows us that the author confirms the claim. Therefore, **F is true**.

Activity

Read the texts below and answer the questions that follow each extract.

Extract 1

Last Lesson of the Afternoon

D. H. Lawrence (1885–1930)

When will the bell ring, and end this weariness?

How long have they tugged the leash, and strained apart,

My pack of unruly hounds! I cannot start

Them again on a quarry of knowledge they hate to hunt,

I can haul them and urge them no more.

No longer now can I endure the brunt

Of the books that lie out on the desks; a full threescore

Of several insults of blotted pages, and scrawl

Of slovenly work that they have offered me.

I am sick, and what on earth is the good of it all?

What good to them or me, I cannot see!

So, shall I take

My last dear fuel of life to heap on my soul

And kindle my will to a flame that shall consume

Their dross of indifference; and take the toll

Of their insults in punishment? — I will not!—

I will not waste my soul and my strength for this.

What do I care for all that they do amiss!

What is the point of this teaching of mine, and of this

Learning of theirs? It all goes down the same abyss.

What does it matter to me, if they can write

A description of a dog, or if they can't?

What is the point? To us both, it is all my aunt!

And yet I'm supposed to care, with all my might.

I do not, and will not; they won't and they don't; and that's all!

I shall keep my strength for myself; they can keep theirs as well.

Why should we beat our heads against the wall

Of each other? I shall sit and wait for the bell.

From statements A to H, select the four that are true according to the poem. Be prepared to justify your answers.

A. At the end of the school day, students are manageable albeit unconcerned with learning.

B. The speaker is willing but unable to teach students anything new at the end of the school day.

C. The speaker hardly sees anything good in attempting to teach a new lesson at the end of the school day.

D. The speaker regards the education system as a complete waste.

E. The speaker thinks that he benefits more from teaching than students do from learning.

F. Although largely uninterested, the speaker is expected to give his all when teaching students.

G. The speaker views attempts to teach students as a never-ending battle.

H. The speaker and the students sit docilely awaiting the end of the school day.

Extract 2

This is not a play; it is not a lecture; it is not an interactive workshop; it is not a physical theatre piece; it is not a public conversation. *How to End Poverty in 90 Minutes* is all of these things. Most significantly, it's an opportunity to challenge a different audience every show with the question: how do you attack the problem of poverty in America? Over the course of 90 minutes, the audience will listen, explore and ultimately choose how to spend $1,000 from ticket sales that will be sitting onstage in cash. It is an experiment in dialogue, in collective decision-making, in shared responsibility and in the potential for art to help us make our world a better place. Spectacularly eclectic in form, often delightful and occasionally uncomfortable, *How to End Poverty* will engage students and Chicago-area audiences alongside community experts. Come spend with us.

Northwestern University, 2013

From statements A to H, select the four that are true according to the text. Be prepared to justify your answers.

A. *How to End Poverty in 90 Minutes* is a theatrical show.

B. *How to End Poverty in 90 Minutes* focuses on the issue of poverty in the world.

C. *How to End Poverty in 90 Minutes* lasts for more than an hour and a half.

D. The audience interacts with the performers.

E. $1000 will be given to the person who chooses how to best spend them.

F. *How to End Poverty in 90 minutes* highlights a number of important competences.

G. The audience is a mixture of community experts, Chicago residents and students.

H. *How to End Poverty in 90 days* encourages thrifty spending.

Defending ticks

When asked to decide whether a statement is true or false and to justify your answer, you need to remember that **the justification you provide has to be an exact quote from the text**. This quote, whether it be a few words or a slightly longer sentence, has to defend your choice of the tick (**true OR false**). Do note that both the correct tick and the correct justification are required. Do not attempt to paraphrase the justification and be very careful when you choose your quote, for sometimes quoting the whole sentence shifts the focus or nullifies the justification. In other words, when writing the justification, be **precise and concise**.

Example

The scrubby desert outside Port Augusta, three hours from Adelaide, is not the kind of countryside you see in Australian tourist brochures. The backdrop to an area of coal-fired power stations, lead smelting and mining, the coastal landscape is spiked with saltbush that can live on a trickle of brackish seawater seeping up through the arid soil. Poisonous king brown snakes, redback spiders, the odd kangaroo and emu are seen occasionally, flies constantly. When the local landowners who graze a few sheep here get a chance to sell some of this crummy real estate they jump at it, even for bottom dollar, because the only real natural resource in these parts is sunshine.

Which makes it all the more remarkable that a group of young brains from Europe, Asia and north America, led by a 33-year-old German former Goldman Sachs banker but inspired by a London theatre lighting engineer of 62, have bought a sizeable lump of this unpromising outback territory and built on it an experimental greenhouse which holds the seemingly realistic promise of solving the world's food problems.

Indeed, the work that Sundrop Farms, as they call themselves, are doing in South Australia, and just starting up in Qatar, is beyond the experimental stage. They appear to have pulled off the ultimate something-from-nothing agricultural feat – using the sun to desalinate seawater for irrigation and to heat and cool greenhouses as required, and thence cheaply grow high-quality, pesticide-free vegetables year-round in commercial quantities.

Jonathan Margolis, *The Observer*, 2012

The sentences below are either true or false. Tick [✓] the correct response then justify it with a relevant brief quotation from the text.

                                                       True False

1. The desert outside Port Augusta is picturesque and tourist-friendly.   ☐ [✓]

   Justification: 'not the kind of countryside you see in Australian tourist brochures'

   > *Tourist brochures normally publicise areas that are of extreme natural beauty. Since the desert outside Port Augusta is 'not the kind of countryside you see in Australian tourist brochures', it is hardly scenic or picturesque. The remainder of the paragraph describes the area but does not allude to magazine-worthy scenic beauty or to whether tourists are interested in it.*

2. Sundrop Farms' vast land is owned by a former banker and his colleagues.   [✓] ☐

   Justification: "have bought a sizeable lump (of this unpromising outback territory)"

   > *The text mentions a former banker and provides a general description of his colleagues: 'brains from Europe, Asia and America', in addition to the lighting engineer. Buying something denotes acquiring/owning it. The remainder of the sentence 'and built on it an experimental greenhouse which holds the seemingly realistic promise of solving the world's food problems', if used, shifts the focus from 'owning the land' to 'what the land is used for', and will result in your not being awarded the mark.*

3. Experiments are still required to determine if Sundrop Farms can produce cheap, high-quality and pesticide-free vegetables.   ☐ [✓]

   Justification: '(is) beyond the experimental stage'

   > *The word 'beyond' means going past the experimental stage. 'They appear to have pulled off the ultimate something-from-nothing agricultural feat', although it emphasizes 'going beyond the experimental stage', does not clearly show that further experiments are not required like 'beyond the experimental stage' does.*

Activity

Read the texts below to answer the questions that follow each extract.

Extract 1

Distance learning requires a virtual classroom that facilitates qualitative higher education where highly motivated students are willing to take advantage of state-of-the-art technologies to ensure knowledge transfer. E-learning consists of both real-time and asynchronous classes, meeting the needs of flexible modern students with multiple extracurricular responsibilities. On-line foreign language programs should provide a virtual community that captures and captivates foreign language learners with meaningful dynamic content while utilizing the target language as the medium of communication.

Foreign language study in a virtual classroom through e-learning offers several advantages over classical mediums for foreign language learning and provides state-of-the-art foreign language training, furnishing multimedia in the classroom previously deemed impossible. Multimedia classrooms armed with the Internet render a historical precedent of a positive language learning environment which celebrates cultural diversity, cross-cultural awareness through cross-cultural exchange, and intercultural communication unlike never before.

Collaboration in the target language within an on-line foreign language program reinforces the concept of a communicative curriculum. Keeping the target audience in mind, educational content providers should heed the adage that content is king. Correct input in the target language diminishes the possibility of future grammatical and phonological errors in addition to cultural misinterpretations. On-line programs for studying foreign languages should manipulate traditional teaching methodologies to construct a positive learning environment where fluency in the target language with native to near native accuracy, according to the foreign language learner's proficiency level, would be the norm instead of the exception.

Eric Paul Monroe, 'Evaluating online programs for studying foreign languages', 2007

The sentences below are either true or false. Tick [✓] the correct response then justify it with a relevant brief quotation from the text. Be prepared to defend your tick and justification.

		True	*False*
1.	Advanced technologies are used in online learning environments.	☐	☐
	Justification:		
2.	E-learning focuses on synchronous communication.	☐	☐
	Justification:		
3.	Using multimedia in the virtual classroom has been achievable in the past.	☐	☐
	Justification:		
4.	Developers of foreign language e-courses should focus on content.	☐	☐
	Justification:		
5.	Fluency in the target language should be achieved by all students in a foreign language e-course.	☐	☐
	Justification:		

Extract 2

It's just past lunchtime on a Friday afternoon and Lansbury opens the cupboard in her compact and modern kitchen. It is stocked with HobNobs and she offers to put some on a plate while explaining why she's going to resist. About a month ago, she woke up with a mysterious stress fracture in her right hip and now, standing in front of the open fridge, she points to the calcium beverage she's had to constantly drink.

"I've put on weight from all the muscle milk," she says, sounding alarmed. "I had to drink more than a pint — twice a day!" Whatever weight she's gained doesn't show. Her trim figure and lively manner betray that of a woman half her age and as she elegantly moves around her kitchen, dressed in a tailored tweed blazer and black slacks, gold earrings that match a gold brooch, it's hard to believe that she's nearly 87.

Lansbury has received numerous lifetime achievement awards and she's earned them. One of Britain's most beloved, durable and revered actors is currently starring on Broadway in Gore Vidal's *The Best Man*, eight times a week. Doesn't she get tired? "I'm the bionic woman," she giggles, picking up the tray with tea and biscuits and moving us into the living room to chat.

Other shows have required a lot more energy, she says, citing her performance as Madame Arcati in Noël Coward's *Blithe Spirit*, as an example.

But then, she prefers hard work and it pays off. She won the Tony Award in 2009 for the role and it was her fifth win, having won previously for *Mame*, *Gypsy* and *Sweeney Todd*.

Ariel Leve, *The Telegraph*, 2012

The sentences below are either true or false. Tick [✓] the correct response then justify it with a relevant brief quotation from the text. Be prepared to defend your tick and justification.

		True	*False*
1.	Angela Lansbury eats some of the HobNobs she offers the interviewer.	☐	☐
	Justification:		
2.	Angela Lansbury is anxious about gaining weight.	☐	☐
	Justification:		
3.	Angela Lansbury looks like an 87-year-old woman.	☐	☐
	Justification:		
4.	Angela Lansbury is currently enjoying her retirement.	☐	☐
	Justification:		
5.	Angela Lansbury won a Tony Award for her role in *Blithe Spirit*.	☐	☐
	Justification:		

A, B, C, or D?

Answering multiple choice questions correctly is not an easy feat. The alternatives given are sometimes so close. Therefore, and after you read the question, you need to re-read the text and the choices while mentally ticking off those that are wrong.

Example

Although we, as a society, have come a long way from the oppression of women in South Africa, there are still instances where gender discrimination in the workplace is an issue. Despite all the efforts being made to stamp out this problem, complaints of gender discrimination in the workplace have in fact increased. Whether this is due to an increase in awareness of a woman's rights or whether the incidence level has increased is hard to tell. It is therefore important for both employers and employees to be aware of what constitutes gender discrimination in the workplace and how this can be prevented.

The first and most prolific form of gender discrimination in the workplace is through the inability of women to enter into management or executive positions in a company. This basically means that men will be placed in higher level positions before a woman is considered for a high level vacancy. Some companies even go as far as the outright refusal of employing women in certain positions within the company. It is important to note here that there is sometimes a reversal of roles here where some companies prefer woman employees and discriminate against men instead.

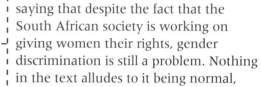

The second factor that is often an issue is the amount of money that a woman will earn performing a certain job when compared to her male counterpart in the same position of employment. Statistics reveal that women earn around 15% less than their male counterparts. It is very important to address the issues of gender discrimination in the workplace as soon as they are detected to eliminate this problem once and for all.

'Gender discrimination in the workplace', SNA Attorneys, 2013

Choose the correct answer from A, B, C, or D. Write the letter in the answer box provided.

1. Gender discrimination in South Africa
   A. still permeates the society.
   B. is the norm.   `A` ← - - - - -
   C. is decreasing.
   D. has been effectively dealt with.

   In the first paragraph, the author is saying that despite the fact that the South African society is working on giving women their rights, gender discrimination is still a problem. Nothing in the text alludes to it being normal, decreasing or dealt with; it is still an issue that more or less 'permeates the society'.

2. Women in South Africa
   A. are in general considered inferior to men.
   B. come second to men in executive positions.   `B` ←
   C. do not apply for executive positions.
   D. discriminate against men.

   The second paragraph specifies the workforce, not the society as a whole. We do not know if women are in general considered inferior to men, but we know that they are not hired if a man applied for the same managerial position. As for discrimination against men, some companies, not women, do it.

3. When employed for similar jobs, women in South Africa
   A. are given the same wages as men.
   B. ask for less money than men.
   C. ask for more money than men.   `D` ← - - - - -
   D. make less money than men.

   In the third paragraph, the author states that women earn '15% less than their male counterparts'. This means that they make less money than their male colleagues. The text does not mention whether women, in fact, ask for more or less money.

Activity

Extract 1

It was a blazing hot day in August. Baker Street was like an oven, and the glare of the sunlight upon the yellow brickwork of the house across the road was painful to the eye. It was hard to believe that these were the same walls which loomed so gloomily through the fogs of winter. Our blinds were half-drawn, and Holmes lay curled upon the sofa, reading and re-reading a letter which he had received by the morning post. For myself, my term of service in India had trained me to stand heat better than cold, and a thermometer at ninety was no hardship. But the morning paper was uninteresting. Parliament had risen. Everybody was out of town, and I yearned for the glades of the New Forest or the shingle of Southsea. A depleted bank account had caused me to postpone my holiday, and as to my companion, neither the country nor the sea presented the slightest attraction to him. He loved to lie in the very center of five millions of people, with his filaments stretching out and running through them, responsive to every little rumour or suspicion of unsolved crime. Appreciation of nature found no place among his many gifts, and his only change was when he turned his mind from the evil-doer of the town to track down his brother of the country.

Sir Arthur Conan Doyle, 'The Adventure of the Cardboard Box'

Choose the correct answer from A, B, C, or D. Write the letter in the answer box provided. Be prepared to justify your answer.

1. Sherlock Holmes is
   A. enjoying the break.
   B. reading the paper.
   C. lying on the couch.
   D. feeling very hot.

2. The narrator can tolerate the heat because
   A. it is better than the cold.
   B. he dreams of his upcoming holiday at the seaside.
   C. his body is used to it.
   D. he can stand it as much as he can stand being cold.

3. The narrator has not gone on holiday because
   A. many people were out of town.
   B. he does not have enough money.
   C. he is not interested in either the country or the sea.
   D. he does not mind the heat.

4. Sherlock Holmes is
   A. obsessed with evil-doers.
   B. obsessed with mysteries.
   C. appreciates natural beauty.
   D. likes the countryside.

Extract 2

Going forward, Saturday nights will keep music enthusiasts occupied, as the much-awaited India in Concert initiative is all set to go live today! An initiative by music lovers for music lovers, India in Concert is the brainchild of Supratik Ghosh, who left his full-time job with an advertising agency years ago and pursued his passion for music through his band, Aurko. The objective is to make music available to all, traversing the boundaries of caste, creed and language.

Anyone with a passion for music can take part in this grand event and showcase his/her skills to the rest of the city. And this time, six contestants will be competing with one another to make their name in the music world: Rahul Sharma, an Infosys employee; Abhilash, a hardcore musician; Pallavi, a relationship manager with IDBI Bank; Reena Hebbar, employee at Airtel, Suraj Biswas, who is quitting his present job to pursue music; Kunal, an employee of Genpact and Rahul Sindagi, who works at Aricent.

Caroline Diana, 'India in concert: Music for a cause', 2012

Choose the correct answer from A, B, C, or D. Write the letter in the answer box provided. Be prepared to justify your answer.

1. India in Concert
   A. started a good number of years ago.
   B. is the idea of Ghosh.
   C. is a week-long concert.
   D. is going live in a number of years.

2. The initiative aims to
   A. unite art lovers worldwide.
   B. ensure the accessibility of music to everyone.
   C. reduce social and linguistic differences.
   D. introduce Ghosh's band, Aurko.

3. Performers in the concert are
   A. professional musicians.
   B. music lovers.
   C. city dwellers.
   D. employees.

4. Contestants are competing to
   A. get a monetary reward.
   B. quit their jobs.
   C. take part in the grand event.
   D. become renowned musicians.

You were saying?

When identifying who says what, you need to read the passage carefully, determine who the speakers are and scrutinize what they say. This need not be in a conversation setting; you may be asked to identify comments or ideas made by the 'speakers'.

Example

Our Readers' Comments

Chris Jones: *Lord of the Flies* is the story of a group of boys who find themselves on a deserted island in the middle of nowhere. The boys convince themselves that they are surrounded by a heinous beast, and work assiduously on shedding all remnants of civilization while on the island. William Golding brilliantly uses imagery to show us how humans degenerate and how easily it is to fall into savagery when our baser instincts are allowed to reign.

Petra Dean: I liked this book because I identified with the characters, especially Piggy. Piggy, one of the main characters, knows exactly what was going on around him and guides Ralph in taking important decisions. However, his general appearance and demeanour make him the last person to be listened to. The most disturbing incident I found in the book was when the boys, encompassed by the frenzy of offering a sacrifice to the beast, all take part in murdering Simon.

Troy Wilkinson: This book is definitely a must read for anyone who is interested in human nature. After reading this book, your understanding of the world around you will change. You will start questioning how much society influences our characters and helps in shaping them. It is really amazing to realise that the boys revert to their original selves – actually act as children rather than savages – at the end.

Read the 'text' and answer the following questions.

1. Who mentions the changing in the children's behaviour? **Troy Wilkinson**

   While the others mention the boys on the island, only Troy Wilkinson highlights the change in their behaviour at the end of the novel.

2. Who comments on the writing style? **Chris Jones**

   Both Petra and Troy mention the book. However, Petra mentions why she likes the book and Troy concentrates on the lessons that can be learned from it. Only Chris comments on Golding's use of imagery.

3. Who makes a specific reference to the novel's characters? **Petra Dean**

   While Chris and Troy refer to the boys, their comments do not specifically mention characters. It is Petra who refers to Piggy and Ralph specifically.

4. Who describes a character's weaknesses? **Petra Dean**

   Troy and Chris do mention how the boys act on the island. Petra, however, refers to Piggy's demeanour and appearance and link them to why the other boys did not see a leading figure in him.

5. Who gives a short synopsis of the novel? **Chris Jones**

   Chris starts by summarizing the novel, while Petra gives her personal opinion and Troy recommends the novel for others.

6. Who makes a personal observation on one of the novel's events? **Petra Dean and Troy Wilkinson**

   Petra mentions how she felt about Simon's murder and Troy comments on how amazing it was that the boys actually behaved as children at the end of the novel.

Activity

Extract 1
What our students say about online learning

Kelsey Winters
Studying Journalism

"The best thing I have found about online learning is being able to create my own schedule. I can take lessons and do homework when I have the time to fit it in. I really benefitted from being able to manage my own time."

Maria Espinoza
Studying Creative Writing

"I felt part of a close community. I really felt as if was connecting with the professor and my classmates, which was helped by things such as being able to see a video display of the professor teaching."

Sarah Mosby
Studying Leadership Communication

"The greatest advantage of online learning for me was flexibility with my schedule. In addition, online learning allows discussions to continue 24/7… and for me, the learning really continued."

Philip Holdsworth
Studying Public Affairs

"I there I were to take any class online, it would be this one. Learning to communicate online on a professional level is a really valuable skill which we'll all need to use in our working lives. Taking an online course is good preparation for that. My only real regret about this class is that it had to end!"

When asked about online learning, who praises:

1. the ability to set one's pace?
2. the chance to communicate with others?
3. continuous learning?
4. their professor's delivery techniques?
5. the type of online course studied?

Extract 2

Interested in taking an online course but not sure what to expect? Below is just a sampling of what some of our online students have to say about the Online Writer's Studio:

Martha L. Henning, Ph.D./ Fiction Writing: The Short Story Cycle: *"I approached the course with a sense of the technology being a brick wall; I emerged from the course with a sense of that same technology enabling rich, personal and small community communications as a benign and transparent tool."*

Melissa Dyrdahl/ The Craft of Poetry: Let's Begin: *"Having never taken an online course before, I was somewhat skeptical about the learning environment and my ability to effectively interact with the instructor and other students. I have to say the OWS (Online Writer's Studio) exceeded my expectations. It was great to be able to work on projects and submit them as my schedule allowed, there was a wonderful and supportive community that developed between the students (who were participating from a variety of countries and time zones) and the instructor was available and responsive throughout the class. I'm looking forward to taking my next OWS class."*

Kim Inman/ Travel Writing: *"While I've been tempted by some Stanford Continuing Ed. offerings in the past few years, none of them were feasible due to the fact that I live in suburban Chicago. The online feature made it both approachable and doable. In my rusty state of mind, an online class seemed safer - if I was too out of my league, dropping out wouldn't be too personal. But once I started the course, there was no way I was going to quit."*

George Patrick Dovel/ Fiction Writing: Voices That Live: *"I expected a high-level learning experience from a Stanford course, and my expectations were not only met but exceeded by a healthy margin."*

Jill Stegman/ Fiction Writing: Voices That Live: *"I just found out that I'm accepted into The Advanced Fiction Writer's Workshop offered by Vermont College. I used the short story submitted here, "Touch," as the admissions piece. I'll be working with Antonya Nelson, one of my favorite short story writers. They even offered me a scholarship!"*

Nicole Harkin/ Creative Nonfiction: Beginning Your Book: *"The engaged, intelligent writers leading the course work at the Stanford Continuing Studies program not only keep me involved in my online course work but also keep me coming back for more."*

Robert Rebele/ Creative Nonfiction: *"I would absolutely take this course again, and I wholeheartedly recommend it to my friends and anyone else interested in a life of writing."*

Miriam Wynn/ Writing for the Movies: Beginning Screenwriting: *"I have a Stanford BA in English/Creative Writing and I can attest to the quality of Stegner Fellows based on my quarterly workshops during my undergraduate career. This online course turned out to be of the same caliber and a great venue to learn and apply new skills."*

Harry Weekes/ Putting a Spin on Science Writing: *"The course was excellent for my work style and my schedule – demanding with deadlines, but not overwhelming."*

Karen Vanuska/ Magazine Writing: *"Thanks to the lead the instructor provided and the writing wisdom she imparted, I've been successfully launched into the world of professional book reviewers. I'm eager to work with her again in the future."*

Stanford Continuing Studies, 2013

In the text above, who:

1. links development to the successful facilitation of the course?
2. was wary of having to deal with technology prior to the commencement of the course?
3. compares the rigour of the course to his university courses?
4. was accepted at another course because of work completed in his/her online course?
5. was not sure s/he would complete the course when registering for the course?
6. will enroll in a future Online Writer's Studio course?
7. found online courses feasible because they do not require presence in a certain physical space?
8. found the course more beneficial than expected?
9. would recommend the course to others?
10. applauds the quality of communication in the online course?

Meaning... something more than meaning!

Not only do vocabulary questions test your understanding of words and their synonyms, but they also require you to show understanding of those words and phrases in context. For example, the word 'glimpse' means 'a brief look' but in a sentence like 'the book gave me a glimpse of what it is like to be physically challenged', it means 'an indication' or 'a clue'. Consequently, even if you know the meaning of a word, re-read the sentence in which the word appears before you determine its meaning.

Example

Along this particular stretch of line no express had ever passed. All the trains--the few that there were--stopped at all the stations. Denis knew the names of those stations by heart.
5 Bole, Tritton, Spavin Delawarr, Knipswich for Timpany, West Bowlby, and, finally, Camlet-on-the-Water. Camlet was where he always got out, leaving the train to creep indolently onward, goodness only knew whither, into the
10 green heart of England.

They were snorting out of West Bowlby now. It was the next station, thank Heaven. Denis took his chattels off the rack and piled them neatly in the corner opposite his own. A futile proceeding.
15 But one must have something to do. When he had finished, he sank back into his seat and closed his eyes. It was extremely hot.

Oh, this journey! It was two hours cut clean out of his life; two hours in which he might have
20 done so much, so much--written the perfect poem,

19

for example, or read the one illuminating book. Instead of which--his gorge rose at the smell of the dusty cushions against which he was leaning.

25 Two hours. One hundred and twenty minutes. Anything might be done in that time. Anything. Nothing. Oh, he had had hundreds of hours, and what had he done with them? Wasted them,

30 spilt the precious minutes as though his reservoir were inexhaustible. Denis groaned in the spirit, condemned himself utterly with all his works. What right had he to sit in the sunshine, to occupy corner seats in third-class carriages, to be alive? None, none, none.

Aldous Huxley, *Crome Yellow*

Find the word in the right-hand column that could meaningfully replace one of the words on the left.

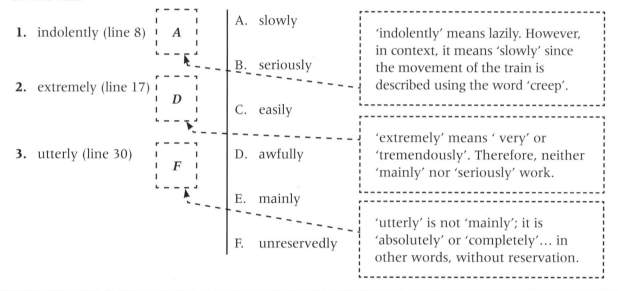

1. indolently (line 8)   *A*

2. extremely (line 17)   *D*

3. utterly (line 30)   *F*

A. slowly

B. seriously

C. easily

D. awfully

E. mainly

F. unreservedly

'indolently' means lazily. However, in context, it means 'slowly' since the movement of the train is described using the word 'creep'.

'extremely' means ' very' or 'tremendously'. Therefore, neither 'mainly' nor 'seriously' work.

'utterly' is not 'mainly'; it is 'absolutely' or 'completely'… in other words, without reservation.

Activity

Extract 1

Tom forgot the ideas of absconding and squinted at the man across from him. "After you, Paragon," he said. No reply came from his cellmate, just quick obedience.

5 Entering the two-way hall, he peered toward the entrance where eleven more guards waited to walk him to his Master. He sighted the fulvous robes of a mage hiding behind a couple of the guards, the

10 choker around his neck glowed like molten gold, his undeniable presence ensuring no disturbances broke out. Taking down twelve well-armored guards would be a feat, but the security of the mage sealed the deal.

15 Not a chance to fight for freedom and come out living.

The two slaves walked the hundred meters to the entrance, passing about fifty slumbering prisoners. Down the opposite way, more than

20 three hundred meters of cells hid in blackness.

The trip elapsed in total quiet. The only noise came from rough footsteps, the shifting of armor, and the clinking of tankards fastened by carabiners at the hips of all the dwarves.

25 The circumstances of the night remained concealed from Tom, and the guards never spoke, except to each other, but even those seldom occurrences were only laconic teasings. The only opportunities to learn

30 revolved around break time in the mines, but even then you had to talk to the right person, and finding someone reliable varied day by day. The shifts in the mines rotated continuously, never the same, always

35 different faces swapping from the compounds of the four other Dwarflords, which made it hard to keep in contact with anyone.

John Hennessy, *A Stalker's Game*

Find the word in the right-hand columns that could meaningfully replace the words on the left.

1. absconding (line 1) ....
2. squinted (line 2) ....
3. fulvous (line 8) ....
4. ensuring (line 11) ....
5. feat (line 14) ....
6. slumbering (line 18) ....
7. elapsed (line 21) ....
8. fastened (line 24) ....
9. laconic (line 29) ....
10. swapping (line 36) ....

A. aimed
B. brief
C. deed
D. escaping
E. guaranteeing
F. hitting
G. interchanging
H. jumped
I. looked
J. passed

K. protecting
L. secured
M. selling
N. sleeping
O. small
P. snoring
Q. tawny
R. voucher
S. walked
T. wordy

Extract 2

The idea of a contemporary Sherlock
Holmes might sound sacrilege to some, but
Moffat manages to update it — with all the
newfangled technologies that our modern
5 world provides — and somehow keep it faithful
to the works of Sir Arthur Conan Doyle.
Technology is often a hindrance to modern
mysteries; DNA fingerprinting, computer
forensics, and GPS often take the fun out of
10 crime solving. With Moffat's *Sherlock*, it only
presents new challenges, challenges that Moffat
stays well ahead of. Contemporary Holmes
doesn't abandon modern tech; he incorporates
it. But it doesn't distract from his deductive
15 skills, his ability to read a person in seconds, or
quickly analyze a crime scene. Modern gadgets
may be able to help answer questions, but it's
always been Sherlock's job to figure out what
questions to ask, and that's where computers
20 and PDAs haven't yet caught up with human
intelligence, and where a detective like Holmes
will always be useful.

Part of the fun, especially in the opening
episode, is rediscovering the Holmesian
25 conventions, now set in modern London.
Watson is a veteran wounded in the
Afghanistan war, where he served as a
doctor. He's also in therapy, suffering from
psychosomatic PTSD. Holmes is a detective's
30 consultant, living at his usual address, 221B
Baker Street (with new London street signs),
only now it's a modern flat. The two are
brought together when Holmes needs a
flatmate, and Watson needs a place to live.
35 The love/hate connection is instant; Holmes
is brilliant but irritating, while Watson is loyal
and tolerating. Freeman is also the best thing
about this show and, like in the novels, an
equal partner and not a sidekick — Holmes
40 may solve the mysteries, but it's Watson who
saves the day.

Dustin Rowles, 2011

Find the word in the right-hand columns that could meaningfully replace the words on the left.

1. sacrilege (line 2) ....
2. newfangled (line 4) ....
3. hindrance (line 7) ....
4. abandon (line 13) ....
5. deductive (line 15) ....
6. served (line 28) ....
7. usual (line 31) ....
8. connection (line 36) ....
9. brilliant (line 37) ....
10. sidekick (line 40) ....

A. bond
B. boon
C. clever
D. contender
E. dated
F. defend
G. desert
H. deterrent
I. familiar
J. follower

K. illogical
L. irreverence
M. kin
N. luminous
O. modern
P. offbeat
Q. officiated
R. reasoning
S. respect
T. sufficed

Pointing the finger at...?

Identifying to whom or to what a certain word refers requires close
reading, understanding of grammatical use as well as semantic
reference. Make sure you read the parts **before and after** the specified
word or phrase before you decide to whom or to what it refers.

Example

The novel begins a few years after 9/11.
Changez happens upon the American in Lahore,
invites him to tea and tells him the story of
his life in the months just before and after the
5 attacks. That monologue is the substance of
Hamid's elegant and chilling little novel.

In 2001, as he explains, Changez was hardly a
radical. Fresh out of Princeton, he was living
in New York City and working as a financial
10 analyst. He appears to have been something of
a cipher, until his reaction to the attacks — that
sudden smile — pierces the shell. It seems to
have come as a surprise even to himself, and
while hardly endearing, it sets his tale in motion.

15 A less sophisticated author might have told
a one-note story in which an immigrant's
experiences of discrimination and ignorance
cause his alienation. But Hamid's novel, while it
contains a few such moments, is distinguished
20 by its portrayal of Changez's class aspirations
and inner struggle. His resentment is at least
in part self-loathing, directed at the American
he'd been on his way to becoming. For to be an
American, he declares, is to view the world in a
25 certain way — a perspective he absorbed in his
eagerness to join the country's elite.

Karen Olsson, *The New York Times*, 2007

Complete the following table by indicating to whom or to what the word(s) underlined refer(s).

In the phrase ...	the word(s) ...	refer(s) to ...	Why?
1. ... the story of <u>his</u> life... *(lines 3–4)*	'his'	Changez	*Who is doing the telling? Changez. Note the use of pronouns: Changez invites the American and tells him about his life. Could Changez be telling the American about the American's life?*
2. ... <u>It</u> seems to have come ... *(lines 12–13)*	'it'	his reaction to the attacks/that sudden smile	*Why are both acceptable? Because the smile summarizes Changez' reaction to the attacks.*
3. ... to join <u>the country's</u> elite ... *(line 26)*	'the country'	The United States of America	*How do you know? From the context and the specific mention of Changez' desire to be American.*

Activity

Extract 1
The farmhouse kitchen probably stood where
it did as a matter of accident or haphazard
choice; yet its situation might have been
planned by a master-strategist in farmhouse
5 architecture. Dairy and poultry-yard, and
herb garden, and all the busy places of the
farm seemed to lead by easy access into its
wide flagged haven, where there was room
for everything and where muddy boots left
10 traces that were easily swept away. And yet,

for all that it stood so well in the centre of
human bustle, its long, latticed window, with
the wide window-seat, built into an embrasure
beyond the huge fireplace, looked out on
15 a wild spreading view of hill and heather
and wooded combe. The window nook
made almost a little room in itself, quite the
pleasantest room in the farm as far as situation
and capabilities went. Young Mrs. Ladbruk,
20 whose husband had just come into the farm by
way of inheritance, cast covetous eyes on this

snug corner, and her fingers itched to make it bright and cosy with chintz curtains and bowls of flowers, and a shelf or two of old china. The
25 musty farm parlour, looking out on to a prim, cheerless garden imprisoned within high, blank walls, was not a room that lent itself readily either to comfort or decoration.

"When we are more settled I shall work
30 wonders in the way of making the kitchen habitable," said the young woman to her occasional visitors. There was an unspoken wish in those words, a wish which was unconfessed as well as unspoken. Emma
35 Ladbruk was the mistress of the farm; jointly with her husband she might have her say, and to a certain extent her way, in ordering its affairs. But she was not mistress of the kitchen.

H.H. Munro (Saki), *The Cobweb*

Complete the following table by indicating to whom or to what the word(s) underlined refer(s).

In the phrase …	the word(s) …	refer(s) to …
1. … into <u>its</u> wide flagged haven… *(lines 7 and 8)*	'its'	
2. … quite <u>the pleasantest room</u> … *(line 18)*	'the pleasantest room'	
3. … that lent <u>itself</u> readily … *(line 28)*	'itself'	
4. … When <u>we</u> are more settled… *(line 30)*	'we'	
5. … in ordering <u>its</u> affairs… *(lines 37 and 38)*	'its'	
6. … <u>she</u> was not mistress… *(line 38)*	'she'	

Extract 2

The United States of America has always been seen as a safe haven of opportunity. For this reason, many immigrants flock to this country in search of new beginnings and
5 better lives. With this belief, when I was two, my family moved to the U.S. from India. My parents were the first of their generation to emigrate to America. Thus, they faced immense pressure getting accustomed to the new land.
10 Initially, my parents wanted to adhere to a traditional Indian way of life, but due to the new atmosphere, they were forced to assimilate into the American culture with the hopes of becoming socially accepted. At the time, they
15 did not realize how it would impact their own Indian culture, but as I grew older, they noticed the changes in my very own lifestyle.

Fearful that I would lose my entire Indian heritage, they sent me back to India to live
20 with my grandparents, hoping that I could build a strong cultural foundation. After returning to America, I entered grade school. At first I felt like an outsider coming from an Indian home. Students used to stare in
25 bewilderment when I brought handvo, a traditional Gujarati snack, to lunch. Pointing fingers, they maliciously asked "Eww what's that? What's it made of? Why does it smell like that?" as I slowly pulled it out of my
30 lunchbox. Slowly I found it easier to disguise my Indian background by eating sandwiches and cookies, what "normal" American children ate for lunch. It was an easier task for me to adapt to my host nation rather than
35 my host nation adapting to me. By doing this, I was assimilating, and this way I felt more comfortable being a part of society and no longer felt like an outsider.

Jay Patel, 2012

Complete the following table by indicating to whom or to what the word(s) underlined refer(s).

In the phrase …	the word(s) …	refer(s) to …
1. … flock to <u>this country</u>... *(line 3)*	'this country'	
2. …<u>they</u> faced immense pressure … *(line 8)*	'they'	
3. … how <u>it</u> would impact … *(line 15)*	'it'	
4. … <u>they</u> maliciously asked … *(line 27)*	'they'	
5. … I slowly pulled <u>it</u> out … *(line 29)*	'it'	
6. … By doing <u>this</u> … *(lines 35 and 36)*	'this'	

Making sense of halves

When asked to match the first part of a sentence with its appropriate ending, do not rely solely on syntactic clues. While grammar and its rules may be helpful, it is your understanding of the text and its context that will allow you to make appropriate matches.

Example

One in eight Australians lives below the poverty line, according to a national analysis by a leading welfare group.

The unemployed, singles over 65, lone-parent families and households reliant on social security were among those most at risk, according to the Poverty in Australia report, released yesterday by the Australian Council of Social Service.

Women were more likely to be poor as they did more unpaid care work, had fewer employment opportunities and lower wages. Sixteen per cent of adults from non-English-speaking countries live in poverty, 5 percentage points higher than those born here.

Vince Chadwick, *The Age*, 2012

Match the first part of the sentence with the appropriate ending on the right. Write the appropriate letter in the boxes provided.

1. Approximately 12% of the Australian population   [D]

2. The sector of the population that is most at risk   [A]

3. The percentage of the poor Australian population that does not speak English as a mother tongue   [B]

A. is the one that is jobless.

B. is bigger than those who do.

C. is comprised of women.

D. is considered poor.

E. is 5% better-off than those who do.

F. is living on social security.

Justifications

1. The first paragraph mentions that 'one in eight Australians lives below the poverty line'. Some of those are reliant on social security but not all of them (at least we do not learn that from the text).

2. Note that the second paragraph specifies the unemployed, the elderly and those reliant on social security. Therefore, we infer that those who do not have secure jobs are more at risk of becoming poor than others. Although women are mentioned in the text, the text does not highlight them as more likely to be poorer than others.

3. The text states that 'sixteen per cent of adults from non-English-speaking countries live in poverty, 5 percentage points higher than those born here'. This means that the number of non-native English speakers who are poor is bigger than the number of poor native Australians.

Activity

Extract 1

Mike used to pride himself on his health, running double marathons and working as a personal trainer, but now he looked painfully thin and nervous. Sat in the bright living room of a safehouse where he lived for three months, he described having to retrain himself to eat properly after being kept in squalid conditions and forced to work unpaid for three years. He was, he said, a modern-day slave.

"Before this happened I never even thought it could happen in this country, or that it could happen to men," he said. "But if you are desperate enough, anyone could find themselves in this trap."

Mike is one of hundreds of men and women who are trafficked into Britain for the profit of their unscrupulous bosses, according to a government report. Estimates released on anti-slavery day suggest the number of people being trafficked into and around the UK is rising, with 946 victims in contact with authorities last year, compared with 710 in 2010.

The report by the inter-departmental ministerial group on human trafficking states that trafficking gangs in China, Vietnam, Nigeria and eastern Europe now pose the biggest threat. But it is not just a foreign national problem, said Helen Grant, the newly appointed victims minister. "This exploitation of vulnerable people by predatory gangs is not something that any civilised society should be prepared to accept," she said. "It is happening to men, women and children, to foreign nationals and to British citizens."

Alexandra Topping, *The Guardian*, 2012

Match the first part of the sentence with the appropriate ending on the right.

1. Mike was ….

2. Trafficking people into Britain is ….

3. Trafficking is mainly dominated by …

4. Civilised societies should …

A. repudiate the idea of trafficking.

B. made to live without food.

C. men, women, and children alike.

D. a scrupulous practice.

E. made to work without pay.

F. embrace the idea of trafficking.

G. on the rise.

H. criminal gangs in different parts of the world.

Extract 2

The decline of a parent's health, death of one parent or financial pressures often mean an aging parent will need increased social and emotional support or services from family—such as help with meals, cleaning, transportation or financial matters. Sue, like many adult children today, is confronted with increased interaction with her aged parent and with decisions that will affect her life and her parent's life.

Quality relationships make for best decision-making and ease the burdens of caregiving. Those adult children and parents who have positive feelings about each other involving mutual assistance and affection are better prepared to deal with the changes and decision of aging.

For other adult children, life-long conflicts and unresolved issues from childhood and adolescence can mean continuing conflicts in later life or reactivation of earlier conflicts and negative feelings. Being called upon to provide support to an aging parent can be particularly difficult.

Feelings in the adult child-aging parent relationship go back many years and run deep. Simultaneous feelings of closeness and conflict may complicate matters.

Texas A&M Agrilife Extension, 2010

Match the first part of the sentence with the appropriate ending on the right.

1. The elderly often…
2. The issues with caregiving can be alleviated by…
3. Unresolved childhood problems …
4. The adult child-aging parent relationship is …

A. need financial support.
B. result in enduring conflicts.
C. affected by complications.
D. spending quality time with the aging parent.
E. result in feelings of hatred.
F. maintaining a good relationship between parents and their children.
G. affected by their child-parent relationship.
H. need the care of family members.

Matchmaking!

Matching headings to paragraphs or interview questions to answers is a skimming exercise. You need to read the paragraph or the answer and understand its overall message before you decide on an appropriate heading or question.

Example

[-1-]

We already have a presence in six states of Punjab, Haryana, Rajasthan, Uttar Pradesh, Tamil Nadu and West Bengal. Our first phase of setting up primary schools is over and now we are moving towards the second phase of setting up senior secondary schools. Initially, we will have 25 senior secondary schools out of which five are already working in Punjab under the PPP model with the government of Punjab. The remaining schools will start in the states of Haryana, Rajasthan, Uttar Pradesh, Tamil Nadu and West Bengal.

[-2-]

One of the biggest challenges is that parents are reluctant to send their daughters to school, though this scenario is slowly changing. Even those who send their daughters to school withdraw them after class V and expect them to start earning a living. However, there has been a major shift, at least in India, where parents want their children to study and make a future and career for themselves. They no longer want their children to live their lives the way they had lived. The second challenge is to provide them with the facility of toilets, which most government schools lack. Other challenges include parents not being able to afford uniforms and lack of mid-day meal facility.

[-3-]

Children drop out because parents feel that they need to become earning hands. Providing vocational training in schools is extremely important to make every child employable after school. This is why, class X onwards, we have decided to provide vocational training in our senior secondary schools. We will also create suitable modules to provide training.

Vishakha Sharma, TNN , 2012

Match the questions on the right with the answers in the text.
Write the appropriate letter in the spaces provided.

1. *Although A also mentions plans, it focuses on academic plans. The paragraph discusses expansion phases rather than academic objectives.*   **D**

2. *The paragraph specifies the challenges facing girls rather than students in general or setting up schools.*   **B**

3. *Although the paragraph begins with the reasons for dropping out of schools, it continues to describe the importance of vocational training and how it can complement formal education.*   **F**

A. **What are your future academic plans for the initiative?**

B. **What are the challenges of female education in India?**

C. **Why do students drop out of school in India?**

D. **Do you plan to spread this initiative in other parts of India?**

E. **What are the challenges facing setting up schools in India?**

F. **Is education enough for children or should it be coupled with skills training?**

Activity

Extract 1

[-1-]

During July, a group of rowers will be setting off on an expedition on the Zambezi to raise money for the charity, Village Water. Included in the team is Antonia van Deventer, born and bred in Zambia and hoping to make it to the 2012 Olympics as Zambia's first and only rowing representative in the Women's Single Skull. We asked them about this trip.

[-2-]

Row Zambezi represents a dream to change the fortunes of thousands of people in Zambia and to complete a world-first rowing expedition. The start of the expedition will see the culmination of over a year's worth of planning and fundraising for this charity expedition. A real family-oriented project, the expedition leader, Tim Cook, and three of his sons will be in the rowing team.

[-3-]

Tim Cook, the expedition leader, wanted to do a rowing expedition to celebrate his 50th birthday. Originally planning to row the Atlantic, one of his sons suggested he do something more original like row the Zambezi River in Zambia. Due to familial ties in the region, this was a perfect opportunity to plan a charity expedition that would help bring support to a very poor nation in Africa.

[-4-]

The team is concerned about wildlife encounters in the last 200 kilometres from Shesheke, especially hippos, crocodiles and elephants. We will have to remain constantly vigilant throughout the expedition to ensure that there are no serious encounters, either on or off the river.

[-5-]

Since the expedition is going to take place in a very remote area, a lot of planning has been done beforehand. With more or less no infrastructure to support an expedition like this, we have had to find out and put in place all the logistics which come naturally to us in Zambia including gathering information on medical facilities, airstrips and fuel availability. We have to feed a team of 31 for 25 days, and will have to bring everything with us.

[-6-]

As a rowing expedition, it seemed best to support a charity that focuses on water. This charity provides sustainable water wells, sanitation and hygiene education to rural villages in Zambia. Since 2007, they have helped over 65,000 people in over 240 villages. They decrease cases of certain diseases, train local people to maintain the wells and encourage crop cultivation.

Lowdown, 2011

Match the questions on the right with the answers in the text. Write the appropriate letter in the spaces provided.

1. [ ]
2. [ ]
3. [ ]
4. [ ]
5. [ ]
6. [ ]

A. How did the Row Zambezi Expedition come to be?

B. How is Row Zambezi accomplished?

C. How will the expedition support sustainable water wells?

D. How will you feed the participants?

E. How will you overcome the challenges?

F. What do you expect will be the major challenges?

G. What has it been like planning the expedition?

H. What is Village Water?

I. Where was the idea of rowing the Zambezi born?

J. Where, when and how was the idea born?

K. Who would row the Zambezi?

L. Why did you choose to support Village Water?

Extract 2

Interview with award-winning ventriloquist comedian Jeff Dunham

Jeff Dunham, the comedian who uses his puppets to spread laughter around the world, is back with another DVD. Amanda Thambounaris spoke with Jeff Dunham recently about his career and his life as an average kid.

Amanda: [-1-]

Jeff Dunham: I think a part of it was maybe lack of anything else that I was good at. I was not one of the popular kids: I was not great at sports, girls didn't pay attention to me – I was just pretty much an average kid, no stand-out abilities, nothing note-worthy. So, when I got the dummy, something about it just fascinated me and I practiced for about a month and got up and did my first book report and got laughs and everybody thought it was great.

Amanda: [-2-]

Jeff Dunham: Whatever pops into my head that will make an audience laugh, that's the first step. And some of those characters, I guess chaotic is a good word, are sometimes extreme or stereotypical. But I think there are pieces of every one of those descriptions that make people laugh.

Amanda: [-3-]

Jeff Dunham: I made my first one in sixth grade, and then there was a bit of a lull, I don't know what happened, I had to wait until I had a little more confidence. It wasn't until college that tried it again and tried my hand at making dummies and I got pretty good at it. So now when I come up with somebody new, if I think it's going to work and the jokes work in my head then I go and create the character myself. Peanut's the only one because he's a more Muppet soft character and I had somebody make him for me.

Amanda: [-4-]

Jeff Dunham: I don't do it for the money, it just so happens that it has gotten to a certain level and certain popularity. I've got a lot of good people working around me, we all think about things really hard and that's the point it has gotten to. You never know how long your fifteen minutes of fame is going to last; I certainly don't take anything for granted. I guess that kind of money is one of the perks that come with a little popularity on the road.

TheCelebrityCafe.com, 2011

Match the questions on the right with the answers in the text. Write the appropriate letter in the spaces provided.

1. [ ]

2. [ ]

3. [ ]

4. [ ]

A. How did you learn to make puppets, and why not Peanut?

B. How did you learn to make such jokes, especially Peanut's?

C. How do you come up with such original and chaotic characters?

D. How do you think of such chaotic ideas?

E. How does it feel to be considered the highest-grossing comedian in the U.S.?

F. How does it feel to be so popular?

G. What were you like as a kid?

H. Why did you take up such a hobby?

Finding concrete evidence (HL only)

Sometimes you are asked to find evidence in the text that supports a certain interpretation. For you to justify an interpretation by locating evidence or key phrases, you have to read the question carefully, understand it, and re-read the text to find the part that corresponds with the claim or interpretation specified in the question.

Example

The Other Hand is an ambitious and fearless gallop from the jungles of Africa via a shocking encounter on a Nigerian beach to the media offices of London and domesticity in leafy suburbia. Part-thriller, part-multicultural Aga saga, the book enmeshes its characters in the issues of immigration, globalisation, political violence and personal accountability. Lists of themes are often review-speak for "worthy but dull", but not in this case. Cleave immerses the reader in the worlds of his characters with an unshakable confidence that we will find them as gripping and vital as he does. Mostly, that confidence is justified.

The book begins in an immigration detention centre where Little Bee, a 16-year-old Ibo girl from Nigeria, has spent the last two years honing skills that point back to horrific past events and forward to a hoped-for future. Making herself look unattractive to men is the first of several mysterious threads that Cleave slowly winds in. Learning the Queen's English (from the quality broadsheets only, she specifies) has a more obvious relevance. "Excuse me for learning your language properly. I am here to tell you a real story. I did not come here to talk to you about the bright African colours."

The colours, when they come – on a beach in Nigeria – are certainly not bright. The route back to them begins with Little Bee's inadvertent escape from the centre with three women, variously cheerful, bewildered and suicidal, and a phone call to a columnist and journalist, Andrew O'Rourke. Little Bee encountered Andrew and his wife Sarah in Nigeria. Now he is dismayed to hear from her.

Lawrence Norfolk, *The Guardian*, 2008

Q: Norfolk compares *The Other Hand* to the way a motivated, daring horse runs. Which phrase in the text supports this statement?

✓ an ambitious and fearless gallop

> *The word 'gallop' is used to describe how a horse runs. Both motivated and daring are synonyms for ambitious and fearless. Should we include the rest of the sentence from 'from the jungles of Africa' to 'domesticity in leafy suburbia'? No. In such questions, only the relevant phrase is required. If you include extra or irrelevant parts, you will lose the mark.*

Q: Which phrase shows that the readers of the novel find the characters fascinating and dynamic?

✓ we will find them as gripping and vital

> *The comparative element of the original statement (as gripping … as he does) is of no importance and therefore should not be included in the answer. In addition, being immersed in the life of the characters does not mean the readers necessarily find them fascinating and dynamic.*

Q: Little Bee does her best to avoid the unwanted attention of men. Which phrase in the text supports this statement?

✓ making herself look unattractive to men

> *'horrific past events' is too general to point specifically to the unwanted attention of men.*

Q: Andrew O'Rourke does not want to renew Little Bee's acquaintance. Which phrase in the text supports this statement?

✓ he is dismayed to hear from her

> *'Dismayed' means 'saddened' or 'distraught'. Its meaning denotes lack of interest, even reluctance and discouragement. Its use shows that Andrew is no longer interested in knowing Little Bee.*

Activity

Extract 1

Nestled at the edge of the Torsa River delta on the border with Bhutan, and against the foothills of the mountain range that will become the mighty Himalayas, Totopara is happily isolated from much of the turbulence of the countries around it. The rains of the monsoon season regularly cut the village off by road, and the electricity supply is not yet so reliable as to seriously disturb the quiet.

The Toto speak their own language, a tongue that shares no close derivation with any of those spoken around — Nepali, Bengali, Hindi or Bhutanese. But the Toto people fear their language, and with it, their culture, history and way of life, is being lost, consumed by an education system that obliges their children to speak Bengali, and an economy that pushes them towards Hindi and English.

Ben Doherty, *The Age*, **2012**

Answer the following questions.

1. Which phrase in the first paragraph shows that countries surrounding Totopara suffer from unrest?

2. Toto is a language unlike other languages spoken in the same area in India. Which phrase in the second paragraph supports this claim?

3. Which word in the second paragraph tells us that children in Totopara are forced to speak Bengali?

Extract 2

The good news is that Canadian children's television, in particular, is frequently a source of good messages. A 2009 study of Canadian TV aimed at youth found that among shows aimed at preschoolers, nearly half focused on social relationships, while a third focused on learning, with none focusing on fighting or violence. These themes did appear in Canadian programs aimed at kids ages 6–12, but represented only one in 10 shows: social relationships, adventure and learning were all found much more often. Canadian children's TV was also found to have a high level of ethnic diversity, with visible minorities represented at a level close to their actual numbers in Canada. Unfortunately, the same study found that fewer children's programs are being made in Canada, falling from half of all kids' programming broadcast in Canada in the 1990s to roughly a third in 2009.

MediaSmarts

Answer the following questions.

1. Fighting and violence appear in Canadian children's TV shows. True or false? Justify your answer.

2. Good messages appear more than negative ones in children shows. Which phrase in the text supports this claim?

3. Representation of ethnic minorities in children's shows is:

    A. high

    B. visible

    C. diverse

    D. accurate

4. Since 2009, the number of children shows produced in Canada has:

    A. doubled

    B. decreased

    C. increased

    D. tripled

Jumping to logical conclusions (HL only)

Inference is making a logical deduction or assumption. The answer is not readily available in the text, but it is alluded to. Therefore, read the question carefully before you decide on an answer. Inference questions come in different shapes: multiple choice questions, short answer questions, gap filling questions, etc.

Example

I did not have lofty dreams of coming to Harvard throughout my childhood. My prime exposure to the institution was the film 'Legally Blonde', which thankfully has not shaped the course of my life.

I applied to Harvard for practical reasons. The courses and professors are brilliant, it is widely respected, and there is funding available. I am sure many other British students have been in my predicament – with a masters offer that will help in the long-run, but financially cripple you in the short-term. In the US, 42 per cent of people repaying their student debt are between the ages of 30 and 50. I was incredibly lucky to receive a scholarship from the Kennedy Memorial Trust.

Jennifer Quigley-Jones, 2013

1. Jennifer's opinion of *Legally Blonde* is
   A. directly linked to her opinion of Harvard.
   B. hardly positive.   **B** ← - - - -
   C. mainly positive.
   D. detrimental to Jennifer's opinion of Harvard.

2. We infer from the second paragraph that some of those who do not receive scholarships are not as lucky as the author. Why?

   The author begins by listing funding as one of the reasons why she applied to Harvard. She goes on to explain how many students feel financially crippled in the short-term because they spend a big amount of time – approximately 20 years – after graduation repaying their student loans.

There is no connection between Jennifer's opinion of Harvard and her opinion of *Legally Blonde*. She merely mentions that her exposure to Harvard was through *Legally Blonde*. However, Jennifer does mention that the film, 'thankfully' has had little influence on the course of her life.

Activity

Read the texts below to answer the questions that follow each extract.

Extract 1

Few military films have been as successful
as 1986's *Top Gun*. It stars Tom Cruise as
Maverick, a US Navy pilot, and it features
dazzling aerial footage that kept audiences
5 coming back for more, eventually making
it the highest-grossing film of the year.
Just as he had done three years earlier in *Risky
Business*, Cruise popularized another
line of Ray-Ban sunglasses, the Aviator.

CNBC, 2013

1. 'Few military films have been as successful
   as 1986's *Top Gun*' (lines 1 and 2). What does
   this tell us about the remaining military films
   that were produced in 1986?

2. *Top Gun* was 'the highest-grossing film of the
   year' (line 6). This means that other films:

   A. made more money than *Top Gun*.

   B. were more popular than *Top Gun*.

   C. were less popular than *Top Gun*.

   D. made less money than *Top Gun*.

3. The Ray-Ban glasses shown in *Risky Business*
   sold well. True or false? Justify your answer.

Extract 2

None of them knew the color of the sky. Their
eyes glanced level, and were fastened upon the
waves that swept towards them. These waves
were of the hue of slate, save for the tops, which
5 were of foaming white, and all of the men knew
the colors of the sea. The horizon narrowed and
widened, and dipped and rose, and at all times
its edge was jagged with waves that seemed
thrust up in points like rocks.

Stephen Crane, 'The Open Boat'

1. From the description of the scene above,
   what was the colour of the sky?

2. What is inferred from 'all of the men knew
   the colors of the sea' (lines 5 and 6)?

Extract 3

And the research also found a downside to the
switch of childcare duties from women to men,
with almost one in five stay-at-home fathers
saying that their role makes them feel 'less of a
5 man', while around one in eight admitted that
looking after children is harder than holding
down a job.

Steve Doughty, *Daily Mail*, 2011

1. Around 80% of stay-at-home fathers do not
   feel their role affects the way they regard
   themselves. True or false? Justify your answer.

2. Approximately 12% of stay-at-home fathers
   considered 'looking after children [...] harder
   than holding down a job' (lines 6 and 7). What
   does this tell us about the remaining 88%?

Showing appreciation (HL only)

Appreciation of a literary work in Paper 1 is shown through
demonstrating understanding of literary features. You will be asked
to demonstrate understanding of imagery, tone, theme, and plot
sequence without necessarily using those words. A word of warning:
when reading a literary text in Paper 1, always remember that literary
analysis and criticism are not required. Even if you know the literary
work, do not rely on previous knowledge of the text. Your answers
should come from the excerpt in front of you; therefore, be sure to
read the passage carefully to answer the questions.

Example

'You will not find your father greatly changed,' remarked Lady Moping, as the car turned into the gates of the County Asylum.

'Will he be wearing a uniform?' asked Angela,

5 "No, dear, of course not. He is receiving the very best attention.'

It was Angela's first visit and it was being made at her own suggestion.

Ten years had passed since the showery day in late

10 summer when Lord Moping had been taken away; a day of confused but bitter memories for her; the day of Lady Moping's annual garden party, always bitter, confused that day by the caprice of the weather which, remaining clear and brilliant with promise until

15 the arrival of the first guests, had suddenly blackened into a squall. There had been a scuttle for cover; the marquee had capsized; a frantic carrying of cushions and chairs; a table-cloth lofted to the boughs of the monkey-puzzler, fluttering in the rain; a bright period

20 and the cautious emergence of guests on to the soggy lawns; another squall; another twenty minutes of sunshine. It had been an abominable afternoon, culminating at about six o'clock in her father's attempted suicide.

25 Lord Moping habitually threatened suicide on the occasion of the garden party; that year he had been found black in the face, hanging by his braces in the orangery; some neighbours, who were sheltering there from the rain, set him on his feet again, and

30 before dinner a van had called for him. Since then Lady Moping had paid seasonal calls at the asylum and returned in time for tea, rather reticent of her experience.

Evelyn Waugh, *Mr. Loveday's Little Outing*, 1935

1. Which words are used to describe the day Lord Moping attempted suicide?

    ✓ confused and bitter

    > *Lord Moping attempted suicide the same day on which Lady Moping held her yearly garden party. The author describes the day as always bitter because of the garden party and confused because the weather turned from sunny to stormy all of a sudden.*

2. From the description of the weather on the day Lord Moping attempted to take his own life, we understand that this suicide attempt was:

    a. planned

    b. impetuous

    c. bitter

    d. irresponsible

    B

    > The sudden change in the weather suggests that the suicide attempt was an impulsive act. Although Lord Moping has always threatened to commit suicide during Lady Moping's garden party, the use of the word 'habitually' suggests that the recurrence of the threat has rendered it ordinary rather than planned.

3. Which word between lines 26 and 33 shows that Lady Moping did not speak about her visits to the asylum?

    ✓ reticent

    > *The first part of the paragraph is devoted to describing how Lord Moping was found. 'Since then' – since the incident or the suicide attempt – Lady Moping pays seasonal (periodic or regular) visits to the asylum, does not stay long (she is usually home by teatime) and is reticent (quiet, reserved) about the visit.*

Activity

Extract 1

As long ago as 1860 it was the proper thing to
be born at home. At present, so I am told, the
high gods of medicine have decreed that the
first cries of the young shall be uttered upon the
5 anaesthetic air of a hospital, preferably
a fashionable one. So young Mr. and
Mrs. Roger Button were fifty years ahead
of style when they decided, one day in the
summer of 1860, that their first baby should be
10 born in a hospital. Whether this anachronism
had any bearing upon the astonishing history I
am about to set down will never be known.

I shall tell you what occurred, and let you judge
for yourself.

15 The Roger Buttons held an enviable position,
both social and financial, in ante-bellum
Baltimore. They were related to the This
Family and the That Family, which, as every
Southerner knew, entitled them to membership
20 in that enormous peerage which largely
populated the Confederacy. This was their
first experience with the charming old custom
of having babies—Mr. Button was naturally
nervous. He hoped it would be a boy so that he
25 could be sent to Yale College in Connecticut, at
which institution Mr. Button himself had been
known for four years by the somewhat obvious
nickname of "Cuff."

On the September morning consecrated to
30 the enormous event he arose nervously at six
o'clock dressed himself, adjusted an impeccable
stock, and hurried forth through the streets of
Baltimore to the hospital, to determine whether
the darkness of the night had borne in new life
35 upon its bosom.

When he was approximately a hundred yards
from the Maryland Private Hospital for Ladies
and Gentlemen he saw Doctor Keene, the
family physician, descending the front steps,
40 rubbing his hands together with a washing
movement—as all doctors are required to do by
the unwritten ethics of their profession.

Mr. Roger Button, the president of Roger
Button & Co., Wholesale Hardware, began
45 to run toward Doctor Keene with much less
dignity than was expected from a Southern
gentleman of that picturesque period. "Doctor
Keene!" he called. "Oh, Doctor Keene!"

The doctor heard him, faced around, and stood
50 waiting, a curious expression settling on his
harsh, medicinal face as Mr. Button drew near.

"What happened?" demanded Mr. Button, as
he came up in a gasping rush. "What was it?
How is she? A boy? Who is it? What—"

55 "Talk sense!" said Doctor Keene sharply, He
appeared somewhat irritated.

"Is the child born?" begged Mr. Button.

Doctor Keene frowned. "Why, yes, I suppose
so—after a fashion." Again he threw a curious
60 glance at Mr. Button.

"Is my wife all right?"

"Yes."

"Is it a boy or a girl?"

"Here now!" cried Doctor Keene in a perfect
65 passion of irritation, "I'll ask you to go and see
for yourself. Outrageous!"

F. Scott Fitzgerald, *The Curious Case of*
Benjamin Button

Answer the following questions.

1. It is trendy to give birth in a hospital.
   What kind of hospital should it be according
   to the author?

2. Which phrase between lines 1 and 13 proves
   that the Buttons were pro modernisation?

3. How does the author describe the Buttons'
   decision to have their baby in a hospital
   between lines 1 and 13?

4. 'This Family' and 'That Family' (lines 17 and 18)
   are capitalised to emphasize:

   A. the relationship of those families
      with the Buttons.

   B. the undesirable social standard of
      those families.

   C. the importance of those families in
      the social hierarchy.

   D. the connection between those families and
      the Confederacy.

5. Which word between lines 16 and 29 shows that Mr Button's nickname was directly related to his last name?

6. What is the 'enormous event' (line 30)?

7. Doctors in Baltimore at the time were officially required to rub their hands. True or false? Justify your answer.

8. How is the second half of the nineteenth century described between lines 36 and 48?

9. The author describes the birth of the Buttons' baby as 'astonishing' in line 11. Find three other words or phrases between lines 49 and 66 that show there was something wrong with the baby.

Extract 2

Months afterward the hope within me struggled to a reluctant death, and I found myself without an ambition. But I was ashamed to go home. I was in Cincinnati, and I set to
5 work to map out a new career. I had been reading about the recent exploration of the river Amazon by an expedition sent out by our government. It was said that the expedition, owing to difficulties, had not thoroughly
10 explored a part of the country lying about the head-waters, some four thousand miles from the mouth of the river. It was only about fifteen hundred miles from Cincinnati to New Orleans, where I could doubtless get a ship. I
15 had thirty dollars left; I would go and complete the exploration of the Amazon. This was all the thought I gave to the subject. I never was great in matters of detail. I packed my valise, and took passage on an ancient tub called the
20 'Paul Jones,' for New Orleans. For the sum of sixteen dollars I had the scarred and tarnished splendors of 'her' main saloon principally to myself, for she was not a creature to attract the eye of wiser travelers.
25 When we presently got under way and went poking down the broad Ohio, I became a new being, and the subject of my own admiration. I was a traveler! A word never had

tasted so good in my mouth before.
30 I had an exultant sense of being bound for mysterious lands and distant climes which I never have felt in so uplifting a degree since. I was in such a glorified condition that all ignoble feelings departed out of me, and I was able
35 to look down and pity the untraveled with a compassion that had hardly a trace of contempt in it. Still, when we stopped at villages and wood-yards, I could not help lolling carelessly upon the railings of the boiler deck to enjoy
40 the envy of the country boys on the bank. If they did not seem to discover me, I presently sneezed to attract their attention, or moved to a position where they could not help seeing me. And as soon as I knew they saw me I gaped and
45 stretched, and gave other signs of being mightily bored with traveling.

I kept my hat off all the time, and stayed where the wind and the sun could strike me, because I wanted to get the bronzed and weather-beaten
50 look of an old traveler. Before the second day was half gone I experienced a joy which filled me with the purest gratitude; for I saw that the skin had begun to blister and peel off my face and neck. I wished that the boys and girls at
55 home could see me now.

Mark Twain, *Life on the Mississippi*

1. Which feeling prevented the narrator from returning home?

2. Which phrase between lines 1 and 25 shows that the narrator has not thoroughly planned out his expedition?

3. To whom or what does 'she' in 'she was not a creature' (line 24) refer?

4. Give one word that describes the narrator's utter joy at becoming a traveller as mentioned between lines 26 and 38.

5. Between lines 26 and 38, what are the narrator's feelings towards those who do not travel?

6. Give two actions the narrator does to attract the attention of the country boys standing on the bank?

7. Why does the narrator purposefully sit in the sun?

Rules... NOT made to be broken!

1. Read the questions carefully before you attempt to answer. Highlight what the question is asking you to do to remain focused.

2. Do **not** rely on subject knowledge when answering Paper 1 questions. All the answers are either found or can be inferred from the text(s).

3. Write legibly. You will not be given the benefit of the doubt if the examiner cannot read what you have written.

4. Be precise and concise. When asked for a word, provide only one word. When asked for a phrase, do not copy the whole sentence in the hope that part of it may include the required answer; this will surely cost you the mark.

   Always remember that better communication does not only entail ability to answer comprehension questions, but also includes improving speaking and writing. When your vocabulary base expands and your knowledge of grammar and sentence structures improves, you will be able to understand writing prompts better and to respond coherently when communicating orally in English.

Writing to convince

Paper 2 SL and Paper 2 HL Section A

In Paper 2 at both levels, you are asked to respond to a writing prompt. The aim is to assess your ability to communicate accurately and effectively in writing for a variety of purposes. Paper 2 HL Section A and Paper 2 SL are based on the options:

- Cultural diversity
- Customs and traditions
- Health
- Leisure
- Science and technology

There will be five tasks, each requiring you to respond using a different type of text such as a formal letter or a report. Each task is based on a different option. You must choose one of the five tasks. You are expected to write 250–400 words. To do this successfully, you will need to identify the purpose of the task in order to use register and style appropriate to the specified text type and audience. To achieve this you must be able to:

- use language accurately and appropriately
- develop and organize ideas relevant to the task and produce the features of the required text type correctly.

Text types

Paper 2 requires you to produce text types from the following list:

- article
- blog/diary entry
- brochure, leaflet, flyer, pamphlet, advertisement
- essay (SL only)
- interview
- introduction to debate, speech, talk, presentation
- news report
- official report
- proposal (HL only)
- review
- set of instructions, guidelines
- written correspondence (letters and emails)

Exam tip ✓

You do not have to limit yourself to the options you have studied in class. If there is a task you know you can confidently address, in terms of content, audience and text type, do it.

The assessments for Paper 2 SL and Paper 2 HL Section A are each out of 25 marks. The following criteria will be used to assess your work:

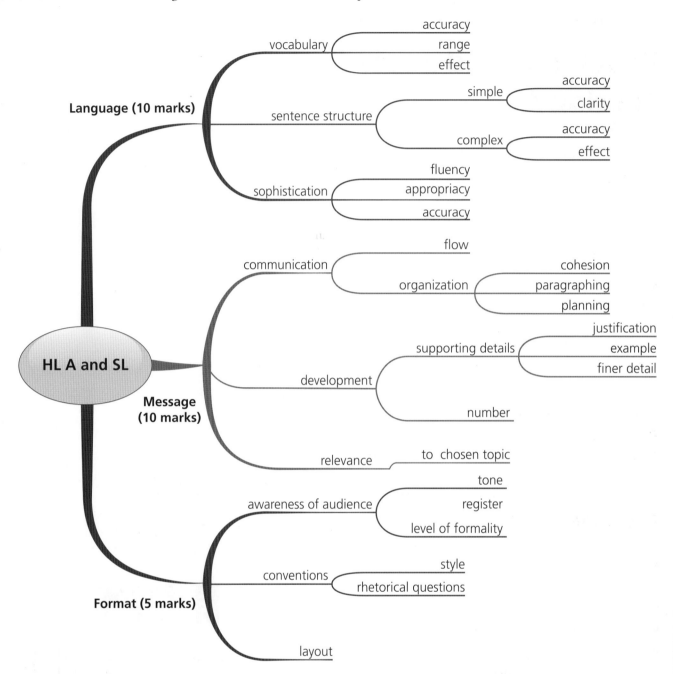

Skills

Skills for thinking: generating and organizing ideas

Make sure you understand the topic about which you are writing. Remember that in Paper 2 you have five prompts, one for each option topic. Choose the prompt for which you are able to formulate the best answer. Here are some questions to help you to decide.

- Do I know enough about the subject matter?
- Do I have the necessary vocabulary?
- Do I understand the purpose of the text?
- Can I handle the features of the text type?
- Can I use the appropriate register?

Look at the practice examinations on page 199 of Chapter 7. Which prompt can you best answer?

Before you even think about starting to write, you will need to brainstorm ideas. To be successful, you must be able to do this quickly and efficiently. There are only 90 minutes in the exam, and at HL in Section B you will also have to write a personal response of between 150 and 250 words in that time.

The purpose of note-taking is to develop enough first thoughts and to help you organize them clearly. You may feel you can just jot down your notes and points. However, as you think about the prompt, you may wish to use mental models such as mindmaps or spider diagrams in order to arrange your ideas as clearly as possible.

Using mental models

Whatever the topic, your text will always need a structure. For example, a set of instructions are set out in a timeline. More complex, thesis-driven texts use ideas to guide your reader along a specific path. In the section below you will find different ways of organizing your ideas using a variety of diagrams. These 'thought pictures' can help you plan your ideas more clearly, and are known as mental models.

Look at each example, and practise making notes using each mental model.

Defining the subject matter

Some tasks require you to define the subject and work out the features of the subject. A definition can be represented like this.

> **Sample question: Science and technology**
>
> Write a review to be published in your school magazine about a film that discusses the importance of technology in our daily lives.

Look at the question, find a suitable film to discuss, and make notes on it in preparation for writing a review.

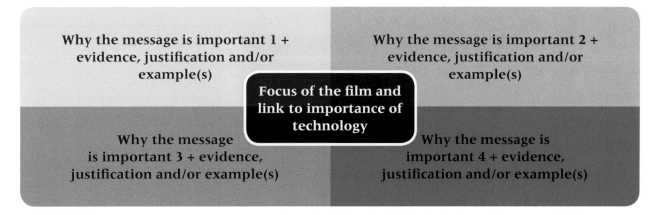

This technique can also be adapted to:

- book reviews
- descriptions of people and/or characters
- descriptions of places
- outlining a problem.

Describing organizations

This method of organization puts the most important item at the top and then subdivides it into different categories and sub-categories.

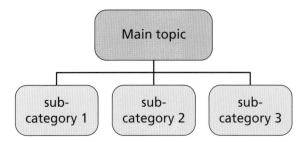

Look at the question on leisure and make notes on the main topic and its sub-categories: buildings, attractions and events. Make notes on each of the sub-categories in preparation for writing a feature article.

Hint: Each sub-category could become a paragraph in your article.

Sample question: Leisure

Write a feature article for your town's tourist magazine persuading tourists to come and visit.

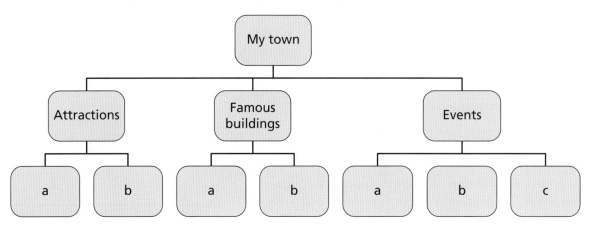

This technique can also be used for:

- describing institutions of any kind
- describing families

Making comparisons

In this kind of task you need to put two concepts side by side and find characteristics that can be compared. These characteristics can be similarities or differences, or both. A diagram can look like this:

	A	B
Characteristic 1		
Characteristic 2		
Characteristic 3		
Characteristic 4		

Sample question: Cultural diversity

Interview a psychologist to establish similarities and differences in cultural attitudes between teenagers and adults. Write an article based on this interview to be published in your school magazine.

Use the table to make notes on adults' and teenagers' attitudes towards the categories below. Comment on your findings.

	Adults	Teenagers
Money		
Clothes		
Leisure		
Relationships		

This technique can also be used for writing about:

- advantages and disadvantages
- positive and negative points
- agreeing and disagreeing with an idea.

Narratives and sets of instructions

Both these kinds of writing tend to be chronological. Therefore they can be represented by a timeline.

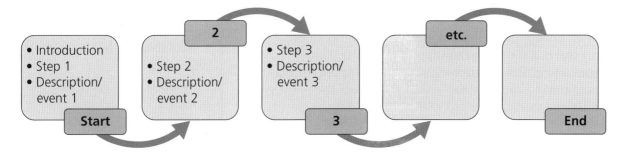

Use the flow chart to map out the events you have witnessed. First write an outline of the action, or the events, or stages that you want to write about. Make it a short list of bullet points and add descriptive detail or comments as you go along.

Alternatively, write ideas out on scraps of paper, and shift them around until you get the order right. Lastly, arrange the points in a final, logical sequence so as to make your narrative coherent and comprehensible.

This technique can also be used for:

- narratives of any kind
- a flow chart for the organization of an event
- sets of 'how to' instructions
- a production process
- a set of guidelines.

> **Sample question: Customs and traditions**
>
> Write a letter to a friend in which you describe the events that took place at a recent festival.

Describing routines

Some tasks require you to describe routines or cycles. In other words they start and develop but end up in (almost) the same place they started. These cycles differ from narratives which start in one place but end in another.

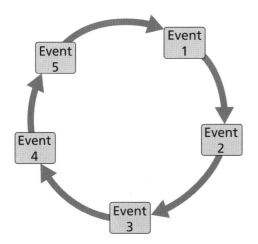

Look at the sample question on leisure and use the diagram to make notes on key moments in the year. Add descriptive detail to each point. Complete your planning by choose a favourite time of the year and explaining your choice.

This technique can also be used for:

- daily/weekly/monthly routines
- describing natural cycles
- an annual event.

Constructing an argument

The strength of any kind of argument rests on the ability of the writer to construct a thesis and make valid supporting points. Plan an answer to the science and technology question opposite. Support your points with evidence, and explain how the evidence explains the point you are making. Having made a series of valid points, it may be necessary for you to rearrange your supporting points into the best order.

MY BIG IDEA
Point A
evidence/example/explanation
Point B
evidence/example/explanation
Point C
evidence/example/explanation

This technique could also be used for:

- identifying a problem and finding solutions
- writing a short report on an issue
- nominating a person for an award
- Paper 2 (HL) Section B, the personal response.

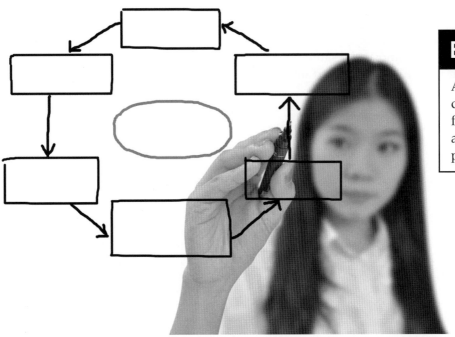

> **Sample question: Leisure**
>
> Write a magazine article describing the natural beauty of your area during the different seasons of the year.

> **Sample question: Science and technology**
>
> There is a meeting against the building of a new nuclear power plant in your vicinity. Write a speech opposing or defending its construction.

> **Exam tip** ✓
>
> Any of the these methods can also be applied to the first draft of the written assignment, or even used in planning your extended essay.

Skills for thinking: writers, audiences and communicative purpose

Writing texts aimed at a specific audience is a very sophisticated task. In English B, you are expected to undertake such writing tasks in your second language. While this might sound difficult, every writing task, like every journey, can be broken down into stages. Once you realize that this task can be planned *before* you start writing, your job will be much more manageable. Here are some steps to follow.

First of all, consider the three elements of the process:

- Your role as the writer of the text
- The audience you are writing to
- The reasons for writing – the purpose of the text

Your role as writer

As an English B student, you will often find yourself writing tasks that require you to pretend to be a specific character, an **implied identity**. For example, you may write a letter of complaint, a feature article or a topical news report. In such instances, you are asked to play a role. Your **implied identity** could be that of an angry member of the public, a journalist, or a technical writer.

Audience

Just as you must assume an identity, you must write your text to an **implied (imaginary) audience**. For example, you could be writing a formal report for a committee or a letter to an editor. You need to choose the appropriate register to make your written English appropriate for your audience. However, as you are writing within the context of the IB Diploma Programme you are also writing for your teacher and examiner (as well as for the imaginary audience). The job of the real audience (your teacher/the examiner) is to assess you on the standard of your work!

Purpose

All messages have at least one communicative purpose. Make sure you understand the purpose of the text you are writing. Here are some of the most obvious ones:

- advise on
- apologise for
- comment on
- complain about
- describe
- enquire about
- explain
- instruct
- narrate
- persuade
- request
- suggest

Activity

Below are some sample Paper 2 questions. Identify the **implied role** of the writer, the **implied audience** and the **communicative purpose** of each text.

1. Four robbers with guns burst into a bank and rob it. As the police officer in charge of the case, write a report of the incident.

2. You are the principal speaker in a school debate in which the motion is: 'Technology is heading in the wrong direction and concentrating on the wrong problems'. Write the text of your speech either agreeing or disagreeing with this motion.

3. Your school needs a new building for after-school clubs and similar activities. Submit a proposal to local business people appealing for financial support. Explain how the building would help solve some of the problems faced by young people.

4. You have been asked by the editor of your school newspaper to write a review of a recent thought-provoking film. Write your review.

5. A travel agency in your hometown or city is running a competition to encourage tourists to visit. Entrants have to write a feature article about the town. Write your article.

Task	Implied author	Communicative purpose	Implied audience
1			
2			
3			
4			

Skills for writing: texts types, features and language

Consider the next two points.

1. What text type are you writing?

2. What are the structural features of that text type?

Text types

In the next section you will find detailed descriptions and analyses of the different text types and their structural features. For the moment, test yourself. Fill as much detail as you can about the specific or unique features of these text types in the chart below. Note the information that you will need to go under each heading.

For example, a newspaper report is:

Text type	Definition	Unique features
Newspaper reports	A short account of the news; basically factual. Audience: newspaper readers who, depending on the type of newspaper, could range from a very specific audience to the general public.	• A lead paragraph: the five Ws (what, when, where, who, why) • Explanatory paragraphs • Background paragraphs • Final paragraph

Text type	Definition	Unique features
Advertising copy		
Blogs		
Brochures/pamphlets		
Diary entries		
Essays		
Feature articles		
Formal written correspondence		
Interviews		
Leaflets/flyers		
Official reports		
Personal letters/emails		
Proposals		
Reviews		
Sets of instructions/ guidelines		
Speeches/talks/ introductions to debates/ presentations		

Language

Once you have decided which question to answer and you have worked out the structure of the information you want to communicate, think about the style.

- How will you address your reader properly? Have you used the correct level of formality?
- How will you choose the right vocabulary appropriate to the text type?

In the box below you can see the possible relationships between different types of written texts and language choice.

	Personal communication	Mass communication	Professional communication
Examples	• Personal letter • Diary • Blogs* • Personal advice	• News reports • Feature articles • Interviews • Reviews • Brochures and pamphlets • Guidelines • Advertisement	• Report • Formal letter • Proposal • Essay • Speech†
Relationship between writer and audience	• Personal	• Can be formal or informal depending on text and purpose	• Always formal

| Register and vocabulary | • Combination of narrative explanation and description
• Frequent use of language involving emotions and perceptions | • Depends on text type, purpose and relationship in the text between writer and audience (informal, formal, personal, etc.)
• Topic-based vocabulary | • Unemotional, formal, factual use of logical argument
• Formal and technical vocabulary |

* Blogs can have the features of both personal and mass communication.

† Depending on context, a speech can be a formal address, a talk to your classmates, an introduction to a debate or a presentation. Determine who your audience is to choose the level of formality required.

Activity

Look at the following tasks and make decisions about the kind of language that you may choose to use.

1. A meeting has been arranged which will be attended by supporters and opponents of a proposal to build a home for the elderly in your area. You have strong views on this issue. Write a speech to be delivered at the meeting.

2. A well-known charity has decided to pay the expenses of one student from your school to do work in another country. Write a letter of application.

3. An alumnus of your school has become famous because of his/her achievements and is visiting your campus. You interviewed him/her. Write an article based on this interview to be published in your school magazine.

4. In a film you have recently seen, there are two characters who are from very different cultures from one another. Write a blog discussing the contrast between those characters.

5. When meeting people from other cultures, we have all had embarrassing moments which often have unexpected results. Write a diary entry of such an incident.

6. Write a magazine feature article: 'Leisure activities are a waste of time and money; we should use every spare moment on work, study or helping others'.

	What is the relationship between writer and audience?	What is the appropriate register and address system?	What vocabulary is used? Give examples.
1.			
2.			
3.			
4.			
5.			
6.			

Skills for communicating: the writing process

Writing a first draft

Before you write, make sure that you know where you and your text are going. Think about the overall structure of your text. Here are three separate structures for writing:

- **Narrative-driven texts:** tell a story, explain the background and the significance of the events
- **Problem-driven texts:** set out a problem, explain the details and offer a solution
- **Thesis-driven texts:** start with an answer to a problem, justify the answer with evidence and make a final point

> **Writing tip**
> Some text types can use more than one kind of structure. The important thing is to plan clearly using one of the three structures.

Text planning

	Narrative-driven texts	Problem-driven texts	Thesis-driven texts
Examples of English B text types	1. Instructions 2. Diary entries	1. Reports 2. Feature articles 3. Interviews 4. Guidelines 5. Letters of application	1. Essays 2. Proposals 3. Reviews 4. Letters of complaints
Opening	• Start by describing the setting or the context for the story: where and when. • If the story has a point, you could state the problem or puzzle	• You can start by describing the context and then explain the issue or the problem. • Sometimes you can state the problem in the headline or title.	• In thesis-driven writing, you state the context or issue and then state your thesis statement in the opening.
Content **Body paragraph 1** **Body paragraph 2** **Body paragraph 3** **Body paragraph 4** **etc.**	Explain: • how the conflict or issue started. • how it developed. • how it reached a climax. • what happened afterwards.	The body of the text analyses the problem. You can: • define the problem and identify different causes and solutions. • break the main problem into smaller components.	• Use the body paragraphs to support your thesis statement. • Each paragraph will make a point, contain evidence for the point and an explanation while linking your evidence to the supporting point.
Structure	• Divide the narrative and ideas into logical sequence. • One clearly stated section per paragraph.	• One clearly stated idea per paragraph. • After you have described each element of the problem, give a solution to each.	• One clearly stated idea per paragraph. • Organize the paragraphs into the best possible order. (e.g. weakest to strongest).

Ending	• State the point of the story. This could be a truth or some aspect of human nature.	• Close by explaining either the benefits or the limitations of your solution.	• Restate the thesis and give a final thought.
			• You might want to add a final thought. e.g.
			  • Which point is the most/least convincing?
			  • Will the situation remain the same? Are your ideas based on logic or emotion?

Activity

Look at the following questions. Which structure should you use for each? Having decided, plan your opening, body paragraphs, and ending.

1. You are the secretary of a school committee established to research students' attitudes to the problem of litter. The Principal asked you to report to the school's governing body, describing the present situation and recommending any changes that should be made.

2. A well-known educational foundation has decided to pay the expenses of one student from your school to do a gap year project in another country. You are interested. Write a letter of application to the foundation.

3. A well-known actor or actress visited your school to promote a humanitarian cause. Write a blog entry of the events.

4. A new community centre in your area boasts that it has 'something for everyone'. Write a promotional brochure aimed at young people.

5. Write an essay examining the statement: 'Wars would never happen if women were in leadership positions'.

6. You are concerned about the problem of traffic congestion in your town. People seem to park without any thought for others living in the area. Write a letter to the editor of the local newspaper, explaining the problem and suggesting solutions.

Having planned a number of Paper 2 answers, write one.

Exam tip

Body paragraphs

Divide your text into a series of sections with supporting material. Each of these points should help you to communicate your purpose to your intended audience. If you are writing a thesis- or problem-driven text, such as a report or a speech, you might give each paragraph a *topic sentence*. This will help the readers (and examiners) to focus on the main idea of each of your points. The topic sentence can come at the beginning or end of a paragraph.

Your ideas within a text should also flow. This can be done through the use of **connecting devices**. It is amazing what a difference the odd 'so' or 'as a result' can make to the quality of your writing.

Self-assessment skills sheet – first draft

Once you have completed the first draft of your answer, use the
self-assessment sheet below to assess your writing for its strengths
and weaknesses.

Name:		Date:	
Title of assignment:		Draft #:	

Message and text type	Inadequate	Adequate	Good	Very Good	Excellent
Use of text type					
Developed ideas/content					
Clear purpose					
Appropriate to the audience					

Organization	Inadequate	Adequate	Good	Very Good	Excellent
Introduction					
Thesis/main idea					
Suitable structure/ paragraph format					
Use of topic sentences/ headings					
Use of examples/quotes					
Conclusion/final thought					

Language	Inadequate	Adequate	Good	Very Good	Excellent
Grammar					
Punctuation and spelling					
Appropriate register for audience					
Appropriate vocabulary					
Well-connected sentences					

Comments:
My targets for next draft
Message and text type:
Organization:
Language:
Time management:

Proofreading and redrafting

Professional writers write many drafts before they allow a document to stand. You should write at least three drafts: a rough first draft, a second draft, and your final draft. Our three tips are: 'Reread! Check! Rewrite!' Be prepared to rewrite even the final draft.

- **Read aloud.** Reading aloud forces you to pay attention to each word. You may hear when the grammar, idiom or vocabulary 'sound wrong'. When you hear your work aloud you can usually hear if there is something wrong with the grammar and syntax. If your text does not 'sound right', fix the sentence.

- **Give yourself some distance.** If possible, leave a day between finishing your first draft and further versions of your text.

Writing the final draft

Now write the final draft. This should be the version that you wish to hand in. Read your work carefully and check everything one more time for sense and errors before you hand it in.

> Some young musicians asked a famous West African musician what advice he would give them. 'I can give you three tips,' he said. 'My first tip is: Practice. My second tip is practice, and my third tip is practice.'

> 'I'm not a very good writer, but I'm an excellent rewriter.'
> **James Michener**

Text types

Why you need to understand text types in English B

You need to be able to understand, analyse and use different types of writing in English. One way of classifying writing is by text type. A text type is a piece of writing that has a specific format, structure, audience and purpose. In English B, there are two tasks that will assess your ability to handle specific text types:

- Paper 2 HL Section A; Paper 2 SL

- The written assignment

As you grow more confident you will discover that there are many ways to write different text types. The advice given here will help you to learn the basics of writing for Paper 2. The ideas are not prescriptive. In time, once you are more confident and more experienced, you may wish to organize and express your ideas in other ways that suit your personal writing style better. However, for the moment the most important thing is to communicate clearly and accurately in your English B assessments.

For the purposes of this guide the text types are divided up into five categories:

Making a point	Personal writing	Journalism	Informative and persuasive texts	Professional texts
• Argumentative essays • Short speeches	• Diaries • Guidance and advice • Personal letters • Blogs	• News reports • Magazine articles • Interviews • Reviews	• Instructions • Leaflets, flyers and brochures • Advertising copy	• Reports • Proposals • Formal correspondence

Making a point: text type – essay (SL only)

What is an essay?

An essay is a piece of writing in which you can state your organized thoughts about a topic. The essay is an essential tool in school and for scoring highly in IB examinations and coursework. Well-written, well-organized essays get good marks. Therefore, you must learn to communicate your ideas clearly and persuade your audience that your opinions and facts are reliable. It follows that badly written, disorganized scripts score badly.

Writing to a specific audience

Decide if your essay is to be formal and academic, or personal and anecdotal.

If the essay question requires you to write about an idea, use the third person. Therefore do not write about 'I', 'we' or 'you'. You will need to use a formal **thesis-driven structure** and will almost certainly need to cite evidence: facts and figures, and use technical language to validate your opinions.

You can create a more personal and humorous tone through the use a first-person narrative. For this kind of **narrative-driven essay** you may wish to make a point and to relate a personal experience or anecdote. At the end it is usual to explain how this made you come to some conclusion. This kind of essay does not necessarily have a thesis: it may have an opening statement and only come to a conclusion at the end. (For more about this kind of writing, see the section on blogs on pages 73 to 77)

Length

While an extended essay may be anywhere between 3,500 and 4,000 words, in Paper 2 (written production) 250 to 400 words will suffice and therefore your thesis-driven essay need only contain three or four supporting ideas.

The structure of three types of essay

	Narrative-driven essay	Thesis-driven essay	Problem-driven essay
Introduction	Setting the scene	Describing the context and stating the thesis	Describing the context and problem
Body	Narrative events leading to climax and resolution	Supporting points with evidence and explanation	Individual elements of the problem, each with its own solution
Conclusion	Point of the story	Restate the thesis	Offer an overall solution and evaluation

A thesis-driven essay could look like this:

- Question
- Introduction and thesis
- Supporting paragraph (1) with:
  - ▶ Point
  - ▶ Evidence
  - ▶ Explanation
    (Add additional supporting paragraphs as necessary)
- Conclusion/final thought

Tone and style

Cohesive devices and discourse markers (e.g. however, nevertheless, insofar as, etc.) help to connect sentences and ideas together, and lend coherence and cohesion to the written piece. Their appropriate use will help you structure your ideas and show how they are connected. The following web pages may help you determine which cohesive devices to use:

Exam tip ✓

You should try to use details and specific examples to make your ideas clear and convincing. In order to do this, remember the acronym **PEE**.

- **Point**
- **Example**
- **Explanation**
  = PEE

Learning English online at Warwick

http://www2.warwick.ac.uk/fac/soc/al/learning_english/leap/grammar/discourse/

BBC

http://www.bbc.co.uk/worldservice/learningenglish/flatmates/episode64/languagepoint.shtml
http://www.bbc.co.uk/worldservice/learningenglish/grammar/learnit/learnitv316.shtml

Oxford University Press

http://elt.oup.com/student/headway/advanced/a_grammar/unit04/?cc=jo&selLanguage=en

Essayzone.co.uk

http://www.essayzone.co.uk/blog/how-to-begin-a-new-paragraph-useful-linking-words-and-phrases/

Study Guides and Strategies

http://www.studygs.net/wrtstr6.htm

In writing, your tone conveys your attitude towards the topic. It is determined by the nature of the task, its implied audience, and your implied identity as writer. It can be garnered from the vocabulary you use and how you structure your sentences. When writing essays, your tone should be assertive but respectful. You are advised to avoid using provocative vocabulary and structures like 'those who believe in this are absolutely mad', for example.

Structure

Introduction

The first paragraph in an essay contains introductory sentences linked to the question. These could be an example, or a definition or an anecdote. The purpose of the opening sentences is to *grab the readers' attention* and to let them know you have something interesting to say on the subject. The introduction may include a *thesis* – a sentence which contains your main idea. A thesis is a provable statement related to the essay question. It may be balanced or one-sided depending on the nature of the essay you are asked to write. The thesis provides the focus for your essay.

The main body

Divide your essay into a series of supporting points. Each of these points should help you to prove your thesis. Each point will focus on a single idea that supports your thesis. You should express each point clearly in a *topic sentence*. This will help the readers (and examiners) to focus on the main idea of each of your paragraphs. The topic sentence can be at the beginning or end of a paragraph.

Conclusion

In your conclusion you might want to add some sentences that emphasize the importance of the topic. State why your thesis is important. In addition you might want to add a final thought.

- Which of your supporting points are the most or least convincing?
- Do your arguments rely on logic, motion or sense perception? (TOK)
- Will the situation change or remain the same in the future?
- How do you feel personally about the subject?

Argumentative versus opinion essays

In Paper 2 SL, you may be asked to write an argumentative or an opinion essay. Argumentative essays require you to write both sides of the topic: for and against, pros and cons, advantages and disadvantages, etc. Conversely, opinion essays require that you state your opinion clearly, and devote the body of the essay to support your opinion with evidence, examples and/or explanations. The figure below shows the organization of paragraphs in both argumentative and opinion essays.

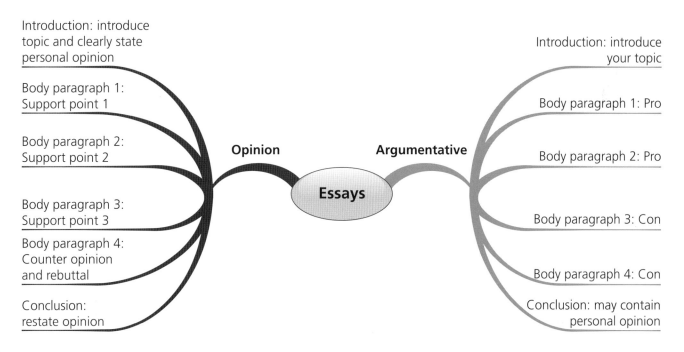

Sometimes, you may mention more than one counter opinion in an opinion essay. However, always make sure that you refute those opinions by mentioning why you think their opposite is more valid.

Sample essay

Animal Testing Has Many Advantages

Medical research involving animals has dramatically improved the health of the human race. Without animal testing, the cure for polio would not exist and diabetics would suffer or die from their disease. Despite those benefits, some people believe that animals should be not be used for testing medical techniques and drugs. This essay will outline the advantages of animal testing.

To begin with, animal testing allows scientists to test and create new drugs. Animals such as monkeys or rabbits have similar physical processes to humans. This allows scientists to test the effects of certain drugs. If a drug produces adverse effects in animals it is probably unfit for human use.

In addition, animal testing is cheap. There is a large supply of animals for medical research. Animals are easily bred, and maintained safely in controlled labs. The costs of testing in humans would be extremely high.

Many people argue that animal testing is cruel. In some cases this is true. However, it would be much crueler to test new drugs on people or children, or to let people die because there was not enough information about a drug. Furthermore, legislation in most countries sets standards for animal treatment, and laboratories have guidelines to prevent cruelty.

Opponents of animal research also say that information from animals does not apply to humans. They point to certain commercial drugs which have been withdrawn because of their side-effects on humans. While it is true that animal systems differ from human systems, there are enough similarities to apply information from animals to humans.

Animal rights campaigners claim that we do not need new tests because we already have vast amounts of information. However, many new deadly infections appear every year and new treatments and drugs are needed to combat these deadly plagues.

Animal testing is needed in the world we live in. Our responsibility is to manage the animals in our care and balance their suffering against the good that comes from them.

Writefix.com, 2013

Analysis

Read the sample on the previous page. Use the following questions to evaluate the essay.

Overview • Is the essay question clearly stated? • What is the thesis/main idea? • Is the conclusion clear? • Does the conclusion match the thesis?	
Structure • Are the paragraphs too long or too short? • What are the main ideas/topic sentences of each paragraph? • Is there a clear logical progression of ideas?	
Paragraphs • Is there evidence to back up each topic sentence? • Are there clear explanations of the evidence? • Are quotes (when needed) used properly?	
Sentences • Is the essay written in a formal style? • Is the meaning of each sentence clear? • Are the tenses correct? • Are sentences too long/too short? • Are the sentences clearly linked?	
Vocabulary • Is there much unnecessary repetition of vocabulary? • Has the writer used the correct vocabulary for the topic?	

Activity

Practise writing thesis-driven essays on the following topics. Plan your ideas before you start to write. You will need to think about the question, brainstorm ideas and decide what your thesis is.

Science and technology

• Is information technology now essential to society? (argumentative)

• Is it worth studying the natural sciences? (opinion)

• Can renewable energy solve our problems? (opinion)

• Are all forms of scientific research moral? (argumentative)

• The study of social sciences is more important than the natural sciences. (opinion)

Making a point: text type – speech

What is a speech?

A speech is addressed to a listening audience. The speaker wishes to make an impact, hold the attention of the audience and convince them of an idea. In order to achieve this, speakers use a variety of techniques that make their speeches convincing. In English B, you may be asked to write a speech, a talk, or an introduction to a longer one as part of a debate.

Writing to a specific audience

When writing a persuasive speech, you must decide what topic you are going to talk about. You must consider who will be listening to you and what aspects of your topic are best suited to meet the needs of your audience. Therefore, you need to consider the angle to best suit this group. Be clear about your purpose. Is it, for example, to persuade, inform, demonstrate, entertain, or welcome? Is it a combination of these functions?

Make sure you connect with your audience. Use direct address but be careful with the use of the pronouns. How you address your audience can radically affect your relationship with them. For example, there are two meanings of 'we'. 'We will solve this together' suggests partnership. On the other hand 'We give you the choice' suggests a distance between you and your audience with you having more power or being different. Which form of address is appropriate for your speech?

Types of speech

Here are four basic methods of arranging the body of your speech. Choose the one most appropriate for your needs.

- **Thesis-driven speeches. Big idea, evidence, final thought.** You have a point of view that you wish to prove.
- **Problem-driven speeches:**
  - ▶ **Cause, effect and solution.** You show event *A*. This results in *B*. This solution is *C*.
  - ▶ **Problem and solution.** You state the problem is *X* and the solution is *Y*.
  - ▶ **Advantage and disadvantage.** You examine the positive and negative aspects of an idea or event and come to a balanced conclusion.

Structure

Introduction

Firstly, greet your audience, grab their attention and make sure they understand the topic! You will then need to give a one sentence summary of your speech topic and your point of view or angle (thesis statement). For example, 'Green politics is no longer just a passing fashion, it is a necessity'. You also want to convince your audience that you have credibility – the right to speak on the topic. You can do this by citing your qualifications or expertise. Next, briefly outline the key points (topic sentences) you are going to cover. Explain the benefit for the audience. What's in your speech for them? Why will they want to hear what you have got to tell them?

The main body

The main body of your speech may well look like an essay or a reasoned argument. It will contain supporting paragraphs with topic sentences (key points), supporting examples or evidence and explanations (see essay section, pages 53 to 57).

Conclusion

This might contain a summary of your key ideas. You can do this by re-stating your thesis statement or question, then restating the key ideas from the body of your speech. Remember to restate the benefit of your ideas to your audience, and end with a bang not a whimper!

> The final sentence should be a clincher or call to action. For example, 'The 21st century awaits us. Let us confront its challenge with confidence, and together give our children the future they deserve' (Tony Blair, British Prime Minister, 1998).

Tone and style – rhetorical devices

The purpose of your speech is to persuade your audience that your ideas are correct and ensure the audience is on your side. Therefore, your tone should be assertive and friendly but still courteous and respectful. Some techniques speech writers use are:

- personal experience
- using statistics
- quoting experts
- lists of three (e.g. tired, hungry and ill OR overpopulation, poverty and unemployment)
- repetition (for emphasis purposes)
- rhetorical questions (you don't need to ask what they are, do you?)

Sample speeches

Speech A

Fellow students

Nowadays, whenever a phone rings, we see people frantically searching to see if it was their mobile that rang.

Mobile phones are everywhere. There are mobile phone adverts wherever we look. How often do we end up on public transport unavoidably listening to our neighbours' conversations? Do you really want to hear someone's latest sales pitch? Or hear the latest gossip about people you have never met? Or, worst of all, listen to sickly love-talk of boyfriend and girlfriend?

On top of all this mobile phones have also become giant money-eaters. People are obsessed with buying the latest phones. New ones come out at an unbelievable rate. And what about the cost of all the accessories? Can we really afford them?

This trend is absolutely unhealthy. Therefore, I believe mobile phones should be banned at school. There is absolutely no need for us to bring mobile phones to school. Are we prepared to deal with the problems in exchange for just a little more convenience?

Remember, mobile phones are not just for making old fashioned phone calls anymore; they have become super-convenient playthings. If we allow phones in school I am certain we will spend most of our time will be spent texting friends, playing Snake, checking e-mails, and being on Facebook. Learning will be forgotten.

If schools allow the bringing of mobile phones to school, they will be supporting this expensive, unhealthy and antisocial fashion.

Ask yourselves. Do we really need them? As students we are not expecting urgent phone calls from our clients overseas, or our brokers telling us when to buy and sell our shares. It is true we may need to make a phone call to our parents now and then. But if there is a genuine need to make an urgent phone call, can't we simply use the phones at school?

Here is the bottom line. There is absolutely no need for students to bring mobile phones to school. All they do is create more complicated and serious problems, problems which are definitely not justified by the minor convenience they bring.

Thank you.

Yannie Fu, 2000

Speech B

Sunday 12th June, 2011 marks the World Day Against Child Labour, and the Board, Management and Staff of The Ghana Cocoa Board (COCOBOD) join with others in the international community to highlight the continued and urgent need to combat exploitative child labour around the world, with a special emphasis on worst forms of child labour in the cocoa sector of Ghana.

It is an undeniable fact that the status of children across the world is a key indicator of whether or not progress is possible in a particular society. However, throughout the world, children continue to be disadvantaged in many ways, including through discrimination, limited access to schooling, and traditional roles that still relegate certain forms of work to children which are detrimental to their wholesome development.

As we mark this day, the Board and Management of COCOBOD categorically condemn the use of children as child labourers in no uncertain terms and will do all in its capacity to facilitate the prosecution of perpetrators of this act especially in cocoa sector. COCOBOD therefore wishes to entreat all cocoa farmers and caretakers to desist from the use of children under 18 years in hazardous work on their farms. Specifically, children should not be engaged in work that interferes in their education, affects their health, morals, safety and their holistic development.

We owe it to the children of today to help them realize their potential to become the adults of tomorrow; and to fully develop their talents and strengths at school rather than endure work which weakens and destroys that potential. We must therefore join in the fight against child labour to ensure they have the childhood to which they are entitled. And by doing so, we lay the foundations for them to have an adult life as full-fledged citizens living in dignity and contributing to the development of their society under decent working conditions.

Ladies and Gentlemen, I would finally like to reiterate COCOBOD Management's resolve to work closely with all stakeholders to eliminate the worst forms of child labour on cocoa farms, because COCOBOD believes that, with commitment from all stakeholders, the child labour elimination mission would be accomplished.

Ghana Cocoa Board, 2011

Analysis

	Essential questions	Speech A	Speech B
1.	Identify: • the audience • the topic • the purpose of the speech		
2.	Is the speech problem-driven or thesis-driven? Can you identify the key features of the structure?		
3.	What techniques does each speaker use?		
4.	What type of speech are they making?		
5.	What key points does the speaker make on the issue?		
6.	How well is each key point supported?		
7.	What is the logic behind the sequencing of the paragraphs?		
8.	Has the speaker written a convincing conclusion?		
9.	To what extent has the speaker used formal English which is clear and easy for the listeners to understand?		
10.	How successfully has the speaker connected with the audience?		
11.	Has the speaker used rhetorical devices?		
12.	How might the listeners react to the speaker's conclusions?		

In your opinion which speech is most effective?

Activity

1. Speech A was written more than ten years ago. Do you think the arguments are still valid? Would you use the same arguments today? Write a speech either supporting or opposing the use of mobile phones in your school today.

2. Practice speech writing on one of the debate topics given below:
   • Our obsession with the Internet is causing a breakdown of social values.

   • Hand-held devices and smart phones are an essential part of our lives. We cannot do without them.

   • Go Green! We must act now or it is our children who will suffer.

   • Subcultures should not be given the chance to thrive; people who look different should be treated differently.

Personal writing: text type – informal letter

What is a written correspondence?

In Paper 2 you may need to write a personal letter in order to narrate an event, give advice, or describe a person, a place or a situation. Keep in mind that you need to be able to open and close the letter correctly.

Following are some functions of the personal letter:

To apologise	Saying sorry and making amends
To describe	Descriptions involve the use of the senses and emotions. They can be physical and/or involve an assessment of character.
To instruct or advise	The writer tells the reader what to do or how to act. The writer applies logic to suggest a series of actions to the reader. The writer uses language to structure these ideas by dividing them into clear steps.
To narrate	The telling of a short story or incident. Setting out events in a clear and logical fashion with a clear beginning, middle and end. Could be amusing or striking.

A friendly letter could be a combination of the above functions, for example 'narrate and describe', 'describe and instruct', 'narrate and advise', etc.

Writing to a specific audience

We write personal letters to someone we know well, like a family member or a friend. You might want simply to keep in touch with people you care about. Many personal letters are written to maintain a friendship or personal relationship. Writing a letter shows that you care about the person to whom you are writing. People tend to keep letters and will sometimes re-read them. Personal letters often contain your latest news and narrate a recent incident. If you want to explain your ideas or your feelings, you will want to make sure that the letter reflects your personality and your exact thoughts and feelings. You could also ask questions of your friend to make sure he/she feels involved in the letter and to make it sound more like a conversation than a speech!

Structure

Keep in mind that you need to be able to open and close the letter correctly. The most frequent salutation is 'Dear,' followed by the reader's first name.

When closing a personal letter, you could end with 'Love', 'Best wishes', or 'Cheers' for example.

Style tips

	Required	Optional	Not acceptable
Form	● Date ● A greeting ● A closing salutation ● Signing off with your name	● Addresses ● Smileys	● Title
Language	● Correct punctuation ● Paragraphing	● Contractions: 'I'll', 'can't', 'doesn't' ● Idiomatic language and phrases	● Abbreviations ● Textese (4 for 'for'; U for 'you', etc.) ● Deliberate misspellings/ slang e.g. 'gonna' ● Swear words

Activity

You were on holiday and visiting a market in an English-speaking country and had a very interesting encounter at one of the stalls. Write a letter to a friend, telling him/her about your experience at the market.

● Start with a greeting and explanation of where you are and what you are doing.

● Tell the anecdote (past tense narrative).

● Add descriptive detail (past tense description).

● Explain why the incident is amusing, striking or noteworthy (present tense).

● Close your letter with a greeting and salutation.

Specific types of personal letters

In the age of the Internet, we tend to write personal letters on special occasions: invitations, thank you letters, and letters expressing congratulations or sympathy. Remember that the person reading your letter will form an opinion of you based upon the way you write and the language you use.

Letter of invitation

If you have to invite someone, you need to explain what the occasion is: birthday, farewell party, or anniversary etc. This means you will need to give information about the time, the date and place, and explain any special arrangements, such as what to bring or what to wear.

Sample letter of invitation

5th April, 2013

Dear Julie,

I hope this letter finds you in the best of health. How are things down south at the moment? I wonder if you might be having a tough time with the crowds and the awful weather in London. You know we talked about meeting up this summer so I was wondering why you don't come here for a change.

Why don't you come over to Saddleworth during the summer vacation? We could have lots of fun here and I am sure that you will like the area. It will certainly be a change for you and we could catch up too.

The moors around here are famous for their hills, lakes, rivers, forests and natural beauty. There are some great picnic sports nearby. Manchester is only half an hour away on the train.

I should imagine that city life is full of tourists, very crowded and probably polluted. You would find peace and quiet, fresh air and lot of natural beauty if you come here for the summer. OK, sometimes it rains too!

Anyway, the main thing is we would be able to get together and have a great time. I'll introduce you to all my friends.

I have already asked my parents and they would be happy for you to come and stay with us.

Send my regards to your parents and love to your little sister.

Missing you like mad,

Suzy

Letter of thanks

You may be asked to write a thank you letter to someone for a gift, a visit or a favour. In such situations, it is important to express your pleasure. For example, it is best to mention a couple of specific details about the event (food, comfort, hospitality might be key concepts here). If you are writing a letter of thanks for a gift, you can say if and when you have used the gift and what you thought about it.

Activity

Write your own letter to a friend inviting him or her to come a visit you at home during the summer holidays. Remember to give a number of reasons for coming and staying.

Sample letter of thanks

January 12th 2013

Dear Mr. Marshall,

Thank you for taking the time to talk with me today. I really appreciate the time you spent discussing my academic goals and recommending strategies for achieving them. Your advice was very helpful and gave me a new perspective on my own direction.

I plan on following up with the contacts you emailed me right away. I will also use the Internet resources you recommended to look at possible university courses. Any additional suggestions you may have would be welcome.

I'll update you as I progress.

Again, thank you so much for your help. I greatly value the assistance you have provided me.

Best Regards,

Dwayne

Activity

1. Read the following letter of thanks and complete paragraphs A–C. You have been given a topic sentence for each.

September 4th, 2012

Dear Mrs. Eliot,

I wanted to thank you for taking our class on a field trip to the IT exhibition at the National University yesterday. I know it must have been such a lot of work making all the transport arrangements, organizing the lunch at the café, and making sure we all arrived back at school safely and on time.

Paragraph (A) The exhibition was much bigger than I expected .... (Describe the exhibition)

Paragraph (B) I learned a huge amount. I had never realized how many new innovations are on the way. (Give examples)

Paragraph (C) I am really grateful I had the chance to speak to so many enthusiastic professionals. (Give examples)

I have always enjoyed working on computers but until now I had never really considered a career in technology. Now I think that is a possible option for me. Maybe I'll try to compete for a scholarship.

If you ever organize another trip like this one next year, I'll be the first one to sign up! Thank you once again for opening up a whole new world to me.

Your student,

Dwayne

2. You have just finished your IB course. Write a letter of thanks to a teacher, counselor or tutor who has been particularly helpful to you over the past two years.

Letter of congratulations

When a friend or relative has been lucky or achieved something, you may want to write a letter to congratulate that person. A letter of congratulations should be to the point.

- Focus only on the recipient and the reason for writing the letter of congratulations.
- Open the letter with the reason for writing the letter and congratulate the recipient for their achievement.
- Express your happiness for him or her.
- End your letter with best wishes.
- Always be genuine in your feelings.

Things to avoid

- Do not exaggerate either the person's achievements or your feelings of happiness; it may sound ironic!
- Do not talk about yourself in the letter.
- Avoid negative thoughts or comments. For example, if you are writing a letter of congratulations to wish your friends for their acceptance at university, do not mention anything about their previous failures to get into better colleges!

Sample letters of congratulations

Letter A

05-11-2013

Dear Kylie,

It is very exciting to hear that your university has named you Sportswoman of the Year and awarded you the achievement medal. Please accept my heartiest congratulations on this superb achievement. The award comes as no surprise because I know that you are an ace athlete.

Having won this recognition, you can now make a name for yourself at national as well as international level.

Hope this is just the beginning and many such awards will follow you.

My best wishes for a wonderfully bright future.

With regards,

Josh

Letter B

May 22, 2013

Dear Jenna,

I was so pleased to hear that you have been offered a six-month internship at Lessing and Kluge solicitors after graduation. I have heard that they are one of the best Law firms in the city and I am sure you will have loads of opportunities to see how a top-class law firm works and make lots of useful connections.

You have my heartfelt congratulations both on passing IB with such splendid grades and your new position. You have worked so hard for the last two years and you really deserve this.

These are exciting developments, and I'm sure you will meet the challenges they bring with your usual optimism and abilities to cope.

I wish you all the best as you move forward in this new phase in your life.

Best Wishes,

John

Expressing your pleasure: useful phrases

- Congratulations on having won the first prize…
- How delighted I am that you've been awarded a scholarship to…
- I am thrilled to hear that your college has named you…
- I'm so happy at your coming first in…
- Imagine how happy I was to learn you passed…
- It is really great to know that…
- It's so exciting to learn that you are on the merit list of…
- Please accept my heartiest congratulations on obtaining…
- It's wonderful news that you've won the first prize in the competition for…
- We are proud to hear that you successfully completed…

Activity

A relative recently won his/her school's best film production award. Write a letter congratulating this person.

Personal writing: text type – diary entry

What is a diary entry?

A diary entry is a personal account that describes what you did, saw or felt on a particular occasion. These entries could be straightforward events outlining what you did in the course of the day. However, at HL a daily routine does not make for interesting writing. A good diary entry is likely to contain your thoughts, feelings and reflections on the events of the day.

Writing to an audience

Unlike most text-types we discuss in Language B, in real life diaries are private, rather than public. Some diary writers like to write to the diary as if it were a good friend. This technique is called *direct address* and allows you to talk to your diary as 'you'. Because you are writing to yourself, a diary can be a place where you can write down your thoughts, feelings in secret and in confidence.

Structure

At SL your diary entries could be a straightforward (narrative-driven) account of a day's events. However, many people keep diaries as a method of examining their lives. So in terms of structure, such diary entries do not have to have a chronological structure.

Frequently the writer's opinions give structure to the writing rather than the events themselves. You might start with a phrase to focus the reader on the main event you wish to relate. You could use an exclamation, 'What a day this has been!' or you could start with an opinion, 'I have never felt so insulted.' Alternatively you might like to start with a rhetorical question that you go on to answer. 'How could I have imagined they could be so cruel?'

Diary writing is spontaneous and therefore the language and the ideas should sound fresh. Nevertheless you should still use the basic rules of paragraphing with each paragraph having a topic sentence and a clear focus. This will help you and your reader to understand your thoughts. (Remember you are writing for an English B examiner).

You could finish either with a final thought. This might be a concluding statement about the events in the diary entry or a question on the lines of 'I wonder what will happen next....'

Style

The most difficult aspect of producing an imaginative diary entry is writing in character. The most obvious point is that diaries are written from a first-person perspective and refer to possibly fictitious events that have just recently 'happened'. But you have to remember you are writing in character to an implied audience (in this case your imaginary self). Your writing should, therefore, try to reflect the personality and mood of the diary-writer.

It is worth noting the tenses for diaries. If you are writing about events that took place the day before i.e. 'yesterday', then you need to write in the simple past. 'I *came*, I *saw*, I *conquered*.' However, you are also writing about events that have taken place earlier in the same day i.e. 'today.' In this case you may need to use present perfect tenses to describe events whose consequences can still be felt. 'Today has been wonderful. I've finally discovered the true nature of the universe.'

> You can be relatively informal with your use of language. After all you are writing to yourself! However you are advised not to use too much slang. If you do feel it necessary, it is wise to put the word in parentheses to show you understand that the word is non-standard English. Swearing is almost certainly unnecessary in your assessed writing, and may be offensive to your examiner.

A note on grammar

Diary writers are not always certain about their ideas so it is useful to begin some sentences with phrases like: I wonder, I suppose, I think, I reckon, I imagine, I hope, I doubt.

You may also want to use verbs in the conditional tenses:

- I wonder what will happen if I go (future).
- I wonder what would happen if I went … (theoretical situation in the present).
- I wonder what would have happened if I had gone … (theoretical situation in the past)

Sample diary entries

Diary entry A

Thursday January 1st

Bank Holiday in England, Ireland, Scotland and Wales

These are my New Year's resolutions:

1. I will help the blind across the road.

2. I will hang my trousers up.

3. I will put the sleeves back on my records.

4. I will not start smoking.

5. I will stop squeezing my spots.

6. I will be kind to the dog.

7. I will help the poor and ignorant.

8. After hearing the disgusting noises from downstairs last night, I have also vowed never to drink alcohol.

My father got the dog drunk on cherry brandy at the party last night. If the RSPCA hear about it he could get done. Eight days have gone by since Christmas Day but my mother still hasn't worn the green lurex apron I bought her for Christmas! She will get bath cubes next year. Just my luck, I've got a spot on my chin for the first day of the New Year!

Friday January 2nd
Bank Holiday in Scotland. Full Moon

I felt rotten today. It's my mother's fault for singing 'My Way' at two o'clock in the morning at the top of the stairs. Just my luck to have a mother like her. There is a chance my parents could be alcoholics. Next year I could be in a children's home.

The dog got its own back on my father. It jumped up and knocked down his model ship, then ran into the garden with the rigging tangled in its feet. My father kept saying, 'Three months' work down the drain', over and over again.

The spot on my chin is getting bigger. It's my mother's fault for not knowing about vitamins.

Saturday January 3rd

I shall go mad through lack of sleep! My father has banned the dog from the house so it barked outside my window all night. Just my luck! My father shouted a swear-word at it. If he's not careful he will get done by the police for obscene language.

I think the spot is a boil. Just my luck to have it where everybody can see it. I pointed out to my mother that I hadn't had any vitamin C today. She said, 'Go and buy an orange, then'. This is typical.

She still hasn't worn the lurex apron.

I will be glad to get back to school.

Sue Townsend, *The Secret Diary of Adrian Mole Aged 13 ¾*, 1982

Note:

The particular point of view of a diary writer can be very limited, as is the case of Adrian Mole above. In his diary, he manages to blame everyone else for his problems, but fails to recognize that he makes things worse too! Because of his age and naivety, he frequently fails to understand what is going on – although we, the readers, understand the bigger picture.

Diary entry B

In the following passage Helen, a schoolgirl in her final year, realizes she is pregnant by her boyfriend Chris.

But I'm not ready for Chris. I'm not ready to share my life with him, and that's what it would mean. The thought of it terrifies me. He's all keyed up for Newcastle, and university life. He's talked of nothing else since I met him. I know he'd stay with me if I asked him to. It would be asking him to make an enormous sacrifice but I'm pretty sure he'd do it. I know we'd find a flat somewhere and maybe his dad and my dad would help us out. I'd lose my mum forever. But we'd do our best to make things right for you.

Yet I hurt inside when I think about it. I wake up in terror, Nobody, and I don't know what it is I'm more frightened –of promising myself to Chris forever, or spending forever without him. I don't know him yet. Six months ago the thought of spending the rest of our lives together had never entered our heads. We were a pair of kids having fun together. And now we've been catapulted into the world of grown-ups. I'm not ready for forever. I'm not ready for him, and he's not ready for me. And more than anything else, I'm afraid of all this hurt touching you. Does it? Can you tell?

I'm going to wait till his exams finish before I tell him.

It would be cruel to do it now, but I mustn't just let it slide, just wait till you're born, just let things happen as if nothing could be helped or stopped or thought about. Chris and I will have a lovely last few weeks together – I'll see him every day if I can.

Berlie Doherty, *Dear Nobody*, 1991

Analysis of the texts

	Diary entry A	Diary entry B
Who is the audience for the text?		
What is the purpose of the text?		
How does the writer start the diary entry?		
How does the writer finish the diary entry?		
What is the core narrative (storyline) in the text? Is the narrative an important part of the diary entry?		
What descriptive details has the writer included in the diary entry?		
What are the writers' main ideas in the text?		
In each text what are the approximate proportions of: • the narrative content • the descriptive details • the thoughts of the character		
How does the text show the personality of the writer?		

Activity

Write a diary entry on one of the option topics given below:
- The celebration of a social or religious event
- A problem with a dress code or school uniform
- An embarrassing event where you or someone breaks the rules of etiquette
- A fashion event you attend
- A great (or disastrous) meal
- You witness an historical event
- An event where people wear national costumes
- An arts event: concert, performance or exhibition

Personal writing: text type – guidelines and advice

Unlike a set of instructions, guidelines and advice are descriptive and can be more personal in style and address depending on the topic and the relationship between the writer and the audience. You can organize guidelines as if you were defining a problem.

Alternatively you can take a big problem and break it down into smaller ones.

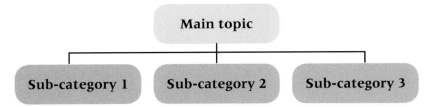

In the ironic short story 'Girl' by Antiguan writer and poet Jamaica Kincaid, a mother is giving advice to her teenage daughter:

Girl

Wash the white clothes on Monday and put them on the stone heap; wash the color clothes on Tuesday and put them on the clothesline to dry; don't walk bare head in the hot sun; cook pump¬kin fritters in very hot sweet oil; soak your little cloths right after you take them off; when buying cotton to make yourself a nice blouse, be sure that it doesn't have gum on it, because that way it won't hold up well after a wash; soak salt fish overnight before you cook it; is it true that you sing benna in Sunday school?; always eat your food in such a way that it won't turn someone else's stomach; on Sundays try to walk like a lady and not like the slut you are so bent on becoming; don't sing henna in Sunday school; you mustn't speak to wharf-rat boys, not even to give directions; don't eat fruits on the street—flies will follow you; ***but I don't sing benna* on Sundays at all and never in Sunday school;*** this is how to sew on a button; this is how to make a buttonhole for the button you have just sewed on; this is how to hem a dress when you see the hem coming down and so to prevent yourself from looking like the slut I know you are so bent on becoming; this is how you iron your father's khaki shirt so that it doesn't have a crease; this is how you iron your father's khaki pants so that they don't have a crease; this is how you grow okra—far from the house, because Okra tree harbors red ants; when you are growing dasheen, make sure it gets plenty of water or else it makes your throat itch when you are eating it; this is how you sweep a corner; this is how you sweep a whole house; this is how you sweep a yard; this is how you smile to someone you don't like too much; this is how you smile to someone you don't like at all; this is how you smile to someone you like completely; this is how you set a table for tea; this is how you set a table for dinner; this is how you set a table for dinner with an important guest; this is how you set a table for lunch; this is how you set a table for breakfast; this is how to behave in the presence of men who don't know you very well, and this way they won't recognize immediately the slut I have warned you against becoming; be sure to wash every day, even if it is with your own spit; don't squat down to play marbles—you are not a boy, you know; don't pick people's flowers— you might catch some¬thing; don't throw stones at blackbirds, because it might not be a blackbird at all; this is how to make a bread pudding; this is how to make doukona; this is how to make pepper pot; this is how to 'make a good medicine for a cold; this is how to make a good medicine to throw away a child before it even becomes a child; this is how to catch a fish; this is how to throw back a fish you don't like, and that way something bad won't fall on you; this is how to bully a man; this is how a man bullies you; this is how to love a man, and if this doesn't work there are other ways, and if they don't work don't feel too bad about giving up; this is how to spit up in the air if you feel like it, and this is how to move quick so that it doesn't fall on you; this is how to make ends meet; always squeeze bread to make sure it's fresh; ***but what if the baker won't let me feel the bread?;*** you mean to say that after all you are really going to be the kind of woman who the baker won't let near the bread?

Jamaica Kincaid, 1983

*Benna = local calypso music sometimes using vulgar language

Activity

1. In the chart below organize the mother's various pieces of advice into different categories.

Category	Advice
Buying wisely	
Cooking	
Domestic chores	
Finding a job	
Friendship	
Gardening	
Health matters	
Money matters	
Morality	
Old age	
Parenthood	
Personal habits	
Relationships	
Superstitions	
The future	

2. Organize the mother's advice identified above to either:
   - define the girl's problems (as seen by the mother)
   - organize the problems into different types.

3. Having completed the chart, what do you infer regarding the points in the table below?

	Relationship with the other person	Personality	Attitude to the other person
Mother/Speaker			
Daughter/Listener			

4. When writing a set of guidelines, an author usually uses bullet points. In the poem above, semicolons were used instead. Re-organize the poem using bullet points. Make sure you group similar problems/pieces of advice together.

5. The mother uses an authoritative tone to give advice. Will the same tone be appropriate if the poem was written by the daughter? Re-write the poem, giving the same guidelines and advice to a friend.

6. What advice would you give to the mother? Using one of the organizational charts, map out a similar set of guidelines and suggestions from the daughter to the mother to improve their relationship.

Activity

Write a set of guidelines and advice on one of the topics below:
- Etiquette: how to behave properly on a certain occasion such as a formal meal.
- Dress codes: explain the dress code for an important occasion, or explain your school's dress code to a new student.

- Social interaction: how to behave politely on Facebook or in a chat room.
- Travel: safety tips for visitors to your country.
- Physical exercise: how to get fit or improve fitness.
- Illness: advice for caregivers looking after old people who live alone.
- Concepts of beauty: fashion and beauty tips for teenagers.

Personal writing: text type – blog entry

What is a blog entry?

A blog can be a sort of online diary. However, whereas a diary is essentially private, you write a blog so that other people can read it. In English B, a blog entry can be a useful way to write well about one of the option topics you are studying. Consequently, a blog can be very suitable for SL students because you can write a fairly straightforward narrative with some descriptive detail and explanation. On the other hand, at a more complex level, your blog could focus on a specific topic rather than a series of events. If you choose to write a topic-based blog, it is also important to write about an issue that interests you; one that you have some passion for. It is also important to have a clear point of view. This will give your blog a focus.

Writing to an audience

Your target audience will be those people who share your interests or ideas. When you write your blog, you can address your audience directly and you can ask your readers to respond to your ideas. The blog will appear on the Internet and is therefore public. You will have to use more formal language than you would use in a diary, but keep it personal nonetheless.

Two types of blog

Like a diary, a blog could be a narrative-driven blog, a straightforward account of what you have done. This kind of blog focuses on narrating clearly a set of events such as an excursion or an important event in the life of the blogger. Alternatively, your blog may focus on something that you have experienced: a sporting event, a wedding or concert.

Still, bloggers often write because they have a particular point of view that they wish to get across to the public. In that respect, a blog can be like an essay. Therefore, this kind of blog may use the same conventions such as a thesis, paragraphs with topic sentences related to the thesis and a final thought or conclusion. Such a thesis-driven blog can be much more informative or opinionated.

Both blog types share one important aspect: **reflection**. As mentioned earlier, you blog because you want to communicate something to your readers/followers; therefore, you should make your voice heard even if you are writing a narrative-driven blog. Your opinions, reflections and feelings should be conveyed to the reader.

	Narrative-driven blog	Thesis-driven blog
Focus	Events	Ideas and opinions
Organization	Chronological account of events	A reasoned argument
Opening	Beginning of the events	Thesis/main idea
Main paragraphs	Different parts of the story with description, explanation and thoughts (reflections)	Ideas to support your main idea: Point, examples and explanations with reflections
Ending	Final thought and reflections	Final thoughts, conclusion and reflections

Tone and style

Normally you would write a narrative-driven blog using past tenses. It is also a good idea to join your sentences using time connectives. You can be quite chatty and informal in your use of language. It is useful to include descriptive detail of the events and write some thoughts and reflections. To achieve this, you need to use imaginative language.

When writing up conversations, you can use reported speech.

A thesis-driven blog is likely to contain more descriptive detail than an essay because it is a more personal form of writing. You may not be chatty but you surely need to describe your reflections.

Sample blog entries

Blog entry A

Monday, October 11, 2010

Floods

A normal day: I woke up at 7am, just in time to get dressed, have breakfast (muesli, banana+ honey yoghurt), wash my face and brush my teeth before it was time to leave. Then it was the regular tuk-tuk ride to Lakeside, to drop off Max and Victor, and then forward to Youth School for Will and I. Once we arrived, the topics for the morning classes would be the letter 'V' and 'Days of the week.' Ah, but someone had other plans.

I should probably have mentioned this previously, but yesterday was approximately one of the lengthiest rainstorms of my life: when we woke it was raining, when we slept it was raining, with not even a sense of a pause in between.

I suppose we didn't really consider the effect this would have, that by this morning, the whole of the area around Lakeside was completely flooded, the people's houses and all. Because of the controversial filling of the lake that is currently happening at Boeung Kok where the Youth School and Lakeside schools are located, the after-effects of a day of rainfall have been catastrophic. As Will said, the water in the lake they are displacing with sand has to go somewhere. And where has it gone? Into the houses of the residents nearby – the people living on so little a day, the ones who could never afford to repair the damage done. They just have to wait for the water to go down.

Due to the floods, both schools were locked and so all four of us – Will, Max, Victor and I – were at a bit of a loss what to do. Of course, the kids always save us. Hanging around outside waiting for their lesson that would never happen, I was immediately brought a 'seo pulng'(book) and asked to 'an' (read) out the words so they could repeat them. So we spent a while identifying the difference between an ostrich and an owl. After some intense grueling of this, I'm pretty sure that they still didn't understand, probably thinking that both just meant 'bird'. Oh well, I tried.

We were also treated to many presents – this time, from the natural world. Yes, flowers in our hair and bracelets made out of leaves and grass, we were treated royally. Although at one point they did try and (quite forcefully) drag us into the volleyball-court-turned-lake that lay only 5 or 6 meters from the classroom entrance.

It's a clichéd phrase that we really do take our lives and our pleasures for granted. And that when you are really there, in the midst of it all – that's when you know what it's really like.

More blogging later.

Juliet

PS: I found a really good blog that updates regularly on the situation at Boeung Kak Lake. To read more about the pumping, **CLICK HERE**.

Posted by Juliet Miriam Clark at 9:37 PM

Juliet Clark, 2010

Analysis

Is entry A a narrative-driven or a thesis-driven blog?

A good narrative-driven blog entry might contain:

- background details to give a context
- a core description of events
- descriptive detail of the people, places and events
- thoughts and feelings about what happened
- a final thought or conclusion.

Analyse how the writer has combined different functions in her writing by completing the table below.

Paragraph	Core narrative	Descriptive detail	Thoughts and feeling
1			
2			
3			
4			
5			

1. What background details does the writer give us so that we can understand where and when the events occur?

2. With what final thought does she finish her blog?

3. Is the blog an effective piece of writing? Give reasons.

4. If you were writing a thesis-driven blog entry about the same events described in blog entry A, how would you organize your text?

Activity

Write a narrative-driven blog entry on one of the topics given below:

- Entertainment: a visit to an exhibition, a concert, a show
- A visit to a sporting event
- A description of one of your hobbies and why it is important to you
- A description of a party, a celebration or a day out
- A personal travel blog
- A school trip
- A visit to a university you are thinking of attending

Make sure to include different elements of the blog in your writing:

Paragraph	Background	Core narrative	Descriptive detail	Thoughts and feeling	Final thoughts
1					
2					
3					
4					
5					

Blog entry B

October 2010

Mudslide in Ladakh

You can never fully comprehend the suffering of people affected by natural disasters until you are the affected yourself. With the Thursday night floods and mudflows stripping the region of Leh, Ladakh in the Jammu and Kashmir state of India, Wallace and I are beginning to comprehend how nature can destroy everything. Although having previously studied the effects of such natural disasters in Geography, I have never grasped their social and emotional consequences.

Since all buildings in Ladakh are constructed from mud bricks, any water (especially in large quantities like floods and cloudbursts) causes immense damage to a building's structural integrity. Since Lamdon Model School in Shey is directly in the wake of Shey Valley River, with no other building in between, it took the full force of the mud. Some rooms suffered significant damage (such as partial wall collapse) as well as the piling of mud one meter deep.

The flooding had been terrifying. Manoj, the headmaster, Wallace and I had the responsibility for 145 students, all under the age of 15. For example, 40 kindergarten students were isolated in their own – extremely vulnerable – building, so we had to work out a way to reconnect with them. This required perfect timing. We had to move them all to the main building between the intermittent mudflows that were already two foot deep and flowing at a great pace. Eventually our solution was to construct a human chain between the kitchen window and the room 10m away. As we did this, we passed the 3 to 5 year olds down the chain all the time avoiding the next surge of mud, trees and boulders. The surges were only a few minutes apart, and to be caught in one would have spelt unthinkable disaster. With the students growing anxious, it did not seem as though they could last much longer before breaking down emotionally. We understood their trauma.

Having said that, even though we have been there and been displaced, we still do not completely comprehend the consequences. We could feel the same emotional distress as the children as we were forced to evacuate to the nearby Thiksay Monastery that is perched on a rocky hill. It seems as though we were not the only ones to seek refuge here as there were over 300 people in the small hall where we stayed.

No matter what happens to us in Ladakh, no matter if we lose all of our possessions, even if the school has been destroyed or the school jeep has been washed away, we still have the security of our perfect, underappreciated first world lives. We will still have our homes and lives in Singapore, Australia and Scotland, to which we will return untouched. However, in Ladakh, the people here will live with the consequences of August 5th, 2010 for the rest of their lives.

Stephen Khalek, 2010

Analysis

Is entry B a narrative-driven or a thesis-driven blog?

To write a clear thesis-driven blog entry, you should have these paragraphs:

- a thesis statement/big idea
- supporting paragraphs (point – example – explanation, see page 54 for PEE strategy)
- a final thought or conclusion.

You need to also include your thoughts and feelings about what has happened as well as giving descriptive details.

Analyse how the writer has combined different functions in his writing by completing the following table:

Thesis-driven blog

	Paragraph	Idea	Descriptive detail	Thoughts and feeling
1.	Thesis			
2.	Supporting paragraph 1			
3.	Supporting paragraph 2			
4.	Supporting paragraph 3			
5.	Final thought			

Activity

Write a thesis-driven blog on one of the topics given below:

- Entertainment: an evaluation of a concert or a show where you explain your attitude to the performers
- A visit to a sporting event where you assess one of the players
- A blog about the importance of hobbies
- A travel blog where an incident makes you think
- A blog about a lesson or lecture or video which made a big impression on you

Journalism: text type – news report

Definition and structure

Newspaper reports require you to write in a different style and use a very different structure to that of a narrative-driven story where the events are in chronological order. When writing a news report, your most important information for the readers comes first. The least important information comes last. A news report is written this way because your readers might not want to read the entire text all the way through to the end. Your **lead paragraph** tells the readers what details they will find further on in the report.

To be newsworthy, the events will have just taken place. Such a report is going to be dramatic, and the journalist is telling the readers something completely new as opposed to a feature article in a magazine which may be more analytical because the writer has had more time to reflect on the events.

> **The features of a news report**
>
> A news report consists of the following items:
> - Headline
> - The lead paragraph: the 5 Ws
> - Explanatory paragraphs
> - Background paragraphs
> - Final paragraph

Sample news reports

News report A

Read the following news report and read the definitions of the news report features before answering the questions that follow.

Dog rescued from five-foot deep rabbit warren

A dog is reunited with its owner after being stuck for almost nine hours down a rabbit warren in Shrewsbury.

1. Firefighters used earthquake rescue equipment to save Cookie, a black Pattersdale Terrier, after she chased a rabbit down a hole and became stuck five feet underground.
2. Owner Kay Barnes, 32, spent more than two hours trying to rescue the dog herself before eventually calling the emergency services on Thursday afternoon.
3. It took a team of ten fire fighters from Shrewsbury, Shropshire, more than three hours to locate and rescue the three-year-old dog using specialist listening equipment which is currently being used in Japan to locate earthquake survivors.
4. Collin Bennet, who recorded the video, said: 'The rabbit warren covered an area of about 20 square metres.
5. 'We were shouting down the holes and we could hear a faint yelp from Cookie as she called for help.'
6. The fire crew placed highly sensitive microphones in various positions on the ground to finally pinpoint Cookie's exact location.
7. After locating her position rescuers dug a trench parallel to where Cookie was trapped and coaxed the terrier out using dog biscuits.
8. A relieved Ms Barnes said: 'I'm absolutely delighted to have Cookie back. We set off for the walk early in the morning but we didn't end up getting back until around 5pm.
9. 'There must have been around 10 fire fighters there and they worked for hours to get her free.'
10. A spokesman for Shropshire Fire and Rescue said: 'We used specialist listening equipment to detect where the dog was.
11. 'It is usually the sort of equipment used in operations where buildings have collapsed.'

Daily Telegraph, 2011

- **Headline:** a short, attention-grabbing statement about the immediate news-worthy event. It gives the outline of the story. The choice of words will indicate the nature of the story e.g. sad, amusing, or shocking. **Identify the headline.**

- **Standfirst:** block of text that introduces the story, normally in a style different to the body text and headline. **Identify the standfirst.**

- **By-line:** The byline comes below the standfirst and states who wrote the report and where. **There is no byline in this news report.**

- The **lead paragraph** grabs the reader's attention by using an opening sentence which is either a vivid summary or describes something unusual. Sometimes, the opening sentence is in the form of a question. In the first few sentences of your lead paragraph, you will need to tell the readers:

  ▸ Who?

  ▸ What?

  ▸ When?

  ▸ Where?

  ▸ Why?

Reporters put the most important information at the beginning because their readers might not want to read the whole text.

- The **explanatory paragraphs** follow and come in the first half of the report: The second paragraph adds more details to the who, what, where, why, and when. After that, make sure that each paragraph in the first half will give further information about those key details. Journalists must make sure that they have given enough information to answer any important questions a reader might have after reading the headline and the lead paragraph. This section can also include direct quotes from witnesses or bystanders. **Identify the explanatory paragraphs.**

- The **background paragraphs** give details that are not necessarily part of the main story. Often included are more detailed interviews and statements from officials. The background paragraphs allow the writer to put the news item into context. This could be by introducing some 'human interest' elements into the article or refreshing the reader's memory of what happened 'yesterday' if 'today's' news is part of a larger story. **Identify the background paragraphs.**

- **Final paragraphs** will either anticipate the next stage of the story or link this story to other similar stories or issues. Additional background information can be given in the final paragraph. This information is the least important. Thus, if the news report is too long for the space it needs to fill, it can be shortened without rewriting any other part. This part can include information about a similar event or puts the story into an even wider context such as annual statistics for road accidents. Additional information, such as the history of an organization or event, should be prominently cited in a story and can be included at the end of the piece. When writing tabloid articles, journalists sometimes end their piece with a catchy phase or a quote.

> 'Most rock journalism is people who can't write, interviewing people who can't talk, for people who can't read.'
>
> Frank Zappa

Language features of a news report

Remember that not all news reports are placed on the front page and so a report may be squeezed into thin columns, so writing using short paragraphs will look more appealing and readable. Most people forget this, and will write long and interesting paragraphs, full of information, but will wonder why so many people skip reading them.

Using quotes and indirect quotes

For the body of the report, you need to find some good quotes from interviews. Readers like quotes. Firstly, they make your report more believable. They will also make it more personable as well as allowing you to break the flow of facts.

- How many quotes can you find in News report A?
- How many people give quotes in News report A?
- For what purpose does the journalist quote the dog's owner?
- For what purpose does the journalist quote the spokesman of the rescue service?

'Quotes can be a news writer's best friend' explained long-time Malaysian journalist Nabila Hassan. 'They can clearly illustrate a person's thoughts or opinion on an issue.'

Sentences

Sentences can be long and complex, however, the meaning of the sentence must remain clear.

- In News report A, only one paragraph has more than one sentence per paragraph. Which one?

Active not passive verbs

News reports are written in the third person. Sentences should be clear and worded in a manner that is appropriate for the audience. Use active verbs; avoid the passive.

Identify the key verb phrases in each paragraph and categorize them into active and passive verbs.

Paragraph	Active verb	Passive verb
1.		
2.		
3.		
4.		
5.		
6.		
7.		
8.		
9.		
10.		

Avoid the use of 'I'

Can you give an explanation as to why the journalist does not mention himself/herself?

Paragraphs

Paragraphs should be no more than two sentences per paragraph. It is a good idea to practise joining sentences together. You can use cohesive devices such as commas and relative pronouns to achieve this.

In News report A, paragraph 7 states 'After locating her position, rescuers dug a trench parallel to where Cookie was trapped and coaxed the terrier out using dog biscuits.' Note that there are at least six different pieces of information in the paragraph:

- The dog's name was Cookie.
- The dog was trapped.
- The rescuers located the dog.
- The rescuers dug a trench.
- The rescuers used dog biscuits.
- The rescuers coaxed Cookie out.

The journalist joined all these different ideas together.

Activity

- How many 'joining' techniques can you spot in paragraph 7?
- Now take these eight simple sentences and create a single paragraph for the news report. Your paragraph should have no more than two sentences.

1. Cookie's owner is Kay Barnes.
2. Kay Barnes was worried.
3. She called the rescue service.
4. She used her mobile phone.
5. She gave the location of the rabbit warren.
6. The rescue service arrived.
7. It took them half an hour.
8. They brought specialist listening equipment.

Writing to a specific audience

Popular tabloid newspapers are written in vivid and often informal language with lots of descriptive adjectives and adverbs. They will also tend to use striking nouns and verbs. On the other hand, broadsheet news articles should sound much more formal, aiming to inform rather than sensationalize the news.

Analysis

Complete the following table by indicating the meaning of the word in the second column. By looking at these words, do you think the *Daily Telegraph* is a tabloid or a broadsheet newspaper? Justify your answer.

In paragraph	the word	means
2	eventually	
3	locate	
4	warren	
5	yelp	
6	pinpoint	
7	coaxed	
8	delighted	

News report B

Down syndrome teenager refused American Airlines seat

A. The parents of a disabled teenager have voiced their anger at American Airlines (AA) after not being allowed to take their seats in first class on a flight out of Newark to Los Angeles. Joan and Robert Vanderhorst, who were travelling with their son, a Down syndrome sufferer, claim they were discriminated against by the airline.

B. As they were preparing to board, they were told by AA staff that they could not fly as their son, Bede, posed a security risk. Matt Miller, a spokesman for American Airlines, said the 16-year-old had become agitated and was running around the departure area.

C. Apparently the pilot observed the behaviour and decided it was not safe for the boy to come on board. His parents claim that Bede was behaving normally and either strolling around the gate with his father or sitting quietly. Mrs Vanderhorst said she has a video of her son on her phone showing him sitting down and playing with his cap.

D. The family was booked onto another plane and placed in the last row of coach where other passengers were not allowed to sit within two rows. Mr Vanderhorst said the family had flown numerous times before and never faced any difficulties.

E. He claims that the pilot did not want other passengers in first class to be disturbed by his son and that he may also have been put off by the boy's size. Although American Airlines is standing by its decision, it said it would be refunding the family's upgrade fee.

Analysis

Essential questions	News report B
Identify the headline, standfirst and byline.	
Identify the 5 Ws in the first paragraph.	
Summarize the content of each of the explanatory paragraphs: B, C, and D.	
Is the news report balanced or one-sided?	
How does the writer finish the report?	
Does the report conclude with a catchy phrase?	
Comment on the language used in the news report. How formal is it?	
In your opinion would the news report have appeared in a tabloid or a broadsheet journal?	

Activity

Write a news report about one of the following topics:

- A Language Day at school
- An important cultural festival that has just taken place
- An accident that has just taken place
- A concert, important sports match, outing
- A new 'green' initiative taken by the school

Journalism: text type – magazine article

What is a magazine/newspaper article?

Unlike new reports which concentrate on events that have just happened, magazine/newspaper articles explore a range of issues, opinions, experiences and ideas.

Whatever the idea or topic, the article writer will have a point of view or angle that makes the article interesting and unique. In the article, you can offer an opinion about current affairs or simply present a personal perspective on modern-day life. Article writers go beyond just the facts and add colour, detail, background and personal comment.

> Magazine/newspaper articles can inform, entertain and persuade readers, or may simply satisfy the reader's curiosity about a particular topic. Professional articles may do all four at the same time.

Writing to a specific audience

If you choose to write a magazine/newspaper article, you must think about the audience. Who does the magazine or newspaper usually target? Articles should appeal to the particular audience of the magazine/newspaper. For example, if a magazine is targeted at teenage girls, then the articles, advertising and pictures within that magazine reflect teenage girls' interest in lifestyles, studying, fashion, health and relationships.

You also need to establish the relationship between you as the writer and your readership, so always keep your reader in mind and remember to use appropriate vocabulary and register.

Types of articles

An article provides more background information and analysis about an important issue than a newspaper report. News reports can quickly go out of date but articles have a more lasting value. Articles can be about people, places, topics or current issues. Some examples of articles that you may be asked to write for English B could be:

- an analysis and opinion on an issue you examined during the course
- a profile of a well-known person or a celebrity. This could be a character from a book
- a personal experience or anecdote related to one of the options: cultural diversity, customs and traditions, health, leisure, or science and technology
- some background information on a local, national or international event
- a human interest story about a strange or unusual event.

Structure

An article should always include a headline, introduction, the main body and a concluding paragraph.

> An article can follow either a narrative-driven, thesis-driven or a problem-driven structure.

- **Title or headline**

  The headline grabs the readers' attention and persuades them to read the article. You will also need to add the by-line (the writer's name) and location at the beginning.

- **Introduction**

  The purpose of the introduction or *lead* is to capture the attention of the readers and make them want to read further. Use an attention grabber (sometimes referred to as a 'kicker'). Here are three ways of doing this:

  ▶ Ask a provocative question. 'Do you really need a university degree?' This question can introduce a problem-driven text.

  ▶ Make a provocative thesis statement: 'In the future, no-one will need to speak English'.

  ▶ Relate a personal experience to introduce a narrative-driven text.

  Depending on the nature of the article you are asked to write, you can further illustrate the narrative/problem/thesis in several ways:

  ▶ Begin with a dramatic moment in a story.

  ▶ Start with a quote or joke.

  ▶ Describe some aspect of a place or a person you are profiling.

- **The main body**

  The middle section consists of a number of paragraphs that expand the main topic of the article into subtopics. The paragraphs should link with your angle and prove your point of view. There are different structures you can use for this:

  ▶ **A 'one-sided' approach**

    Each section of the feature emphasizes a single point to support your angle. For example, your angle might be 'X is a great but vulnerable character'. Make sure you give examples for each point you make.

  ▶ **A 'balanced but undecided' approach**

    There are two sides to the issue/problem. Give both sides of the argument with supporting evidence.

- **Conclusion**

  A conclusion should tie everything together and sum up the article. The concluding paragraph should leave a lasting impression by:

  ▶ reminding the reader of the article's main idea; you can return to your problem/thesis statement at the start of the article

  ▶ suggesting an appropriate course of action or make a recommendation

  ▶ explaining a person's future plans if you are writing about a person

  ▶ saving an unexpected piece of information until the last paragraph.

Tone and style

You need to establish the relationship between you as the writer and your readership, so make sure your language is suitable for the magazine's/newspaper's audience.

In an article, you can use a more personal approach than that of the news report. You can relate personal experiences and anecdotes. These will help you to maintain interest in the article. The use of quotes personalizes the topic and adds life and colour to your article.

A more personal tone is created through the use of informal language, for example, contractions, and a first-person narrative. If you wish to be humorous, try mild exaggeration or understatement.

> A magazine writer can use 'I' in certain circumstances. However, you must decide whether the readers are more interested in you or the subject of the article.

Sample magazine articles

Article A

Growing Up Deaf – Discovering Sign Language – My Introduction to a Different World

By Jamie Berke

Every formerly 'pure oral' (what we called it in the '70s) deaf person has his or her own tale to tell of how he or she came to begin using sign language. Here is mine:

Sometime in the late 1970s, I discovered sign language. Or more precisely the sign alphabet.

My mother was working as an oral interpreter at a mainstream program in another state. Some of the kids she interpreted for knew sign language, and she told them she had a deaf daughter. One day she brought home a card with the sign language alphabet on it.

What was this? I was excited and set about learning the alphabet quickly. I carried that card with me on the school bus, where I sat alone and practiced my fingerspelling.

The kids at her school began to invite me along to their activities. They all signed and talked, and for the first time I got a taste of what my life could have been like.

When I was 14, I took my first sign language class at a local community college. What I did not know then was that the class was not teaching ASL but signed English! To this day my sign language is very 'English' in nature. That class was followed by another class when I was 15. After that I had to stop because no more classes were available.

My hearing classmates found out I was learning sign language, and asked me to teach them the alphabet. I did so, only to find that they weren't interested in communicating more efficiently with me, only in being able to curse in sign language!

With no-one to practice my signs with, my sign skills deteriorated. I had no sign classes the year I was 16. Then the following year I went to college, and re-discovered sign language. I still remember how it felt that very first day in the cafeteria at the Rochester Institute of Technology/National Technical Institute for the Deaf, looking around me at all the sign language and feeling as if I had entered a different world.

Jamie Berke, 2009

Manchester

My home town of Manchester has changed beyond recognition in the last few years. After the IRA bombing in 1996, Manchester turned a negative into a positive and created a new blueprint for the city. Now with its great combination of style and culture, it has become one of the most vibrant places in the UK.

Manchester's Metrolink tram system is easy to use and makes getting round the city easy. There are even free shuttle buses waiting at Piccadilly Station to transport you to the city's leading attractions.

The museums such as the Lowry Centre, at the revamped Salford Quays, which is a tribute to L S Lowry, the artist famous for his matchstick men, and the multi-award winning Imperial War Museum North are excellent.

Of course, if you are like me a Manchester United fan, then it would be sacrilege to go to Manchester and not pay a visit to the Manchester United Museum & Tour Centre where you can brush up on your history of the club as well as seeing the spectacular Trophy Room.

There are other great buildings worth seeing such as Manchester Cathedral, which has an amazing interior, Manchester Town Hall and John Rylands Library, both built in Victorian Gothic style.

Manchester is also a shopaholics' paradise. The city centre is compact so it is easy to walk round. I think it is altogether a much more pleasant shopping experience than London. Now that Virgin Trains have converted to me to using the train, I will be flexing my credit card here more often as it only a two-hour journey from London and so therapeutic.

You'll find all the usual high street names as well as a Harvey Nichols and Selfridges. If you are feeling flush then pay a visit to Flannels in Spinningfields, one of the city's chicest districts. This independent boutique, packed with luxury labels including Prada and Marc Jacobs, is a favourite with Manchester's fashion cognoscenti. If you like malls visit The Trafford Centre. It's huge. The Northern Quarter is great for quirky boutiques, art galleries and tea shops such as Teacup.

The five-star Lowry Hotel is the preferred address of stars and captains of industry and my favourite place to stay. The place radiates northern charm and the service is always good.

Manchester does have some great eateries including El Rincon de Rafa, which serves rather good Spanish tapas and Panacea, one of the haunts of the rich and famous. Deansgate is also crammed with plenty of cool bars where you can sit outside, if the weather is good, and watch the world go by.

The place I always head to when I am in town is the Lowry's River Bar and Restaurant. The food is always delicious. Looking out on to the River Irwell and chic apartments, it reminded me of being in Chicago. And just like being in the Windy City, where you have to scratch beneath the surface to discover its throbbing pulse, the same is true with Manchester.

Daralyn Danns

Analysis

Essential questions	Article A	Article B
What is the topic?		
What is the writer's chosen angle?		
How does the writer get the reader's attention?		
Is the article balanced or one-sided?		
How is the article structured?		
How does the writer finish the article?		
Who is the audience?		
How does each writer connect with the readers?		

Activity

Write an article about one of the general topics given below:
- entertainment
- exhibitions and shows
- games
- hobbies
- recreation
- social interaction through leisure
- sports
- travelling.

Journalism: text type – interview

What is an interview?

A variation on the magazine article is the personal interview. An in-depth interview is a technique that allows you to write a person-to-person discussion. An interview can give increased insight into a person's thoughts, feelings, and behaviour. This type of text permits you to encourage an interviewee to talk at length about the topic of interest. Your interview with an individual could appear in a magazine as a transcript of the interview or could be embedded in an article.

Structure

The interview is directed at understanding the issues you want the interviewee to talk about. To do this, you could use either a thesis-driven or a problem-driven structure. In the case of the former, you start with an idea and structure the questions to prove your point. Therefore, before the interview, decide which topics you would like the interviewee to talk about. There are no fixed rules for structuring the interview but it makes sense to start with general questions and move to more specific ones.

Avoid 'closed' questions (questions that require yes/no answers); ask 'open' questions instead: 'Could you tell our readers about ....?' or 'Could you explain/describe/tell, etc.'

- **Introduction**

In your introduction, you need to establish rapport with the interviewee, for example, 'Thanks for coming in today to talk to XXXX magazine', introduce the interviewee and, in the case of a problem-driven text, pose the question to be solved. 'Wycliffe Mangala, you are known as the pioneer of the village mobile phone in Kenya. Where did the idea come from?'

- **The main body**

If you want your interview to cover personal issues, you should ask about less sensitive issues first and then move to specifics. For example, first ask about some facts. With this approach, respondents, or the interviewees, feel more comfortable in the interview before warming up to more personal matters and move on to questions about the present. It is usually easier for people to talk about the present and then work into the past or future. Next, ask questions about matters such as feelings, perceptions and conclusions.

- **Conclusion – 'Wrap-Up'**

Your last question could allow the respondent to provide information about future plans: 'So what do you see as the next stage?' The interview could be concluded by you thanking the respondent.

> **Writing tip**
>
> When creating the interview, make sure that your interviewer appears to listen to the interviewee's answers by asking follow-up questions. This will make the interview appear to flow and can add depth to the discussion.

Tone and style

In real life, we do not speak the way we write. However, if you are presenting the interview as a written text it is best to write your interviewee's responses in complete, grammatically correct sentences.

Sample interviews

Interview A

Interview with Anita Patel Jusnes, a former IB student

Q: Tell us about yourself.

A: My name is Anita Patel Jusnes. I'm 36 years old, married and have two kids. I met my husband when we both attended IB at Berg. Even though I am born and raised in Norway, my parents are Indian. I've never lived abroad for very long, but I feel like a world citizen. After IB, I went to the University of Oslo to get my master's degree in pharmaceutics. I am also working on a master's degree in business management from BI. For the past twelve years I have put these skills to use through working in a pharmaceutical company called GlaxoSmithKline. However, I just started working for a Norwegian company called Pronova Biopharma.

I'm currently part of a programme started by NHO called Global Future. This is a new programme for people with leadership ambition and minority backgrounds. It's an 18-month long process where I have my own mentor etc. I am very excited about it. The newspaper Dagsavisen did a case on this back in October, where I had my picture taken along with Councilman for education in Oslo, Torger Ødegård, and Olaf Stene from NHO.

Q: When did you go to Berg, and what are your fondest memories from that time?

A: My Berg career was from 1989-1991. Even though it was hectic at the time, I look back at the experience with no regrets. I remember I got to choose my own six subjects. There was little time for being idle, and just before my graduation, we had an exam on May 17.

I remember the teachers very well, and the student community was great. Those of us who went to IB were quite international, and all classes were taught in English, except for Norwegian A1, of course.

Q: How has IB shaped you as a human being?

A: Well, I met my husband here, so that's the obvious answer to the question. With my international background, I felt that going to IB was very natural. I mentioned earlier that I felt like a world citizen, and IB helped me develop that side of myself. Even though the people from my graduation class currently are spread all over the world, we actually managed to gather for a 15-year reunion last summer. I didn't think about it at the time, but the network of people I met then has been great to have after I became a career professional. As a serendipitous fact, I incidentally just started working with an old co-student in my current job.

Q: Has your experience from IB been useful in later studies and professional career?

A: IB, and particularly chemistry class definitely laid the foundation for my subsequent academic career. The knowledge and skills I picked up from chemistry class made the first year at pharmaceutical at University in Oslo seem easy. Also, us having had Theory of Knowledge in IB enabled us to bypass the otherwise obligatory preparatory philosophy courses at University.

Even though I chose the sciences, I still have very fond memories from Norwegian and English. I love to analyze literature, and there was a discipline to it that made me feel great respect for that art. I also enjoyed CAS quite a lot, and I think that was particularly useful for growing as human beings.

Q: Finally, what would you say to all the young people who are considering coming to Berg and IB?

A: Without a doubt, I can wholeheartedly recommend it. Today's society has become very globalised and it will only continue. IB is a great course as a foundation for building a career. As a student now, there are so many choices to be made, and so many options on the table. In my opinion, IB will prepare you well for whatever you decide to do. In my experience, getting out of the comfort zone and learning to interact and cooperate from people with different backgrounds will be incredibly valuable later in life.

Anita, thank you so much for taking the time to speak with us about this.

Analysis

Essential questions	Answers
Is the text a thesis-driven, problem-driven, or narrative-driven text? Prove it.	
How has the interviewer explained the background and the reason for the interview?	
How has the interviewer organized the questions to lead the reader into an understanding of the subject or the personality of the interviewee?	
How does the interviewer wrap up the interview?	
Comment on the language used by the interviewee: how, do you think, has the text been changed from actual speech?	

Activity

1. Write an interview on one of the topics below. Your interview could be imaginary, such as one with a favourite sports, media or entertainment personality, or with a friend/classmate.
   - Why beliefs and values are important
   - Why culture is important
   - Growing up in different cultures
   - Being bilingual or multilingual
   - Migrating from one country to another
2. Now transform the interview into a magazine article.

Journalism: text type – review

What is a review?

A review is a form of journalism found in magazines, newspapers and blogs. In a review, you share your opinions about a new book, a new film, a video or a recent concert. Your opinions should be based on evidence: facts and details.

Audience

You need to think about the type of mass audience and the type of publication you are writing for. You can write reviews in either a formal style or use more familiar diction. This will depend on your readership and the publication. If you are writing for a school magazine and your peer group, you will want to sound chatty and still show that you have insightful ideas. If your task involves writing for a magazine, and you do not know the audience or readership personally, then you have to be more formal.

Language and style

English has different registers or levels of familiarity; they range from the formal: 'A most enjoyable musical experience' to the informal and familiar: 'A totally cool show – a total blast!!' If your review is to sound authentic, you need to get the register right. However, this does not mean that you have to lose your sense of humour! You can sound smart and clever and yet be quite formal in your language.

A review of a film or book is an analysis, so it is usually written in the present tense. However, you should write a review of an event, such as a concert or performance in the past tense as it has already taken place.

Structure of the film review

A review is almost always a thesis-driven text. It starts with an opinion (often found in the headline) and supports it.

A film review is divided into different parts.

1. Grab the readers' attention with some information or question to connect them to the film.

2. Introduce the film. This gives an overview of what the film is about. You should include the name of the film, the type of film (comedy, adventure, drama, etc.) the prominent stars, basic setting (time and place).

3. Describe the plot and the action in the present tense while informing the reader which actor plays which role. Do **not** reveal the ending.

4. Analyse the film, talking about the director and then the actors, looking at good things as well as bad things. Depending on the information provided in the question, consider the following:

    ▶ the acting

    ▶ direction

    ▶ costume design

    ▶ photography

    ▶ background music

    Be sure that you are specific and cite examples from the movie.

5. Recommend the film to your audience. Describe your overall reaction to the film as well as your opinion on the quality of the film.

Sample reviews

Review A

Freshman Disorientation

The Perks of Being a Wallflower nails teenage alienation.

Has there ever been a time when you were among friends and felt as if you truly belonged, yet were aware at the same instant that the joy was fleeting and you'd soon be alone—and that the pain of loss would be almost as intense as the bliss? That's the feeling Stephen Chbosky captures in *The Perks of Being a Wallflower,* his exquisite adaptation of his best-selling YA novel about a Pittsburgh high-school freshman who doesn't fit in and then all of a sudden does, for a spell.

The movie is set in the early nineties, before widespread Internet and texting, back when alone meant unconnected, and misfits had no instant access to others of their ilk. (Chbosky was born in 1970.) Charlie (Logan Lerman) arrives in high school having lost his best friend the previous spring to suicide, and he's literally counting the days until college. Casually bullied, snickered at by girls who liked him fine before puberty, he tries not to speak—he's so conscious of his classmates' ridicule he doesn't raise his hand when he knows the answers to questions posed by his English teacher (the ever-boyish Paul Rudd). Charlie has deep funks, blackouts, and mysterious visions of the doting aunt (Melanie Lynskey) who died when he was 7. He can only share his heart in anonymous letters to an unnamed recipient chosen because Charlie heard about him (or her) from a girl: 'She said you listen and understand and didn't try to sleep with that person at that party even though you could have.' It's not much of a connection, but Charlie is desperate to unload.

Chbosky co-created the postapocalyptic TV series *Jericho,* and early in the film he has a hard time cramming so much information into so little screen time. But the emotions are all there. At a football game, doleful Charlie musters the courage to sit next to Patrick (Ezra Miller), a fast-talking clown from his shop class sitting with his stepsister, Sam (Emma Watson). 'What's your favorite band?' she asks Charlie. 'The Smiths.' 'Best breakup band ever!' For Charlie, it's *loooove.* For Sam, it's … strong like, maybe more. Before Charlie knows it, he has been adopted by the stepsiblings and their friends. It's magic—but every emotion, happy and sad, is so heavy.

Watching Lerman in the bland *Percy Jackson & the Olympians: The Lightning Thief,* I thought him one of the few young leads I'd seen in years with no evident talent. I guess context is all. With his thick, dark hair and puppy eyes, he's probably too handsome for Charlie, but he knows the value of stillness: His movements suggest not just wallflower reticence but paralysis. Pale, stringy-haired Ezra Miller is the dynamo. His Patrick has too much crazy energy to leave his school milieu unmolested—or his gayness in the closet. He and his stepsister have their own screwball ecosystem.

And Watson? She's visiting royalty trying like mad to be lusty and forward and a fun person. My ideal Sam would be scruffier, her diction less crisp, but Watson is admirably game, and she brings enough movie-star glamour to make Charlie's longing palpable. All the actors seem like cool people to spend time with. I wanted even more of Nina Dobrev as Charlie's older sister, Mae Whitman as the senior who puts the moves on Charlie (he doesn't know how to say no), and Johnny Simmons as the jock who takes up surreptitiously with Patrick. The grown-ups—among them Dylan McDermott and Kate Walsh as Charlie's parents—are neither a positive nor negative force. They have no impact on Charlie's self-esteem. At this age, it's all about his peers.

Chbosky lingers on objects that are, culturally speaking, on their last legs: 45-rpm singles, manual typewriters, mix tapes passed from boys to the girls they want to reach. It's nostalgia with an emphasis on nostos, pain. My favorite shot: Charlie leaving the wall at the homecoming dance and moving toward Sam, head bobbing as if to propel himself forward as Dexys Midnight Runners' 'Come On, Eileen' begins to accelerate. The music is from so long ago, the feeling of transcendence eternal.

David Edelstein, 2012

Now answer these questions:

1. What is the reviewer's attitude to the subject matter?
2. What is the thesis of the review?
3. How does the writer support the thesis?
4. What can we guess about the audience/readership for this review?
5. What technique does the reviewer use to close the review?

Analysis

Re-read Review A and fill in the chart below.

Paragraph	Content	Functions of each paragraph*	Examples of the functions
1.			
2.			
3.			
4.			
5.			
6.			

* the function could be instruction, description, narrative, explanation, persuasion

The book review

A book review should be a description and an evaluation of the quality, meaning, and significance of a book. Do not retell the plot or spoil the ending for the reader! The chart below can help you to understand how a book review works. To what extent does the review on the next page conform to the guidelines of writing a film review discussed on pages 90 to 92?

A Review: *Pigeon English* by Stephen Kelman

'In England there's a hell of different words for everything. It's for if you forget one, there's always another one left over. It's very helpful.' Stephen Kelman achieves something wonderful in his debut novel, *Pigeon English*, which has been shortlisted for the 2011 Man Booker prize: Kelman reawakens the reader's awareness of language and its possibilities, via a young Ghanaian transplant in London named Harri.

Using Harri's efforts to acclimate to English life and to accept (and investigate) the murder of another young boy—the novel's jumping off scene—Kelman demonstrates how vital language is to everyday life and how personal words can be. Harri, who narrates most of the story in a simple but open manner, as an eleven-year old might, peppers the pages with Ghanian dialect, and we (English readers) can see our language bending. By pushing together 'donkey' and 'hours,' we have a new way to say 'a long time.' Common phrases are elided, 'go away, you' becomes 'gowayou.' Harri never explains his words because there are that: *his*.

Kelman deftly creates a novel that is as much about language as it is about youth, and Henry's two languages neatly reflect both his naïveté and his confidence. Harri is still adjusting to life in London. He has made some bad friends, the type of friends who defile churches, harass the elderly, and may very well have murdered 'the dead boy,' as Harri calls him throughout. Kelman emphasizes the dichotomy of Harri's two lives, two countries; half of his family remains in Ghana, waiting. Harri, aware of his own weakness and the weaknesses in others, consistently translates English words and idioms for the reader. He explains that AKA 'stands for also known as' and that superheroes are 'special people who protect you.' Harri wants so much to understand his new world and to be a part of it that he cannot stop voicing his discoveries. Conversely, Harri never explicates the pieces of his Ghanian dialect. This, he understands. Here, he is confident. One must admire the author's ability to weave this pidgin language—not his own—into the novel. A literary maxim insists that most first novels are rooted in autobiography; Kelman's work defies that, and he should be admired even more for his ability to give a believable voice to such a compassionate young boy.

With endless aplomb, Harri and his best friend resolve to illuminate the truth behind 'the dead boy's'—simply because it must be done. Their confidence is beautiful and naïve, like that which we have in our native languages. We understand how our own language is supposed to work, though often only implicitly. Harri asks, 'Who'd chook a boy just to get his Chicken Joe's?' Such an act represents a grave disturbance, and even Harri, coming from so far away, knows this.

Kelman created a fine first novel, worthy of its Man Booker prize nomination. In a recent article in *The Guardian*, former UK Poet Laureate, Andrew Motion accused the prize judges of focusing their nominations on readability rather than quality. Kelman countered, 'I don't get the idea that readability and quality should be mutually exclusive. I think they should be combined.' Which is exactly what he has done.

Tiffany Gibert, 2011

Read Review B and use the chart below to find the features of
a book review.

Paragraph	
	Tells the reader the title of the book and the name of the author
	In one or two sentences explains very simply what the book is about
	Connects the readers with the book
	Gives an opinion about the book
	Describes the setting
	Gives the plot outline
	Describes a central character
	Explains the central character's problems
	Describes the supporting characters
	Describes a special moment in the book
	Discusses the style of the book
	Gives a clear recommendation

Now answer these questions:

1. What is the reviewer's attitude to the subject matter?
2. What is the thesis of the review?
3. How does the writer support the thesis?
4. What can we guess about the audience/readership for this review?
5. What technique does the reviewer use to close the review?

Activity

Imagine that you were asked to write a review about a novel that you have recently read.

Paragraph 1: Introduction	• Tells the reader the title of the book and the name of the author. • In one or two sentences, explain very simply what the book is about. The introduction, therefore, should state a central thesis, and set the tone of the review. • If you like the book, convince people to read it; but if you didn't like it, your introduction should show this. • You could open your review by retelling a typical moment from the book that conveys your opinion.
Paragraph 2: Describe the plot	What happens in the book? You should not spoil the ending for the reader. But you may want to summarize the basic setting and plot. An alternative way might be to write a sentence about each main character.
Paragraphs 3 and 4: Analyse the book*	How does the book affect you? Are the events and characters believable? Is the style effective? Are there any special moments? How is the book related to your own experience?
Paragraph 5: Recommendation	Would you recommend this book to others? Why?

*Remember that while the structure is similar for all reviews, the content depends on the focus provided in the question. For example, if you are asked to focus on a certain theme, you should not analyse what affected you in paragraphs 3 and 4; you should analyse the theme of the novel instead.

Other considerations for writing a review

Questions	Notes
Think about the kind of publication you are writing for	
What is your role as writer: superior, expert, peer, friend, advisor?	
Think about the kind of audience you are writing for	
Figure out your attitude: clever, humorous, intelligent, opinionated, balanced?	

Activity

Take one of these items: video game, book, film, CD, concert, restaurant or café and write a review. Before writing use the table below to help you to plan your ideas and get your message across clearly.

	Video game	Concert	Song or album	Restaurant or café	Music video
1.		Atmosphere		Food	
2.		Songs		Service	
3.		Quality of the performance		Price	
4.		Length of show		Atmosphere	

Remember:
1. Communicate a clear opinion about the subject matter.
2. Make sure you sound knowledgeable.
3. Make sure your language is appropriate to your audience.

Informative and persuasive writing: text type – written instructions

What is a set of instructions?

A set of instructions explains how to make or produce something. You do this by making sure that the reader can complete the task you have described. Instructions can be a set of procedures, such as a recipe, or guidelines for assembling a product from a kit. They are set out in a logical step-by-step fashion to enable the reader to complete something successfully.

Writing to a specific audience

When giving instructions, you are writing in the role of 'expert' and your readers are the 'learners'. When writing a set of instructions, address the readers directly but politely. You may want to use a more chatty style if you are addressing friends or classmates. However, make sure that your instructions are always clear. There are a number of different strengths for the advice you want to give so you may want to qualify your verbs: 'You may / might / can / could / ought to / etc.' These modal verb phrases can help you to achieve the correct level of politeness towards your audience.

Structure

Instructions are clearly based on a timeline. They are problem-driven and answer a question: How do I achieve X, Y or Z?

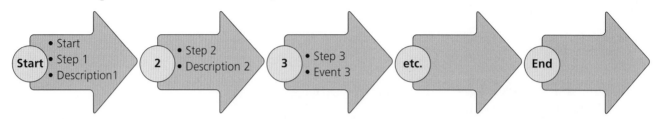

Instructions should have four parts: title, introduction, main body and conclusion.

- **Title**

    Your title should explain in plain language what you are writing about and why your readers should read the document. Include significant key words that alert readers to the content, for example, 'Installing and Operating a Printer Cartridge' or 'Making Spinach Rolls'. This will help your readers decide whether the text will help them or not.

- **Introduction**

    The introduction may include the topic you will discuss and the background. This is particularly important when giving advice. For a set of operating instructions, impatient readers will skip the introduction and start reading the numbered steps, so keep it simple. You may need to give a list of the ingredients or equipment required.

- **The main body**

    This will give your readers a roadmap to follow and will explain to them each step to follow. The body of your instructions should be organized chronologically. It may help you to plan this section by sketching a flow chart to make sure that you have all the steps in the right order.

- **Conclusion**

    Your conclusion should tell the reader what they can do once they have finished making/assembling the product. If you think the whole process is very complicated, your instructions might state how to get further help.

Tone and style

Be careful to give your readers polite but friendly instructions. Do not sound too bossy! In the real world a lot of people hate reading instructions, and will only do so when they are hopelessly lost. Your readers may become impatient, frustrated, or even angry. Therefore:

- explain each step of the operation
- limit the amount of information in each step
- use bullet points or numbers.

Phrase each step as if your reader had just asked, 'What should I do next?' Answer directly with a simple verb phrase 'Add two cups of flour.' A precise verb helps the reader know what to do.

'*In a bowl, **combine** cooked spinach, sour cream, mayonnaise, dressing mix, onions, and water chestnuts. **Mix** well. **Spread** evenly over tortillas and **roll** tortillas tightly. **Chill** the mixture overnight. **Slice** into 1-inch pieces.*'

Avoid passive statements like 'Two cups of sugar are added'. The reader may well ask 'Added to what?' or 'Added how?'

Sample sets of instructions

Instructions A

A simple recipe (A)

Scrambled eggs are simple and quick to make and can be eaten for breakfast, lunch or dinner.

Method

1. Take two eggs and break them **(B)**.

2. Add salt and pepper to the eggs in the bowl and 1 tablespoon of milk per egg and then the mixture is beaten **(C)** for around 2 minutes with a fork until the eggs have blended.

3. Meanwhile warm a saucepan over a moderate heat. Once the pan is warm, add 1 teaspoon of butter per egg and melt the butter by tilting the pan, so that it **(D)** melts evenly.

4. As soon as the butter turns to liquid, add the beaten eggs and allow the eggs to set slightly. The eggs are not stirred **(E)** at this point.

5. As soon as the eggs start to solidify, take a wooden spoon and scrape the eggs from the sides of the pan and **(F)** fold the solidifying mix into the middle taking care not to burn the eggs. This should take about 4 minutes. **(G)**

6. Serve. **(H)**

7. Remove the pan from the heat. The eggs will continue to cook due to the heat from the pan.

8. Break up any lumps of egg.

Variations to the recipe

There are a number of different ways to make your scrambled eggs more exciting. Try adding some chopped onion and garlic in the butter. Fry a few mushrooms in the melted butter before pouring in the raw egg mixture. Alternatively, you might like to try adding grated cheese or a few chopped herbs to the egg mixture.

In Instructions A, there are a number of problems (A–H). Make changes to the text so that the meaning becomes clearer.

	Problem	Solution
A	The title is vague	
B		
C		
D		
E		
F		
G		
H		

Activity

Write a set of instructions on one of the topics given below:

- Fashion: how to apply make-up for a certain occasion
- Food: a recipe for a favourite dish
- Sport: how to play a game
- Hobbies: instructions on how to make an object using origami or paper folding
- Social interaction: give a set of directions for getting from one place in school to another

Informative and persuasive writing: text type – brochure, flyer, leaflet and pamphlet

What are they?

Businesses, clubs, organizations and government bodies use **leaflets, flyers** and **pamphlets** to communicate information. **Brochures** have a similar function but are longer, running to several pages. These texts can advertise a service or a product, or draw attention to a cause or event. One key feature is that they focus on one key theme, idea or range of products. The information is set out in a simple but attractive format. This encourages the reader to focus on the key message.

Writing to a specific audience

You should know who you are aiming your brochure/leaflet/ pamphlet at so you can write your text from the reader's point of view. In deciding to use a leaflet/brochure/pamphlet to communicate your message, you should ask yourself the following basic questions:

- Who is the audience? What special interest do they have in your information, service or product?
- What does the audience want to know? What are your readers' concerns?
- What does the audience already know, and how much more do they need to know?

Types of texts

The **informative text** is factual. In it you present facts previously unknown to the audience, and it attracts readers by satisfying curiosity. For example:

- a health authority explains how its services work
- a new school club introduces itself: what it does, when and how frequently the members meet.

A **persuasive text** uses reasoned argument. You have to present information and convince the audience to reach certain conclusions, for example to ask readers change their behaviour by using or buying certain products. This could be:

- a leaflet by a medical practice on healthy lifestyles
- a leaflet from a shop or business asking the audience to buy its products.

Instructional texts ask people to take certain actions. They may be used to give advance warning of a problem. These are used by authorities to direct and control activities, such as in emergencies. Alternatively an instructional pamphlet will give clear steps about how to solve a problem. For example:

- what to do in case of a power shortage
- how to apply for a place at university.

Also some leaflets/pamphlets/brochures will use a mixture of information, persuasion and instruction.

Understanding the texts

On the following pages you will find four very different flyers, brochures and leaflets (A–D). Analyse each one noting in particular the features shown in the table below.

	Sample A	Sample B	Sample C	Sample D
Subject matter				
Purpose of the text				
Role of the author of the text				
Target audience				
Use of language				
Use of layout and structure				
Other comments				

Once you have completed the table, decide which of the flyers you think is most effective. Give reasons.

Sample A

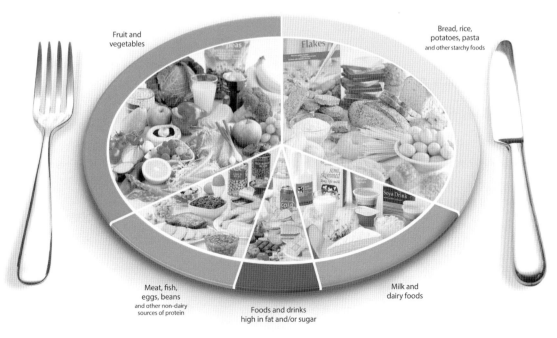

The eatwell plate

Use the eatwell plate to help you get the balance right. It shows how much of what you eat should come from each food group.

Fruit and vegetables

Bread, rice, potatoes, pasta and other starchy foods

Flakes

Meat, fish, eggs, beans and other non-dairy sources of protein

Foods and drinks high in fat and/or sugar

Milk and dairy foods

© Crown copyright 2013

Public Health England in association with the Welsh Government, the Scottish Government and the Food Standards Agency in Northern Ireland

Sample B

Food Choices

When your appetite is poor   Information for Patients and Carers

Is this leaflet for you?

If you have lost weight or your appetite is poor, making simple changes to your meals and snacks may help. This advice may not be suitable for some people with conditions such as swallowing difficulties or diabetes. Ask your doctor or nurse for further advice if you are unsure.

Eating well when your appetite is poor

- Eat little and often - 3 small meals a day with 2-3 snacks in between meals

- Include meat, fish, chicken, eggs, milk, cheese, yoghurt, beans or lentils at each meal

- Avoid low fat, sugar-free, diet foods and drinks

- Try ready made meals if you don't feel like cooking

- Having your drinks after meals may prevent you feeling full

- Try to have a pint of full fat milk every day. You can enrich this by stirring in 2-4 tablespoons of dried milk powder. Use this instead of milk or water in drinks, cooking, cereals and puddings.

Eat what you enjoy most!

Ideas for meals and adding extra calories

Breakfast

- Cereal or porridge with milk, cream or sugar

- Roll or toast thickly spread with butter or margarine and jam, marmalade or honey

- Bacon, egg or sausages

Lunch or Dinner

- Soup - add milk, cream or grated cheese

- Sandwiches with meat, fish, cheese or eggs. Add mayonnaise, salad cream or chutney.

- Meals with creamy or cheese sauces such as macaroni cheese, lasagne or fish in sauce

- Pies, pastries, pizza, sausages

- Chips, roast potatoes or mashed potatoes with butter, milk, cream or cheese

- Vegetables with white sauce, butter or cheese

Puddings

- Milk puddings with extra jam, sugar or cream

- Cakes, pastries, jelly or trifle. Add cream, ice-cream or evaporated milk.

- Creamy, full fat yoghurts with extra sugar

Snacks and Drinks

- Crackers, crumpets, toast, pancakes or teacakes. Add butter, cheese or jam.

- Biscuits, chocolate, crisps, nuts

- Milky drinks such as coffee, hot chocolate, milk shakes, malted drinks. Add sugar and cream.

- Nourishing drinks such as Complan or Build-up can be bought in supermarkets or pharmacy shops.

If you continue to lose weight after following this advice, contact your doctor or nurse.

Developed by the Tayside Nutrition Network with contributions from patients and carers. Feb 2010

NHS
Tayside

Sample C

A road to child safety

Safe Play

Children need a SAFE PLACE TO PLAY, such as a backyard, fenced park or recreational area. They should always be ACTIVELY SUPERVISED by an adult.

Passenger Safety

Whenever children are in a car they should be buckled-up in CHILD RESTRAINTS that are correct for each child's size and weight.

For more information on the correct restraint for your child call the RTA HOTLINE on 1800 042 865. Check all restraints have the 🔲 AUSTRALIAN STANDARDS mark and that second-hand restraints are not damaged in any way. It is recommended that all restraints are properly fitted and checked by an Authorised Restraint Fitter.

If possible, place children in the BACK SEAT of the car and encourage them to use the 'safety door' which is closest to the footpath (and away from the road).

Bicycle Safety & Small Wheels

A young child's skull is soft and easily injured from a collision or fall.

Whenever children are riding wheeled toys or bicycles, it is important that they are wearing a correctly fitted and 🔲 AUSTRALIAN STANDARDS approved HELMET. This is an ADULT'S RESPONSIBILITY.

Young children who wear helmets from the moment they start riding their first wheeled toy are more likely to continue the helmet wearing habit.

Driveway Safety

Small children can move surprisingly quickly and can be impossible to see from inside a car, especially if they are immediately behind it.

ALWAYS SUPERVISE children whenever a vehicle is to be moved - hold their hands or hold them close to keep them safe.

Pedestrian Safety

HOLD HANDS with children in and around traffic, until they are at least 10 years old. If your hands are full, make sure children hold onto a trolley or pram, a bag, or even your arm or sleeve.

Kids are always watching - they want to be just like adults - so make sure you SET A GOOD EXAMPLE.

While walking, TALK WITH CHILDREN about why it is necessary to stop, and what you need to look and listen for. Explain where it is safer to cross and why.

Remember that WHEREVER A CAR MAY BE MOVING CAN BE DANGEROUS. This includes quiet and busy streets, traffic lights and roundabouts, pedestrian crossings, footpaths, driveways, car parks, and around schools.

Parked Cars

Parked cars can heat up very quickly, even with windows wound down, and older children can touch controls and may set the vehicle in motion.

ALWAYS TAKE CHILDREN WITH YOU; leaving them alone in cars, even for a short period, is illegal and dangerous.

MOTOR ACCIDENTS AUTHORITY

Kidsafe
Child Accident Prevention Foundation of Australia
NEW SOUTH WALES

For more information
Any questions? Please ask Kidsafe staff or see our selection of brochures.
Ph: (02) 9845 0890   website: www.kidsafensw.org

Sample D

Sample Information and Support Leaflet:

Support Leaflet for Children and Young People

We know that because you have been courageous enough to talk to us you might have remembered some bad experiences. So you *may* be feeling angry, frightened, unhappy or lonely.

You don't have to cope with this by yourself. There are people and organisations that can help you.

We want to help you find the help you need. You may want to speak to an adult you trust such as a parent, your Children's Support Worker or someone else.

This leaflet gives some places you can to get in touch with to find people to speak to and get information.   These include *phoning* a helpline, looking at *websites* and *email*. There is also information from people who have gone through the same kind of thing as you.

Remember all these methods are here to help you.

Don't be embarrassed, don't think you can only talk about one part of your life, don't think anything that you want to ask is stupid. *You can talk about anything.*

It could be about your experiences, your home, your family, your friends, your school or anything else that is on your mind. *You can get in touch with them as many times as you want to*. They are there for you.

There are lots of organisations that are able to provide you with the support, advice and any information you need. We have given the phone numbers, email addresses and websites of a few organisations below. A lot of the websites have a homepage for everyone but they also have special pages for people that are your age.

Over the page, after the contact information, there are *Top Tips*. They are worth reading because they will tell you things that might be helpful including what a freephone number is and how to hide the websites you have looked at from anyone else that uses the computer.

Childline
Phone (freephone number) number: 0800 1111
Website Homepage: www.childline.org.uk
Web page for You 1: www.childine.org.uk/Helpandadvice.asp
Web Page for You 2: www.childine.org.uk/Just4U.asp

Women's Aid
Website: www.womensaid.org.uk
Website 2: www.scottishwomensaid.co.uk
Web page for You: www.thehideout.org.uk

NSPCC

The NSPCC has a few different websites you might be interested in. If you have a look at each of them you will probably find one that suits you more than the others.

Phone number: 0808 800 5000 (freephone number)

Textphone number (for deaf people): 0800 056 0566 (freephone number)

Website 1: www.NSPCC.org.uk

Website 2: www.nspcc.org.uk/kidszone

Website 3: www.worriedneed2talk.org.uk

Website 4: www.there4me.com

www.thereforme.com has an online advisor who you can talk to live by email if you want to. Just follow the link above and on the purple menu on the left of the screen there is a line that says 1-2-1. Click on this and then follow the simple instructions).

Refuge

Website Homepage: www.refuge.org.uk

Domestic abuse Helpline

Phone Number: 0800 2000 247 (freephone number)

Cool 2 Talk

Website Homepage: www.cool2talk.org

Samaritans

Phone number: 08457 90 90 90

Website Homepage: www.samaritans.org

TOP TIPS

Here are some tips about the information we have given you.

Phone Tip: After the phone numbers you may see the words freephone number. This means you can call this number from any phone and nobody will have to pay for it. This includes home phones, a mobile phone, even a phone at school or in an office.

Website Tip: If you want to you can make it a secret that you have looked at any website. This means you can use any computer to look at it (including home, school or an office) and no one will ever know you have been on a website. Here is a link to the instructions that tell you how to do it.

http://www.worriedneed2talk.org.uk/cover_your_tracks.htm

Structure

Informational texts are problem-driven. The problem is stated or implied. In the samples above, what problem does each leaflet address?

Despite their short length, there must be an obvious beginning stating the issue, a middle that illustrates a number of possibilities to solve the problem and a conclusion explaining what further action to take.

Make sure that the information is of real importance to the audience.

- **Opening/heading/title**

  The title should be brief, summarizing the point. Try to use a short, memorable phrase.

  Because you will want your readers to read further than this:

  - ▶ give the name of the organization or company that has produced the text

  - ▶ write a clear focused heading/title

  - ▶ state the purpose of the leaflet

  - ▶ state your message.

- **Sub-headings**

  Use sub-headings to give further explanation. You can also use headings to separate your ideas. Sometimes the sub-headings are questions.

- **Body text**

  - ▶ Use short paragraphs and mark them with headings.

  - ▶ Make sure your first sentences contain the point of the message.

  - ▶ Begin with the benefits of your message.

  - ▶ Organize your paragraphs/headings from most important to least important.

  - ▶ Use bullet-pointed lists that are easy to read.

  - ▶ Highlight single lines in a different font size or colour to make a strong point.

- **Close**

  Make sure your readers know what to do next. Include an email address, telephone number, website, or some other form of response mechanism such as a reply coupon.

Tone and style

- Write your text with your imaginary audience in mind.

- Always show respect for your readers and use appropriate language.

- Your vocabulary should match the formality of the message and the audience; use appropriate register.

- It is perfectly acceptable to use a familiar tone, including jargon and slang, in order to sell your product to a teenage audience but a leaflet about healthcare for the elderly, for example, should be informative and formal.

Exam tips ✓

Because space and word count is limited in Paper 2, your text should be simple and to the point. In the Language B Paper 2 assessment you will be marked on the quality of your texts, not the overall layout. Nonetheless, you might like to plan the format of your leaflet and indicate where you would place your images. This might make your text easier to understand.

Understanding the text

Re-read Sample D. Analyse the content in the table below. You can add your own comments about the effectiveness of the elements of the text.

	Text	Effectiveness of the elements
Structure: thesis-driven or problem-driven?		
What is the subject matter?		
What is the purpose of the text?		
Who is the potential audience?		
How does the text grab the readers' attention?		
How many ideas are in the body text? How are the paragraphs organized?		
What is the order of the main ideas in the body text?		
How does the flyer close?		
How suitable is the language of the text for its intended audience?		
Other comments		

Activity

Write an informative leaflet, brochure, pamphlet or flyer on one of the following topics:

- concepts of beauty and health: eating disorders
- diet and nutrition: healthy living
- epidemics: what to do in the case of an outbreak of flu
- health services: a guide to local services
- hygiene: a guide for working in the kitchen
- illnesses: a brochure explaining the services of a doctor's surgery/clinic
- mental health: coping with stress
- physical exercise: a guide for physical fitness.

Informative and persuasive writing: text type – advertising copy

What is advertising copy?

Advertising aims to grab the interest of the prospective customers and to persuade them to make a purchase, all within a few short seconds. Advertising copy can be found in print, radio, or television advertising messages and is used to grab the attention of potential customers. Adverts use both linguistic and visual text. Full-page colour ads can be found in feature magazines. Advertising copy is the written or spoken part of an advert. Remember that the magazine readers do not have to look at the advertisements, so your copy needs to persuade your readers to take an interest within a few short moments.

Magazine ads do more than just sell products; they also promote ideas, reinforce public opinion of a brand, and are fun to look at. Those ads often depict a specific modern culture, relate to current events, and reflect the values and culture of the times. For example, what does the advert opposite tell you about life in the USA in the 1940s?

Writing to a specific audience

For advertising copy to be effective, somebody must read what you write, understand it and then do something. It is important that you write as if you are talking directly to your customer, so use a level of formality they would accept, use vocabulary and if necessary jargon and slang they would know and would probably use. Always visualize the kind of people you want to buy the product. Write down what you know about those people and think about how to sell your product to them.

Techniques and structure

- Some advertising copy is thesis-driven: 'Manchester is a great place for a great day out'. Some advertising is problem-driven: 'Tired of false promises advertisers make?' In either case, the copy will support the thesis or answer the consumers' question.

- Give your message a more personal tone. Use the words 'you' and 'your'.

- If you want your readers to react quickly, use command forms of verbs to make your writing more direct: 'Call now!'

- If you want to suggest an action, be more polite: 'When you want to order, just give us a call.'

- Make an emotional appeal to the readers. The faster the reader feels the need to own the product, the faster they will decide to buy.

- Support your emotional appeal with logic. Concentrate on your readers' needs, and stress how your product or service will benefit them.

From Bean to Bar

When making our products, we believe that every step from bean to bar is equally important. That's why we make sure we use only the finest organically grown Trinitario cocoa beans to make our chocolate or taking that extra time conching (stirring constantly) our chocolate to bring out the intense flavour that has become our trademark.

More techniques for writing advertising copy

Body copy is what really sells a product. It contains the product details and stresses the benefits of the product to the customer. This copy uses emotional and logical appeal to create a desire for the product.

- Grab the readers' attention.
- Promise a benefit.
- Talk about what job the product does and how it does it.
- Keep the readers' interest.
- Make the product sound attractive. Describe it using sense perception: the looks, feel, taste, smell of the product.
- Associate positive emotions with the product.
- Convey the meaning that 'you [the reader] will be happier if you buy our product.'
- Mention any special offer or free stuff that comes with the product or the service.
- Explain what to do: where to buy the product or find more information.

> **Writing tip**
>
> Here are two mnemonics to help you write advertising copy.
>
> ANSVA
>
> grab Attention, create a Need, show how to Satisfy it, Visualize the benefits, call for Action
>
> AIDA
>
> Attention, Interest, Direct, Action

Tone and style

- Keep sentences clear and simple.
- Use lots of one- or two-syllable words.
- Use short paragraphs.
- Keep in mind the ideal reader that you defined at the beginning.
- Use appropriate language and address systems.
- Revise, revise and revise your copy.

Samples of advertising copy

Copy A

Warwick Castle, UK

Medieval England is bought back to life at Warwick Castle but the history of the castle dates back to the 11th century when it was built by William the Conqueror. Warwick Castle offers something for everyone, young or old. This is a typical castle with a Great Hall, state rooms, Chapel, Ghost Tower and dungeons.

Outside there is a Victorian rose garden, conservatory and peacock garden and in the summer there is a full programme of activities. There are live shows demonstrating jousting, archery, falconry and combat as well as a huge reconstructed trebuchet (the largest catapult in the world) that is fired twice daily.

Visitors can watch a film called Dream of Battle that tells the story of one of the Castle's greatest conflicts through the eyes of a 12 year old preparing for battle. The Ghost Tower hosts a chilling live-action experience with actors and effects to recreate the murder of Sir Fulke Greville.

With so much to see and do the Castle also offers plenty of places to eat and a gift shop.

Tourist Information UK

Copy B

The Valleys of South Wales – Naturally speaking

You might already have a picture in your mind of what holidays in the South Wales Valleys are all about. It probably needs an update. We'd like to introduce you to The Welsh Valleys of today.

We are very proud of our Industrial Heritage, The Valleys were at the heart of the Industrial Revolution. Today you can follow the great stories and achievements of that age, history is all around, and on show in a range of Visitor Attractions, the only coal mine is Big Pit in Blaenavon where you can take a tour with an ex miner. What you will also see are country parks, lakes and forests, open hillsides and green mountains.

And here's another surprise. The world is just waking up to the fact that The Valleys are home to a captivating choice of attractions and places to visits, like Caerphilly Castle or Blaenavon, a World Heritage site. Not to mention the wide range of activities and events that can be played out against our terrific landscape.

So you'll find that things have changed. But what hasn't altered is the strong Valleys spirit. Walk into any hotel or restaurant and you will find that Valleys folk are genuinely warm and friendly. It all comes naturally in the South Wales Valleys – the Heart & Soul of Wales.

For holidays or short breaks in South Wales, The Valleys make a refreshing change.

The Valleys

Analysis

The two texts (Copy A and Copy B) are advertising copy for tourism destinations in the UK. Read them again. Which is the most effective? Look at the following points to help you decide.

Structure

How good is:

- the headline?
- the copy?

Techniques

Does each text:

- state a clear thesis or pose a clear question?
- grab the readers' attention?
- promise a benefit?
- keep the readers' interest?
- make the product sound attractive?
- describe it using sense perceptions?
- associate positive emotions with the product?
- mention also any special offer?
- explain what to do next?

Tone and style

Would you say that the text:

- is clear and simple to read?
- uses lots of one- and two-syllable words?
- uses short sentences and paragraphs?
- uses appropriate language and address systems and conveys the meaning 'Visit us and be happy'?

Activity

Look at these adverts below and write suitable advertising copy for these social causes. In each case you have the visual. Complete the advertisement with a headline and copy.

A. Anti drinking and driving campaign, Australia

B. Healthy diet, New Zealand

C. Anti-smoking campaign, UK

> **Advertising social causes**
>
> Social advertising is a process for influencing human behaviour on a large scale. It uses advertising techniques to benefit specific groups within society rather than to make profits for commercial companies. For example, governments and non-governmental organizations (NGOs) use advertising to promote health and social issues and to bring about positive change. This could be:
> - adopting a new behaviour pattern (Donate now)
> - rejecting a potential behaviour pattern (Say no to drugs)
> - modifying a current behaviour pattern (Eat more vegetables)
> - abandoning an old behaviour pattern (Stop smoking).

Professional writing: text type – official report

What is a report?

A report is a presentation of facts and findings, usually as a basis for further action. It is written for a specific readership and may be kept as an official record. Reports can be written about events that have already taken place. They can tell the reader about a problem that existed, what action was taken to solve the problem, what new information (if any) was discovered and how this relates to the original problem. Such a report might suggest any further steps that must be taken.

Alternatively, reports can be written about present issues and future solutions. They can set out an existing problem, discuss different solutions and come to some recommendations as to which solution would work best.

Writing to a specific audience

Reports are written for a specific audience for a specific purpose. Therefore, report writing requires careful planning. You should always keep in mind what the reader needs to know. Anticipate and answer clearly any questions that the reader may have. To write a successful report, ensure that your intended audience:
- understands everything you have written without difficulty
- accepts your facts, findings, conclusions and recommendations
- decides to take the action you have recommended.

Structure

A report should start with the statement of a problem and end with a conclusion about what action to take. Here is a possible structure:
1. Define the problem
2. Present the information: define, categorize, compare, prioritize
3. Analyse the information
4. Write your conclusions

Tone and style

The relationship between you as writer of the report and the audience is very formal. This means that the language you use must be formal too.

Simplify

Reports are written for people who have limited time. You should write a report that it is easy for the reader to understand and to act on. Nevertheless, you are supposed to write a report using formal English. Keep the language as straightforward as possible.

Active and passive voices

In formal written English, it is advisable to avoid 'I', and 'we'. For example, you might want to write, 'I investigated the level of factory pollution in the river'. Some report writers tend to use the passive form instead: 'The level of factory pollution in the river was investigated'. But now it is not clear if the author did it, someone else, or another group!

To convey the same information it should be 'The level of factory pollution in the river was investigated by the author', which is rather untidy. A trick some people use is 'The author investigated the level of factory pollution in the river'. Sometimes a sentence can be changed from the passive form to the active form by rearranging the words. Instead of 'The pollution level was doubled by the factory's discharges', you can simply write 'The factory's discharges doubled the pollution'.

Often a sentence can be changed from the passive form to the active form by rearranging the words. Instead of 'Social conditions can be improved by the provision of preschool facilities', you can simply write 'Providing pre-school facilities can improve social conditions'. Also, instead of 'Water evaporation is likely to occur in deserts', it is better to write 'Water may easily evaporate in deserts.'

Different types of report

Your purpose and aim will determine what kind of report you write. Here are some basic types of report.

Observation – the police report

The first form of report is the **observation** (police report, also known as eyewitness account) which presents the facts of a situation in a plain narrative. This kind of report does not necessarily offer reasons, or causes and effects. This is a factual report. Its purpose is to inform, to give an accurate and objective statement of the facts. It is an obvious example of a narrative-driven text.

The most important part of police report writing is obtaining all the facts about the incident that has occurred. A person may have a complaint, for example, being threatened or intimidated, or being the victim of a theft. This person is known as the complainant. The complainant may have the most accurate information about the incident. Alternatively, a person may be a witness to an incident. A witness may have seen the events but is not necessarily involved personally.

When police officers arrive at a crime scene, they immediately begin to gather information. This can be harder than it sounds. If the complainant or the witness is upset, confused or in a state of shock, they might not be able to give a coherent, chronological statement of events. All information gathered for a police report must be sorted into a logical narrative. This is achieved by carefully organizing the information chronologically. This can require careful and sensitive questioning.

This information from the complainant and witnesses makes up the basis of the report. The police will need to gather information such as names, dates of birth, residence, place of the occurrence, dates and times of the occurrence, and facts about the incident.

Police reports follow a basic format to ensure that all of the important information is included. The written portion of a report will need to include the following:

- **A synopsis**

  This establishes what the complaint is, and where and when an incident occurred. For example, a police officer might start a report by writing 'At 10:15 AM on September 12, 2012, I responded to a call from police headquarters to go to Bright's Laundry at 123 Lime St. in reference to a complaint of a theft.' Here, in the first sentence the writer has established the date, the time, the location and the reason for the report.

- **Crime scene**

  Here the officer describes what was observed at the scene, what evidence has been recovered.

- **Witness statements**

  The report could continue, 'Upon my arrival, I met with Tim Johnson, date of birth 01/02/1987, who stated that an unknown person had taken $500.00 from his desk without his consent.'

- **Case status**

  Finally the investigating officer would add information about the case status, what they did to resolve the incident.

Activity

Construct a police report around this crime scene photograph. Remember to include a synopsis, a description of the crime scene, witness statements and the crime status.

The evaluative report

Another kind of report is the **appraisal/evaluation**. For example, the author of a report for the consumer will inform the reader about the purpose of a product, its uses and limitations, coming to some conclusions about the product's value and making recommendations about whether to buy the product or not. It is therefore a problem-driven text. The writer of the appraisal should have more knowledge than the reader. Therefore, the purpose of the appraisal is to inform, to make a judgment and help the reader to decide what action to take.

The report for the consumer helps potential buyers to choose between products that are very similar. Such reports give the advantages and disadvantages of different varieties of particular goods or services. Look at the example below.

ConsumerReports.org

Five questions to answer before buying a toaster

It's not a new car or flat-screen TV, but the next toaster you buy could be with you for a long, long time. Choose wisely and the small appliance will help your mornings run smoothly, while maybe adding a nice visual accent to the kitchen. The wrong toaster, however, might make you hot under the collar. Here are five things to ask yourself before getting your next toaster.

How many slots?

Toasters come with one, two, or four slots. If your countertop is crammed, a single-slot toaster has a slim profile, plus it can accommodate oversize items, say a long slice of artisanal bread. Four-slot toasters claim the most real estate, though they're helpful if you're often toasting for a crowd. Two-slot toasters, the most common option in our Ratings of several dozen models, combine versatility in a fairly compact housing.

What's my price range?

You can spend $15 on a toaster or 15 times that amount. The majority of models on our recommended list fall in the $30 to $60 price range. Spending more generally gets you additional features, such as a bagel setting, countdown timer, and slide-out crumb tray. Depending on how you plan to use the toaster, it might be worth spending an extra $20 or so for these conveniences.

Would I be better off with a toaster oven?

If you all you want is toast, buy a toaster, since this appliance still delivers the fastest, most consistent results. But a toaster oven might make sense if you also do a lot of countertop baking, broiling, and reheating.

A handful of models in our Ratings handle these tasks well while also doing a relatively good job of toasting.

Is it safe?

There have been several recalls of toasters in recent years due to fire hazards and other safety-related issues. These recalled toasters should no longer be in stores, but it's still worth running a background check on toasters you're considering on recalls.gov and saferproducts.gov. The latter will include consumer complaints against models that may not have been recalled. Also, make sure any toaster you choose features automatic shutoff, which will turn off the heating elements in the event of a jam.

Does style matter?

Unless you plan to keep it in a cabinet, your toaster will be a visually prominent appliance. Models with stainless-steel housings could coordinate well with your other appliances. KitchenAid is one of several manufacturers that offers toasters in an array of bright colors. One of the most interesting designs in our Ratings belongs to the Magimix Vision Toaster, whose clear side walls allow you to watch your toast turn brown.

Daniel DiClerico, 2012

Activity

Draw up a results table and invent four brands of toasters. Using the criteria below, identify the strengths and weaknesses of each toaster.

Name of toaster model	Slots	Price range	Additional functions	Safety features	Stylishness
A					
B					
C					
D					

Write your report for the consumer based on your findings.

The leading report – problem and solutions

A third kind of report is the leading report. It examines a problem or explains a situation and leads the readers to a specific conclusion. It is used for making plans and solving problems. Usually, an organization commissions someone to research and write a report. As a result of the report, the reader(s) will decide whether to accept the recommendations. Therefore, the purpose of the leading report is to persuade. It is another example of a problem-driven report.

An effective leading report…

…can be written using the following structure.

- Define the problem.
- Present the necessary information.
- Analyse the information.
- Write your conclusions.

You can practise further report writing on one of the following topics:

- Surgery: an accident report (observation)
- Concepts of beauty and health: beauty products (an evaluative report)
- Diet and nutrition: a leading report on the food available from school caterers
- Mental health: a leading report on stress among Diploma Programme students at your school or college
- Physical exercise: an evaluative report on different forms of exercise

> ## Activity
>
> As a member of the student council, you have been receiving complaints about sightings of snakes on campus. Write a report for the college management.

Professional writing: text type – proposal (HL only)

What is a proposal?

The general purpose of any proposal is to persuade a sponsor to fund a project. For example, you can ask for funds to buy goods and/or services. Alternatively, you can ask for a grant for a project that you would like to undertake, such as sponsorship for an educational visit that you would like to make but cannot afford. However, sponsors do not just give money away.

> Your proposal must explain what you are planning, how you plan to do it, when you plan to do it, how much it is going to cost and what the benefit will be.

Writing to a specific audience

Your sponsor can be an individual, a business or any organization you hope will contribute money or equipment to support your project. Your relationship is very formal and so your language must be very formal too. You may need to cite facts and figures as evidence and use technical language, if and when appropriate. These can add authenticity because concrete information will support your request.

Techniques and structure

There is no single formula for a proposal but you should break down your text into clear sections each with a heading. However, unlike a thesis-driven essay, a proposal is problem-driven. First you state the problem, explain the background to it, offer details of how to solve the problem and conclude by asking for help. Here are some headings you may wish to use:

- **Introduction**

  Give a concise introduction to your project. In it you should identify the aim of the project. State clearly the problem to be addressed and why it is important. Use supporting information such as statistics to make your point. Explain why a sponsor should give you funding.

- **The main body – the statement of need**

  You should now explain how you intend to get the job done, how long it will take and how much it will cost. The statement of need should also address who will benefit. Make sure to include the following points:

  - ▶ **Objectives**

    Indicate the expected outcomes of the project, preferably in measurable terms. This shows what you will do, for whom, by how much, and by when. When the project is completed, you will be able to evaluate it and determine whether the project succeeded or not in achieving its objectives. Identify short-term and long-term objectives.

  - ▶ **Methods**

    Describe your plan of action for how the objectives will be achieved and which stages you will use to make the plan succeed.

- **Timetable**

  Describe how long (days, months) specific tasks or components of the project will take. If possible, include a timeline with milestones here.

- **Budget**

  Present the overall cost of the project. A detailed budget should be divided into categories such as salaries, travel costs, supplies and equipment.

- **Conclusion**

  The proposal is different to other forms of writing and requires no formal conclusion. However, you could emphasize any benefits of your proposal for the sponsor. In addition, you might like to draw the sponsor's attention to any material which illustrates your project or the social background in which the project operates.

Tone and style

- Take a clear stand in your proposal and set a positive tone.
- Avoid verbs such as: might, could, ought, may, should, hope, it appears.
- Remember: point, example and explanation; support your argument with evidence.
- Use formal language and be very polite.
- Avoid exaggerated or emotional expressions.
- Use headings to help the reader understand the proposal.

Sample proposals

Proposal A

Proposal for new whiteboards at the Aziza School, Phnom Penh Cambodia

Introduction

I am writing to seek sponsors to solve a simple but recurring problem at The Aziza School where I recently volunteered as a classroom teacher. The Aziza School provides supplementary education for marginalized Cambodian communities. The school is located in the slums of Tonle Bassac in Phnom Penh, the capital of Cambodia. It has been providing free English lessons, leadership training, computer training, life skills, and medical services to nearly 250 young people since May 2005.

Objective

The problem is that the whiteboards in all five classrooms are very old and teachers cannot use them effectively any more. Students and teachers continually become frustrated because it is difficult to write on them. For a school without adequate numbers of text books, whiteboards are crucial for effective learning. The school would like to replace the whiteboards for each classroom, so that the teachers have writing surfaces that work well so that students (aged 6 –16) are able to learn much more effectively.

Statement of need

There are currently 247 students at The Aziza School. These students occupy 5 classrooms each day. The current whiteboards have been in the classrooms since the opening of the school in 2005. They do not work well because they have been in use for so long. As a result they can no longer be cleaned and anyway the poor lighting makes it difficult for the students to read what the teachers have written on the damaged surface of the boards.

None of these classrooms has a whiteboard that works well; due to their extensive use it is now impossible to clean the boards for each new lesson. It can take an average of ten minutes to remove the latest layer of writing all before we can start teaching. This time takes away a great deal from lesson time. Because of the length of time it takes to clean a whiteboard, the teachers have continuous interruptions in their lessons. Almost all classroom learning at The Aziza School requires a whiteboard, and it is difficult to get anything done without this basic classroom tool.

Solution

I propose that we purchase new whiteboards for each classroom. They can be replaced quickly, cheaply and effectively. There are many suppliers of whiteboards in the city and I am certain we can obtain a very competitive price. Therefore, I propose to purchase 5 whiteboards on behalf of The Aziza School. The old boards can be recycled for displays of students work.

Budget

New 2m x 1m whiteboards cost $30.00 each. Moreover, I am sure we can obtain a small discount if purchasing five or more, reducing the total cost to $147.50. Some whiteboards cost less than this price, but on the recommendations of others, I believe that purchasing a middle-priced whiteboard will be a wise and sustainable choice for The Aziza School. There will be no transport costs as teachers will be able to collect directly from the local supplier or manufacturer.

Conclusion

I think purchasing new whiteboards for each classroom would be of tremendous benefit to The Aziza School. It would put an end to the constant frustration of teachers and students losing lesson time and would drastically improve the quality of learning.

If you would like to donate please give your contribution to Annie Ang in Senior School Section.

I thank you in advance for considering contributing to this important purchase.

Analysis

Essential questions	Can you suggest any improvements to this section of the text?
Who is the audience for this proposal?	
Has the writer stated the problem clearly?	
Has the writer stated the cause of the problem clearly?	
Has the writer offered a clear solution?	
Has the proposer set out a series of clear points on the issue?	
What points does the writer make to support the proposal?	
Has the writer fully supported each point with appropriate factual information?	
Has the writer used formal English which is clear and easy for the sponsors to understand?	
What next step does the writer propose for the readers?	
Do you think the potential sponsors will accept the proposal?	
What improvements to the text would you suggest? How would the suggestions make the proposal more effective?	

Activity

You are working on a CAS social services project which is short of funds. Write a proposal for funding for a specific project. Here are some examples:

- Diet and nutrition: buying educational material/sponsoring a community health care project
- Health services: buying a specific piece of equipment
- Hygiene: sponsoring dental care
- Symptoms of good health: sponsoring a child immunization programme
- Health education
- Sports: buying equipment
- Travel: sponsoring an educational visit

Professional writing: text type – formal written correspondence

What is formal written correspondence?

With the coming of email, it is becoming less and less necessary to write letters of any kind, but the formal letters that you will write will probably be very important ones. You may need to write formal letters to different recipients for a number of reasons:

- an application for a job or internship to a company's human resources officer
- an enquiry to an academic office about a course of study and/or the facilities available at a specific college
- a covering letter for some research requesting an addressee to answer a questionnaire or a survey
- a letter of complaint to a customer relations officer or a local government official
- a letter to the editor of a newspaper or magazine commenting on an article that has appeared in the magazine or newspaper
- a letter of apology to an individual for any inconvenience/ embarrassment/damage/offense caused.

Some key functions

Function	Features
Apply	For example, writing to obtain a place at college, an internship, a job
Comment	Agreeing, disagreeing or offering a balanced opinion. In all cases, presenting a reasoned argument for your opinions. There should be direct references to and possibly quotes from the original article
Complain	<ul><li>Explaining a problem and the outcome you want</li><li>Outlining the steps you will take if you cannot resolve the problem</li><li>Asking for a response within a reasonable time</li></ul>
Explain	Linking causes and effects, using evidence, giving reasons and justifications
Enquire	Asking for more information concerning a product or service that interests us
Persuade	Writing in order to change a readers' behaviour. Appealing either to the reader's logic, senses or emotions (or a combination of these)
Request	<ul><li>Asking someone for permission to do something</li><li>Asking someone to do something for you</li></ul>

> **Note:**
>
> A letter could be a combination of functions, for example, you may be asked 'to narrate and describe'.

Style

It has been said that a formal letter is like a wedding; there are certain conventions that have to be followed. One set of conventions relates to form and layout. The other conventions relate to language and register.

	Required	Not acceptable
Form and layout	• Addresses • Date • A greeting • A closing salutation • Signing off with your name	• Smileys
Language and register	• Correct punctuation • Paragraphing • Formal vocabulary and phrasing	• Contractions • Idiomatic language • Abbreviations • SMS words or textese • Deliberate misspellings and slang e.g. 'gonna' • Swear words

Structure

A formal letter should be well presented and in the correct format. It is likely to have either a thesis- or a problem-driven structure.

- **Introduction**
  - ▶ If you do not know the name of the person, begin with the addressee's title above the salutation line. For example:

    The Personnel Manager,

    Name of company

    Date

    Dear Sir or Madam,

  - ▶ If you do know the name of the addressee, make sure you address the person appropriately (using Dr., Sir, Mr., Ms., etc.) and tailor your vocabulary to the purpose of the letter. You may still wish to write the person's job title above the salutation. Use the appropriate language register (formal, not casual). In English B, it is not necessary to include addresses but you must write the date.

  - ▶ If you know the name of the person you are writing to, it is acceptable to address the person by their last name: *Dear Mr/ Mrs. _____, Dear Dr. _____ .*

  - ▶ State the purpose of the letter: to make an enquiry, complain, request something, etc.

- **The main body**

  The paragraph or paragraphs in the middle of the letter should support the relevant purpose of the letter. Organize paragraphs into a clear and logical manner (PEE = point, example and explanation).

- **Conclusion**

  Before the closing, remember that it may be appropriate to thank the reader in some manner: 'Thank you for your time and consideration' (if you are making a request of some sort), or simply end with 'Thank you for your time'; 'I look forward to hearing from you'; 'I thank you in advance for your consideration of this matter'. If you do not know the person, it is usual to close with 'Yours faithfully'. If you have written the addressee's name, close with 'Sincerely,' or 'Yours sincerely'.

KISS = Keep it short and simple

Tone and style

The reason for writing formal letters is often to make an impression and have the desired effect on the reader. You may need to be able to express an opinion, to defend an argument, to sell yourself as a good candidate for a job, or to increase awareness of an issue. Therefore, you will have to communicate your ideas in a clearly organized manner. This will need much planning. In order to achieve this, the formal letter should be free of grammatical or spelling mistakes. Keep in mind that you need to be polite and formal at all times.

The tone and style should suit the addressee. In a personal letter, you would naturally use informal address. In the formal letter, the tone will be much drier, like that of an official report or proposal. However, even in a letter of complaint, where you might be justifiably angry, you should give an unemotional, logical account of the problem. Never swear or use exaggerated language.

Types of formal letter – the letter of enquiry

An example of a letter of enquiry is when you are applying to an organization speculatively, that is to say you are making an approach without them having advertised or announced a specific vacancy. This is also known as an unsolicited application and is a thesis-driven text, your main point being 'I am potentially a wonderful employee'.

Opening paragraph

Introduce yourself briefly and give your reason for writing. Let the reader know the kind of position you are seeking, why you are interested and how you heard about them.

Middle paragraphs

Show why their company in particular interests you, mention your qualifications and experience along with any further details that might make them interested in seeing you.. Refer to your enclosed CV and draw their attention to any particularly important points you would like them to focus on in it.

Closing paragraph

Thank them, explain your availability for interview and restate your enthusiasm for the organization and desire to be considered for posts that might as yet be unavailable.

Activity

Research into volunteering work available and find an organization for whom you would like to work. This could be at home or overseas, if you are thinking of taking a gap year.

Apply to the organization of your choice. Remember first to find out what kind of volunteers they need and what kind of work they offer. Complete the sample letter of enquiry below:

Name of addressee

Title of addressee

Name of organization

Date

Dear .....,

I am currently an IB student in (name of school /college) and I am writing to inquire about the possibility of a volunteer position in your organisation. I plan on graduating in June, 20XX and I would be interested in beginning between June-September of the same year. I am hoping to volunteer for a period of about nine months.

As part of my International Baccalaureate diploma I have taken X Y and Z as higher subjects. As a result I have some knowledge of A B and C. Therefore I feel I would be able to contribute to .....

For social service I have volunteered at .... As a result I have experience of ..... This might enable me to ....

In addition I am a keen (hobby/ interest /skill). Therefore I would be willing to ....

During the course of my senior school, I have become very interested in working in not for profit organizations in developing countries. I have been especially intrigued by (name of organization) and its work in the area of .... Thus, I am very interested in the work going on.

I am planning a visit (the name of the city /state / country) sometime early this summer. If possible, I would like to visit (name of the organization) at that time. I would be happy to discuss my application with you.

Enclosed is a copy of my CV. I have asked two of my teachers to write references on my behalf. I look forward to hearing from you.

Yours sincerely,

James Wu

Activity

What company or organization would you most like to work for? What department would you most like to find out about? What sort of work would you enjoy doing? Imagine applying for an internship with that company. Write a letter of enquiry asking about possible internships or paid work for the summer holiday with the employer of your dreams.

Types of formal letter – the letter of application

A letter of application is the one that accompanies your CV when you are applying for a job. Here is a fairly conventional plan for the layout of the paragraphs. Notice it is very similar to the letter of enquiry and is also a thesis-driven text.

Opening paragraph

Briefly identify yourself and the position you are applying for. Add how you found out about the vacancy.

Middle paragraphs

Give the reasons why you are interested in working for the company and why you wish to be considered for that particular post. Make a series of points:

- State your relevant qualifications and experience as well as the personal qualities that make you a suitable candidate.
- State what experience you have, what skills you have developed and why these are applicable to the position on offer. Do this for each relevant experience you have had.
- Inform the reader that you have enclosed your current CV and add any further information that you think could help your case.

Closing paragraph

Give your availability for interview, thank them for their consideration, restate your interest and close the letter.

Sample letter of application

Harvard Medical School

Boston, MA 02115

Dear Dr. Tsushima,

I am currantly a student at Anytown High School, where I have been studying biology. I plan to graduate next month and I am intrested in your work. Therefore, I am applying for an internship with you in your lab. My CV is enclosed. Please write soon back.

Best wishes and hugs

Willem van Hasselt

What is your opinion of this letter? Good, bad or indifferent? How many weaknesses can you find? List and categorize your findings.

Format	Content	Language	Attitude/other issues

Re-write the letter on behalf of the sender.

Activity

Look at the advertisement below for volunteers and write a letter of application for one of the posts.

Volunteers Wanted

We are currently seeking volunteers to provide a highly valued service to our patients. You may be a student or retiree, or just someone who has some time to give. Volunteers come from many backgrounds and walks of life and we recognise and value every volunteer's unique ability. The role of a volunteer at Chorlton Private Hospital is to help provide a positive experience for patients and to make a significant difference daily to them, their family and friends and staff. The volunteer recognises diversity by treating all people with dignity and respect.

Who can volunteer?

- People who have some available time and who wish to help others.
- People with a happy enthusiastic approach to life.
- People who enjoy chatting or being with others.
- People who enjoy being part of a team.
- People who care about others.
- People who want to make a difference.

What are the benefits of volunteering?

- The ability to work as valued members of the team.
- Experience new challenges, share and learn skills and abilities.
- Having fun, meeting new people and building friendships.
- Enrich the world of others whilst enriching your own.
- Satisfaction from doing something different to make a difference!
- Confidence.

What are some of the volunteer roles?

- Talking with patients.
- Assisting with patients' meals.
- Arranging and refreshing patients' flowers.
- Delivering newspapers and magazines.
- Escorting patients from Reception.
- Making up patient information packs.
- Tidying patient rooms.

How do I become a volunteer?

Contact the Clinical Services Manager – Linda Felix on (08) 4255 XXXX. You will be asked to come to the hospital to meet with us to talk about:

- Your interest in volunteering.
- What you hope to gain from your volunteer experience.
- Your preferred areas of service.
- Your available time and how best we can help you to become a part of the Chorlton Private Volunteer family.

Types of formal letter – the letter of complaint

Opening paragraph

The letter of complaint is an obvious example of a problem-driven text in which you address the reader in the hope of finding a solution to your problem. Therefore, introduce yourself briefly and give your reason for writing. Explain the exact nature of your complaint.

Middle paragraphs

Set out the exact narrative sequence of events that led to you receiving a faulty product or poor service. Explain what outcome or action you want.

Closing paragraph

Explain what action you will take if you do not receive satisfaction. Explain what specific action you want the addressee to take to resolve the problem.

Sample letter of complaint

Dear **(Contact Person)**

Re: **(account number, if applicable)**

On **(date)**, I **(bought, leased, rented, or had repaired)** a **(name of the product, with serial or model number or service performed)** at **(location, date and other important details of the transaction)**.

Unfortunately, your product **(or service)** has not performed well **(or the service was inadequate)** because **(state the problem)**. I am disappointed because **(explain the problem: for example, the product does not work properly, the service was not performed correctly, I was billed the wrong amount, something was not disclosed clearly or was misrepresented, etc.)**.

To resolve the problem, I would appreciate your **(state the specific action you want – money back, charge card credit, repair, exchange, etc.)**. Enclosed are copies **(do not send originals)** of my records **(include receipts, guarantees, warranties, canceled checks, contracts, model and serial numbers, and any other documents)**.

I look forward to your reply and a resolution to my problem and will wait until **(set a time limit)** before seeking help from a consumer protection agency or the Better Business Bureau. Please contact me at the above address or by phone at **(home and/or office numbers with area code)**.

Sincerely,

Activity

Use the template above to write one of the following letters of complaint.

1. You bought a faulty product from a store. Write a letter of complaint to the store demanding action.

2. You have just spent a weekend at an amusement park. You paid the full entrance fee. On arriving you discovered that many of the attractions and rides were out of action for maintenance. Write a letter of complaint asking for compensation.

3. You enrol at a local sports centre and health club to take a particular course or fitness programme. The facilities are unsatisfactory. Complain.

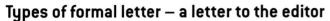

Types of formal letter – a letter to the editor

In many ways a letter to the editor is very similar in structure to an essay. It is therefore a thesis-driven text.

Opening paragraph

Identify the article and the issue you wish to discuss. Give a brief summary of your opinion on the matter. This is your thesis. Alternatively, you might be writing about a general problem or issue that concerns you, for example, 'The big jump in the cost of transport fares is of great concern to me.'

Middle paragraphs

Defend your main idea (thesis) with a series of supporting points. (Remember PEE = point, example, explanation.) You could also praise or criticize what someone has already said or done about the issue. Explain what will happen if something is not done to solve the problem.

Closing paragraph

Make a closing remark (a clincher) to summarize your point of view. One way of doing this is to state your opinion about what should be done. Explain why you think this approach would work. Another way is to evaluate to what extent we should be governed by emotions or logic in the matter under deliberation.

Sample letter to the editor

24th April, 2013

Dear Editor

The Department for Education's current review of the National Curriculum is a vital opportunity to ensure that all young people in England receive quality cycle training.

Like swimming (which is already on the curriculum), being able to ride a bike confidently on the road is an essential skill for an active and healthy lifestyle.

Most children have a bike and want to cycle to school, but only 2 per cent actually do so. With childhood obesity rising and physical activity levels falling, encouraging active travel is vital to the nation's future health and well-being.

'Bikeability' sets the national standard for cycle training, which gives participants of all ages the skills and confidence for everyday cycling. At the moment only half of children in England have access to Bikeability. It's a postcode lottery that means some children will learn to cycle safely and confidently, while others won't.

MPs and peers today call for action to 'get Britain cycling', including cycle training in the National Curriculum; this would help revolutionise children's health, independence and well-being.

The Telegraph, 2013

> **ANALYSIS**
>
> In the letter to the editor opposite can you identify the writer's thesis, main supporting points and final thought. How could you improve the quality and effectiveness of the letter to the editor?

Activity

Imagine you had read the article on page 82 *Down Syndrome teenager refused American Airlines Seat* in your local newspaper. Write a thesis-driven letter to the editor of the newspaper expressing your opinion of the airline's treatment of the boy.

Defending your opinion

HL Paper 2 Section B

At Higher Level, Paper 2 is divided into two sections:

- Section A (covered in Chapter 2)
- Section B – the personal response

As you know from Chapter 2, Section A prompts ask you to write about a certain topic, to assume the role of author and write for an imaginary audience using a certain text type. By contrast, Section B includes one stimulus text and you are asked to provide your opinion in relation to the stimulus text and justify it, irrespective of text type and audience. As its name suggests, the personal response is essentially your own opinion about a topic or an issue.

In Section B, you are expected to write between 150 and 250 words. If you write below the minimum required (150 words), you will lose one mark from the Language criterion. There is no penalty for writing more than 250 words; however, always keep in mind that the more you write, the more mistakes you might make, such as grammatical errors or the repetition of ideas.

The personal response is worth 20 marks. It is assessed using two main criteria: Language and Argument.

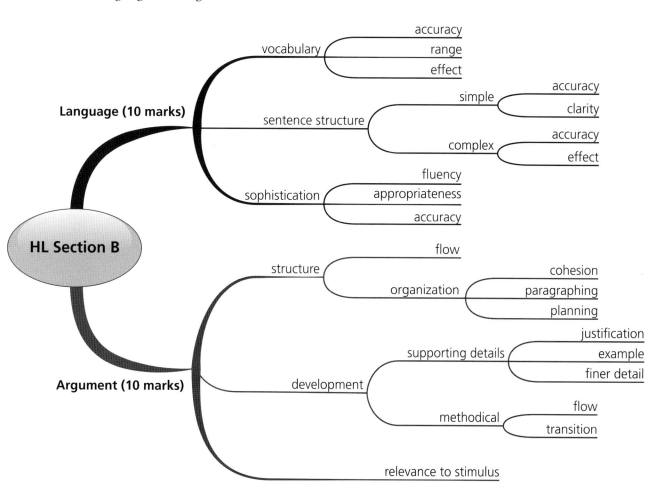

HL Paper 2 Section B: Skills

Skills for thinking: understanding the stimulus

The first step towards completing the task successfully is to understand the ideas that the stimulus text communicates. Although the personal response concerns itself with your opinion about the stimulus text, it is still important to understand what the main idea in the stimulus is in order for you to base your argument around it. Many students do not understand the holistic point in the stimulus and end up writing partly successful, mostly superficial responses.

Take a look at the stimulus text below:

It is said that 'respect for one's parents is the highest duty of civil life'. We celebrate days honouring our parents such as Mother's Day and Father's Day but do we really focus enough on respecting them?

What ideas does the stimulus above communicate? Is it:

a. how we celebrate our parents?

b. how we respect our parents?

c. the lack of balance between celebrating our parents and respecting them, and the importance of respecting our parents?

The answer is: c.

When the stimulus above was tested, many students wrote letters to their parents expressing their love and detailing ways in which they will celebrate upcoming events with them. What those students failed to realize is that their argument should have been based around the importance of respect and how we ignore it. Needless to say, those students did not score high marks in Criterion B: argument. Therefore, it is of utmost importance to understand the stimulus as a whole, not to concentrate on certain parts and ignore others.

Activity

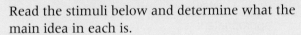

Read the stimuli below and determine what the main idea in each is.

1. 'Books are better than television, the internet, or the computer for educating and maintaining freedom. Books matter because they state ideas and then attempt to thoroughly prove them. They have an advantage precisely because they slow down the process, allowing the reader to internalize, respond, react and transform.' **Oliver DeMille**

2. 'The media's the most powerful entity on earth. They have the power to make the innocent guilty and to make the guilty innocent, and that's power because they control the minds of the masses.' **Malcolm X**

3. 'Education is what remains after one has forgotten what one has learned in school.' **Albert Einstein**

4. 'Anger is an acid that can do more harm to the vessel in which it is stored than to anything on which it is poured.' **Mark Twain**

Skills for thinking: choosing an approach

An opinion need not always be one-sided. More often than not, we find ourselves in situations where we cannot determine whether we fully agree or fully disagree with something. The same applies to Section B. Here are three approaches:

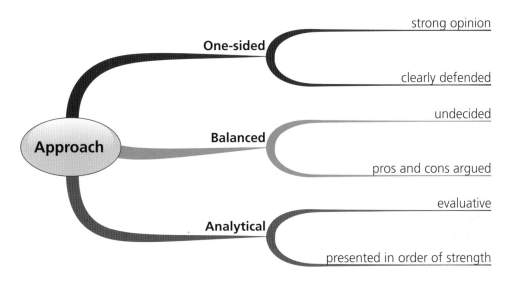

The one-sided approach: you provide a strong opinion, either agreeing or disagreeing with the idea presented in the stimulus, and defend it.

Example

'Anger is an acid that can do more harm to the vessel in which it is stored than to anything on which it is poured.' **Mark Twain**

General opinion: strong agreement with the statement; anger harms the angry person more than it does the recipient of this anger.

Support: 1. negative effect of anger on psychological wellbeing
2. time and effort spent on being angry
3. irrevocability of angry words or actions

The balanced but undecided approach: you see the pros and cons of an issue and appreciate both. You may be drawn to one but you feel you need to explore both.

Example

'Books are better than television, the internet, or the computer for educating and maintaining freedom. Books matter because they state ideas and then attempt to thoroughly prove them. They have an advantage precisely because they slow down the process, allowing the reader to internalize, respond, react and transform.' **Oliver DeMille**

General approach: mildly agree that we learn more from books than we do from television, the Internet and the computer; however, these three also allow us to internalize, respond, react and transform.

Support: 1. educational benefits of books
2. thinking processes and reading
3. freedom and reading
4. educational benefits of television, the Internet and the computer
5. thinking processes and the use of technological devices
6. freedom and technology

The analytical approach: you adopt this approach when you want to evaluate the argument presented in the stimulus. You have several points you want to make so you start with the strongest and finish with the weakest, or the other way round.

Example

'The media's the most powerful entity on earth. They have the power to make the innocent guilty and to make the guilty innocent, and that's power because they control the minds of the masses.' **Malcolm X**

General approach: analyse what is meant by the power of the media and its ability to control the minds of the masses.

Support:
1. bias or sensationalism in the media
2. logic or reason versus media projections
3. individual perception versus media projections

Activity

Read the following stimuli and provide general plans (general approach and support) using the three approaches outlined earlier for each stimulus.

1. 'We are apt to forget that children watch examples better than they listen to preaching.' **Roy L. Smith**

2. 'Environmental concern is now firmly embedded in public life: in education, medicine and law; in journalism, literature and art.' **Barry Commoner**

3. 'By and large, language is a tool for concealing the truth.' **George Carlin**

4. 'The thing that we are trying to do at Facebook is just help people connect and communicate more efficiently.' **Mark Zuckerberg**

Skills for thinking: generating and organizing ideas

In Chapter 2, you learned many ways in which you can generate ideas. Those ways will help you generate ideas for different tasks using different text types. In Section B, you are **not** assessed for your ability to produce a certain text type; you are assessed for your ability to produce a coherent and convincing argument. Therefore, the best mental model to use may be 'constructing an argument' see page 44.

Even though you may resort to comparison (pages 42 to 43) when tackling Section B, you will still have to do this under the general umbrella of 'constructing an argument'.

The one-sided approach: you feel strongly about one side of the argument; you have a strong opinion and you can defend it.

Structure

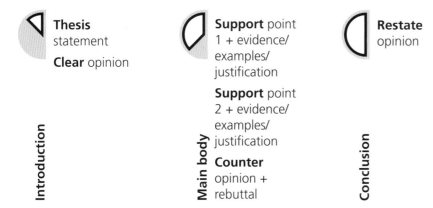

Introduction

◖ **Thesis** statement
Clear opinion

Main body

◖ **Support** point 1 + evidence/ examples/ justification

Support point 2 + evidence/ examples/ justification

Counter opinion + rebuttal

Conclusion

◖ **Restate** opinion

Example

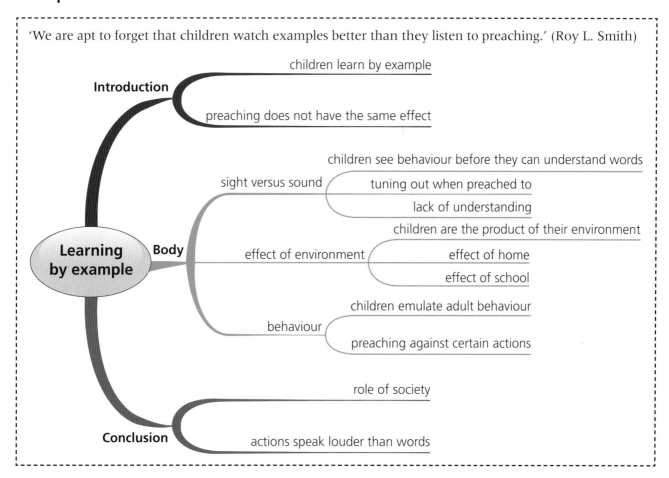

'We are apt to forget that children watch examples better than they listen to preaching.' (Roy L. Smith)

Introduction
- children learn by example
- preaching does not have the same effect

Body
- sight versus sound
  - children see behaviour before they can understand words
  - tuning out when preached to
  - lack of understanding
- effect of environment
  - children are the product of their environment
  - effect of home
  - effect of school
- behaviour
  - children emulate adult behaviour
  - preaching against certain actions

Learning by example

Conclusion
- role of society
- actions speak louder than words

Activity

1. The mind map above can be strengthened by adding more examples drawn from personal experience. Add an example next to each body branch.

2. Adopting the one-sided approach, generate and organize ideas for the following stimuli:

   • 'A child who is allowed to be disrespectful to his parents will not have true respect for anyone.' **Billy Graham**

   • 'We assume that everything's becoming more efficient, and in an immediate sense that's true; our lives are better in many ways. But that improvement has been gained through a massively inefficient use of natural resources.' **Paul Hawken**

The balanced but undecided approach: you see the pros and cons of an issue and appreciate both. You may be drawn to one but you feel you need to explore both.

Structure

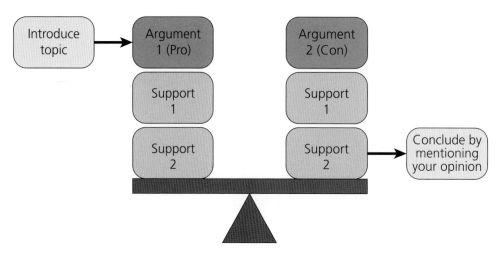

Example

'The thing that we are trying to do at Facebook is just help people connect and communicate more efficiently.' **Mark Zuckerberg**

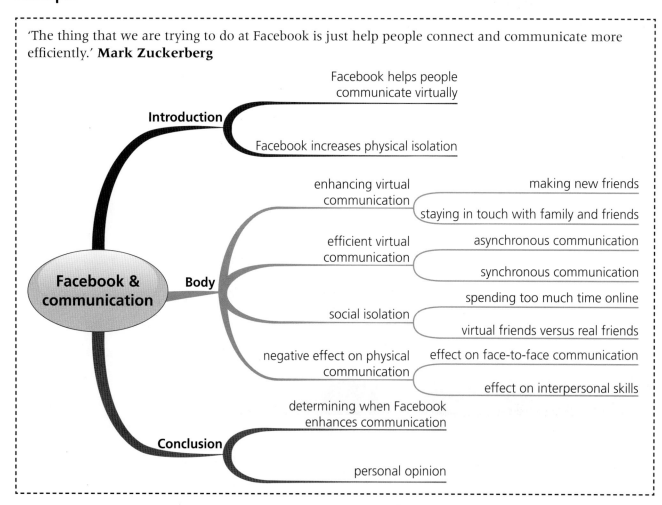

Activity

1. The mind map above can be strengthened by adding more examples drawn from personal experience. Add an example next to each body branch.

2. Adopting the balanced but undecided approach, generate and organize ideas for the following stimuli:

- 'Television is a medium of entertainment which permits millions of people to listen to the same joke at the same time, and yet remain lonesome.' **T. S. Eliot**

- 'Capital punishment is as fundamentally wrong as a cure for crime as charity is wrong as a cure for poverty.' **Henry Ford**

The analytical approach: you adopt this approach when you want to evaluate the argument presented in the stimulus. You have several points you want to make so you start with the strongest and finish with the weakest, or the other way round.

Structure

Conclusion
- mention the ideas you would support and why

Discussion point 3
- support point 1 (explanation/ example/ justification)

Discussion point 2
- support point 1 (explanation/ example/ justification)

Discussion point 1
- support point 1 (explanation/ example/ justification)

General argmuent
- define the main argument

Example

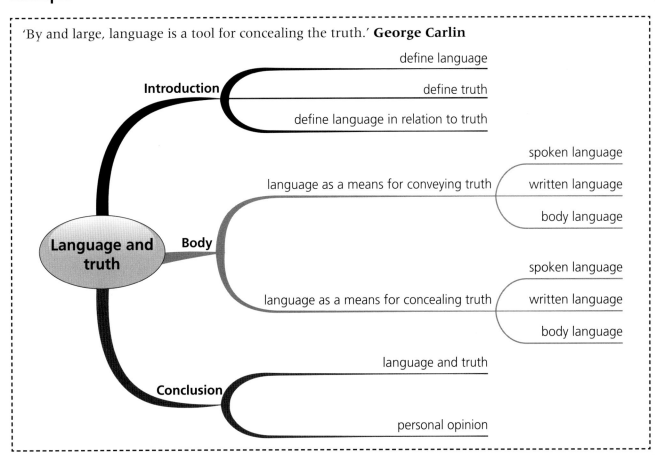

'By and large, language is a tool for concealing the truth.' **George Carlin**

Introduction
- define language
- define truth
- define language in relation to truth

Language and truth

Body
- language as a means for conveying truth
  - spoken language
  - written language
  - body language
- language as a means for concealing truth
  - spoken language
  - written language
  - body language

Conclusion
- language and truth
- personal opinion

Activity

1. The mind map above lacks specific explanations and examples of spoken, written, and body language. Add an explanation and an example next to each branch.

2. Adopting the analytical approach, generate and organize ideas for the following stimuli:
    *   'Poverty is the worst form of violence.' **Mahatma Gandhi**
    *   'It is time for parents to teach young people early on that in diversity there is beauty and there is strength.' **Maya Angelou**

Tips: When writing, make sure you use the appropriate parts of speech. 'Me and my friends went to play' is wrong; the accurate usage is 'My friends and I went to play'. When using vocabulary, make sure that your words are appropriate and meaningful. Writing 'we were surrounded by the enemy' is accurate, but 'the enemy persevered, and the siege lasted all day' is more effective.

Simple structures are sentences that convey one idea. They are usually short, like 'John went to school'. Complex structures combine ideas to emphasize meaning, for example, 'Having gone to bed very late at night, John was sleepy at school'.

Skills for writing: deploying language for effect and cohesion

Like any written piece, the language you use in Section B to convey your ideas is of utmost importance. When writing, make sure you use a wide range of vocabulary both accurately and effectively. Unlike Section A, register is not assessed in Section B. Therefore, make sure you write formally and use a variety of words to communicate your message effectively.

In addition, you need to effectively use a variety of sentence structures, ranging from simple to complex. Make sure you use linking words, adjectival and adverbial clauses, and a number of conjunctions appropriately to lend cohesion to your response.

The following online resources may help you improve your use of vocabulary, grammar and syntax:

*   **University of Ottawa – The Writing Centre**
    http://www.writingcentre.uottawa.ca/hypergrammar/partsp.html
*   **English Grammar 101**
    http://englishgrammar101.com
*   **British Council – English Grammar**
    http://learnenglish.britishcouncil.org/en/english-grammar

*   **Vocabulary.com**
    https://www.vocabulary.com
*   **Daily Writing Tips**
    http://www.dailywritingtips.com/how-to-improve-your-vocabulary-steadily
*   **Building a Better Vocabulary**
    http://grammar.ccc.commnet.edu/grammar/vocabulary.htm

Student samples

Based on the following stimulus, give a personal response and justify it. Choose any text type that you have studied in class. Write 150 to 250 words.

"I'll admit sometimes I do miss the simple life before mobile phones existed. Being connected to the world at all times comes with an incredible number of perks, but it has huge disadvantages too."

IB English B Course Companion, **Oxford University Press, 2012, p. 346**

Response A

> ### New York Times
> ### Mobile Phones; a blessing or a curse?
>
> The simple life of the past has magnificently changed into what is viewed by some as the complicated life of today. And the one to blame in the eyes of many is the mobile phone. As its viewed by some as a curse complicating their lives, many view them as the finest invention of the century.
>
> Mobile phones has enabled many to communicate with their families and friends from all around the globe. Thanks to mobile phones, a mother can today, easily call her son that might just be in the second half of the world.
>
> Furthermore, Mobile phones have also made it cheaper for us to get in touch with people. As with the increasing prices of petrol and gasoline, mobile phones have made it possible to congratulate each other on special occasions without stepping out of our homes and for nothing but a couple of pennies.
>
> Although this seems to be a blessing, many people find it to be a curse, as they seem to decrease the social relationships within the community, and make life more complicated. Many argue, that mobile phones have decreased visits, as many got to see calling their parents on Christmas enough.
>
> This however depends on the person's own perspective of what should or should not be done and not on because of mobile phones. And this is just why I personally support using mobile phones and take it more of a blessing than as a curse. As many however oppose this opinion, the question remains: mobile phone; a blessing or a curse?
>
> Word count: 259

The first paragraph indicates that the student is using the 'balanced but undecided' approach. Although the language used is good, there are a number of errors.

Point (1) supporting the benefits of mobile phones with an example.

Point (2) supporting the benefits of mobile phones with an example. Note the use of 'furthermore' to link Point (1) to Point (2).

Point (3) discussing the disadvantages of mobile phones with an example. Note the use of 'Although' to indicate the shift from advantages to disadvantages. There are many errors in this paragraph though, and those render the message somewhat incoherent.

Conclusion in which personal opinion is mentioned.

General comments: The student manages to outline some advantages and disadvantages for using mobile phones in our daily lives. Ideas are relevant. Although somewhat balanced, the number of advantages discussed exceeds the number of disadvantages. Try to avoid this when adopting the 'balanced but undecided' approach. In addition, lend more depth to your argument giving specific examples to illustrate your argument. Some language errors affect the strength of the response because they render the argument incoherent at times.

Activity

Rewrite Response A to improve it. Make sure you retain the ideas but build on them. Correct language mistakes and make sure that you use a wide range of vocabulary and a variety of sentence structures both accurately and effectively.

The following responses are based on the same stimulus as Response A.

Response B

Does Mobiles Improve our Live or Just complicate it?

It is a strange feeling to try and remember what life was like before the internet, the iPhone, and social networking. I remember how the mailman used to be one of the most important people in our life. Every day, we white hem to deliver a letter from friends or family who were far away, after five or more days from the day they wrote this letter. Gut with mobiles you can easily send a letter via email that won't take seconds to deliver to your phone.

Back then, news was old by the time we read them in the newspaper, and the only way to stay up to date was to keep the radio on through the day, but nowadays everything changed, you can easily check the latest news using your smart phone or the internet. This technology made our knowledge to what is going around this glob, easy to know.

Now, we can contact every one through video calling, or you can include any one to your party even if he or she lives in other country. For instance, I can include my dad who works in Florida in family events that he cannot attend. He get a chance to see and talk to everyone –and it feel like he is there in person. Hence, mobiles let everyone far to be near to his friends as well as his family.

To conclude, mobiles made a huge change in our life, from that old life were everything was complicated. Currently we can send, call, share, and read whatever we want at any time. Mobiles have changed my life for the better. I am so thrilled to be in immediate contact with those I love all the time.

By: Zac Bobby

7th of April, 2013

New York City

Word count: 288

Response C

Are Mobile phones a Blessing?

Written by: Dana Simon

Discover Magazine

We love our smart phones so much that the thought of losing them is enough to bring a cold sweat. They are our digital comfort blankets, the last thing we look at before we go to sleep and the first thing we reach for when we wake up. I do agree that mobile phones have disadvantages and that life was much simpler before the invention of mobile phone, but still I believe that mobile phones are essential now a day.

To begin with, mobile phones have opened doors that were previously unheard of. In the past, if you ended up stranded in the middle of nowhere, you had to find a way to get in touch with help. These days, mobile phones allow us to be in touch with emergency personnel, family, friends, and loved ones in an instant. For example if one is on a trip in an unfamiliar place while needing help, mobile phones allow us to remain in touch and letting them know we are safe. In addition, it is a huge advantage for businesses for example using call or video phone, text message; it became possible to keep in touch together despite the long distance and also some office applications for mobile phones such as Microsoft Office are helping employees do their business more effectively.

Furthermore, with the significant development of mobile phones people are now able use the internet and sending photos or downloading videos and games. According to research, the numbers of people accessing the web through mobile phones are over 22%. Mobile phones are taking over laptops and computers. For example; if one wants to download a song or even research they do so by their mobile phones it is much easier since they are with you wherever you go.

Although it is true that people are now getting a number of advantages from mobiles, these communication technologies also have several disadvantages. Firstly, using mobile phones too much will cause harm for human's health as it can increase the risk of brain cancer. Secondly, children are spending their free times using mobile phones by chatting or playing games instead of going out with their friends and playing Soccer or any other activity.

To conclude, mobile phones have both pros and cons on our society. They make people's life and work become much easier. Yet, they have a negative impact on health, time and communication of individuals. To avoid these problems each person should manage their time effectively.

Word count: 416 words.

Response D

How important mobile phones in an individual's life?

Life was simpler before mobile phones exist. As we can see nowadays mobile phones are playing a major role in our lives today, mobile phones connected us to the world and introduced us to many varieties, life became easier with mobile phones. However, it also complicated our lives.

Mobile phones have its effects on the society in both positive and negative way.

To begin with, mobile phones made our lives easier due to it connected us worldwide.

For example, today we are able to talk around the world through mobile phones. It helped us to stay in touch with our friends and family around the world, and stay updated with latest news with our family.

Moreover, mobile phones sometimes can be important for people as it can help them if a problem occurred. For example if someone got into a car accident, they can call police or ambulance to help them. At those cases mobile phones is a need and should be carried around for emergencies.

However, mobile phones can limit our face to face times with our family and friends, and this might lead family in the country to get apart from each other and not have this family quality time with each other. For example today having quality time with our family members is limited due to the use of mobile phones with each other.

In addition, mobile phones can distract people and some people can misuse mobile phones. For example, it can be a distraction for kids while studying and they might achieve low marks and it might cause car accidents as people use it while driving and this is a misuse for mobile phones.

To conclude, mobile phones have its advantages and disadvantages on our society and individuals and people should find the right way to use it.

Word count: 302

Response E

Biggest Invention Humanity Ever Had

Has it happened to you that you went out and forgot your mobile at home and so you are not feeling comfortable? You fell that you are missing something, you fell that you are not complete. I think that mobiles made life simpler and easier to be lived.

Cell phones are having a great influence on our life. Cell phones are a faster and more effective way to transfer information and a good way to communicate with people. Also, its user can use it in other ways, such as browsing the internet or playing games.

Nowadays even kids find mobile a necessity of life. Parents can be a less worried about their kids by being in constant contact with them.

The more you talk, the more you know how to talk and the better your communication skills will be. Cell phone will teach us the communication skills.

Nothing more than a cell phone comes to great help in emergency. For example, you are driving on the highway and your car breakdowns, the only way to save yourself is by taking your phone out and call somebody and ask him to help to you.

Nowadays cell phones are not just used to contact with others; they are about video, songs, games, alarm clock, notes, calendar and reminder. So it is one machine, but can be used in many ways.

Many people think that cell phones complicated our life, but I think that nowadays we contact anyone we want in any palace and at any time we like to do so.

Because of everything I said about cell phones, I think they are one of the biggest inventions we humans made. If used properly, cell phone can be a wonderful piece of utility in life and most of its disadvantages will simply be insignificant.

Word count: 302

Activity

1. Which approach is adopted in each of the responses you have just read?
2. Are the ideas relevant to the main idea in the stimulus text?
3. Have appropriate examples and explanations been used?
4. Using a table similar to the one given below, evaluate Responses B, C, D and E.

Response

....

Message	Inadequate	Good	How response can be improved
Number of ideas			
Relevance of ideas			

Organization	Inadequate	Good	How response can be improved
Introduction			
Thesis			
Paragraph format			
Topic sentences			
Use of examples			
Explanation of examples			
Well-connected paragraphs			
Conclusion			

Language	Inadequate	Good	How response can be improved
Grammar and sentence structure			
Punctuation and spelling			
Vocabulary use			

Exam tips

- Read the stimulus carefully and determine the main idea it communicates.
- Choose an approach and plan accordingly.
- Make sure your argument concerns itself with all the aspects of the stimulus; do not concentrate on **one** part and ignore the other.
- Remember that your ability to produce a certain text type is not assessed. Do not waste time thinking of a text type.
- Use language (vocabulary and sentence structure) both accurately and effectively.

The written assignment – HL

In your Language A course you are learning about reading and appreciating literature, and you can use similar skills in your Language B course at Higher Level. While literary criticism is not essential in English B, you should feel encouraged by your developing knowledge of how writers of fiction use language. The *Language B guide* talks about understanding fiction 'in some depth', and the written assignment is your opportunity to combine reading fiction with creativity. Here, creative does not mean artistically inventive but refers to the freedom you have to choose the focus of your task. Compared to writing an essay or another factual text, you can use a range of text types and have much more freedom of expression.

The written assignment
- is a chance to reflect on one or both of the literary works read during the course
- draws on both receptive and productive skills to produce a well-planned and coherent text in the chosen text type.

Exploring a literary work is a multi-layered process, and your contribution is required at each level:

- Comprehending the language = What does the text mean?
- Identifying key features and their effects = How does the text work?
- Understanding and interpreting meaning = What does the text say?
- Reflection for intercultural understanding = What does the text say about the English language and/or the anglophone culture?
- Receiving and responding to the work = What does the text say to/about me?

Step 1: active reading

When you are studying the work, gather information which helps you describe it. Make a list of typical features, identifying details and characteristics. Make notes (page numbers make the task of revising easier), and revisit them to check how your understanding of the work is developing.

While reading, pay attention to:

- Language
  - vocabulary, grammar including spelling, sentence structure, word order, register, tone, repetition
  - paragraphing, organization, cohesion
- Literary features
  - characterization
    - who are the characters?
    - how are they introduced?
    - how do they interact with each other and with their environment (protagonist, antagonist, fall character) and how do they look, speak, think, move, etc.?

- ▶ how is the plot organized and delivered through the narrative?
  - ■ who is the narrator (whose point of view is revealed to the reader)?
  - ■ what is conveyed, what is left unsaid (or is implied)?
  - ■ how are descriptive language and dialogue used and what is their relationship?
  - ■ how is time used (foreshadowing, flashback)?
  - ■ what patterns are there in the rise and fall of intensity (rising action, falling action, climax)?
  - ▶ what roles do imagery, symbolism, setting (time and place), names and other details (allusions) play in the text?
- ● Theme(s)
  - ▶ what is the work's take on life; what is seen as valuable, what is emphasized?
  - ▶ what messages can you deduce from reading the work?
  - ▶ how does the context in which you read the work affect your understanding of it?

You may notice that your initial feelings for the literary works you are studying change as you progress and develop your understanding. Take the opportunity to discuss your reading inside or outside the classroom. Keep a journal, revisit it to make amendments as necessary. Do not accept 'truths' or ready-made interpretations without personal involvement and evaluation – be wary of online study guides, as your interpretation must be personal and convincing.

Step 2: choosing aims, a focus, and the text type

Do you feel you now know the literary work well? Look at your notes to assess the best angle for your next step. What feature – or **focus** of the assignment – of the literary work appeals to you most? Can you establish a clear link between your focus and the theme of the work? Try out a couple of ideas to see if you have enough material to support your focus.

Next you will need to choose a **text type** that best meets your objectives. Remember you will have to explain your choice in the **rationale** and justify the link between the text type and the focus you have chosen. Does the text type help you achieve your aim(s)? How? Again, you can try different options and see which works best for your focus.

Here are some examples based on Shakespeare's *Romeo and Juliet* – despite the challenging language of the original text, we are using the play here because many English B students worldwide will have read the story. Look at the examples below and determine, which ones you think would lead to good written assignments and why. If you are familiar with the play, which ones do not convince you? How would you recommend the student to modify his/her plan to show that they could complete a satisfactory written assignment?

> The examples of text types included in Language B are 'writing a new end to a novel, an interview with a character, or a diary entry by one of the characters in a story or play, a news report about an event in the story'.
>
> Note that a formal (literary) essay is not an accepted text type as the assignment must be a creative piece of writing.

	Focus of the assignment (or topic)	Links to the literary work	Text type of the assignment
A	Juliet reveals her love for Romeo to her family and explains why she cannot consent to marrying Paris.	To show the depth of Juliet's emotions and her desperation in the face of the two families' feud. To highlight the tragedy of the unnecessary deaths.	A letter from Juliet to her family; to be read out by Lord Capulet before he prepares for his meeting with Lord Montague in the final act.
B	An account of the escalation of scandalous events resulting from feuding families.	To emphasize the families' vanity and greed and how the ignored emotions of teenagers led to a catastrophe.	A gossip-page column in an online magazine.
C	A pastiche of Romeo and his friends meeting up in town and discussing last night's events (e.g. Act 1, scene 1), delivered in modern rhyming language. Attention to the boys' verbal interaction and humour.	Romeo starts out as an ordinary young man who enjoys life and all it has to offer and who falls easily in and out of love.	A dialogue between Romeo, Mercutio and Benvolio.
D	Benvolio records his friend Romeo's most recent crush in his diary/blog.	The caring Benvolio feels uneasy about reckless Romeo's escalating obsession and shows awareness of the families' power over the lovers.	Three diary/blog entries by Benvolio.
E	A new scene to replace Act 5, scene 3 where Romeo revives Juliet and the lovers happily reunite.	To show that true love conquers all and death is not the only way out in a dispute – a happy ending is always attainable.	A dialogue between Romeo, Paris and Juliet.
F	The bitter Nurse, full of hatred for the Capulets, sets out to destroy the family by creating a scandal between Romeo and Juliet.	To reveal how the devious and scheming Nurse put Romeo and Juliet together to further her own cause.	A monologue by Nurse, to take place directly after the prologue before Act 1.

Step 3: drafting a rationale

Now you have chosen your focus, it is time to start drawing the map leading from your notes and observations to your finished assignment. The body of your assignment is a creative piece which allows you to engage with the literary work and choose the way in which you interpret it. Therefore, your **rationale** is essential to a high assessment score. It introduces your aims and explains the choices you have made in your creative text. Even an artistically brilliant piece of creative writing will not be completely successful as a written assignment if it is not accompanied by an informative and thorough rationale. On the other hand, a focused rationale can produce good results, even if you feel creative writing is not among your strengths.

Your rationale is a sketch map which you should keep at hand when writing your assignment. Like all first maps, you may check its accuracy as you proceed. Be prepared to amend and correct your work but do not omit or erase your central ideas.

Exercise 1

Before you start drafting your own rationale, let's spend some time examining two samples. Study the first rationale below and answer the following questions.

Rationale

"Mr. Loveday's Little Outing" is a short story written by Evelyn Waugh, which starts by Angela going to the Asylum in a visit to her father "Lord Moping". There, Angela gets to meet Mr. Loveday and tries and succeeds in releasing him out of the asylum, as he seems sane, only to find out that a murder had occurred at his time out.

In this written task, my aim is to furtherly explore Mr. Loveday's character and feelings towards the crime he has committed. This aim is to be achieved through a letter he sends to Angela, expressing his gratitude and joy to her succeeding in releasing him in addition to those towards the crime committed.

The reason behind committing the crime is not mentioned though as Mr Loveday is an insane inmate who takes murdering young ladies as a hobby and a source of joy not more. As this appears to be his "secret ambition" that he dreams of doing before he gets "too old to enjoy it".

For that, this written assignment's register is quite semi formal for Mr. Loveday, seems to be well educated, but still is an insane person that writes his letter to thank Angela and to express his feelings of joy and relief towards the crime he finally got to commit.

- **Does the rationale have 150–250 words?**

    A very short rationale is probably thin on essential details, whereas a rambling rationale can lack focus and include unnecessary information, such as a simple retelling of the plot.

    Write down the number of words and comment on the length.

- **Is the selected aspect from the literary work introduced early in the rationale? How is it done?**

    Introducing the work does not mean paraphrasing the plot or superficially summarizing the work. The purpose of the rationale is to help the examiner understand the point of view adopted in the written assignment: what aspect of the literary work does the creative piece explore and how is this topic treated? A good rationale is like a signpost for the reader pointing to the goal ('where to?') and suggesting the means of reaching it ('how?').

    Write down the aspect or the focus of the assignment.

- **Does the rationale state the aim(s) of the piece?**

  This can be done as a straightforward announcement ('I will show how…' / 'I want to illustrate the similarities between…' / 'I wanted to explore…') or the purpose of the creative piece can be expressed or implied more indirectly ('The diary points out…' / 'The letter illustrates…' / 'The dialogue reveals how…'). The choice of text type should also be justified convincingly and in sufficient detail ('A diary entry allows me to show how…' / 'I chose to write a letter from X to Y to counteract…').

  It is important to assess the validity of the aim(s) in relation to the original text or the literary work: Is your approach convincing? Does your text demonstrate a sound understanding of the literary work and its themes and ideas? For example, a light-hearted, jovial dialogue between Romeo and Lord Capulet would hardly convince us that the two men are enemies. It is important to establish clear links between your main ideas and the literary work. Remember that only the points listed and explained in the rationale will be taken into account when assessing your written assignment.

> **Tip:** Treat your rationale as a key to decoding the creative text.

- **Does the rationale explain how the piece works?**

  Does the writer of the sample rationale above clearly identify the means of achieving his or her aims? In other words does the writer link the purpose of the piece with the choices they have made. This could include identifying techniques used in the text and explaining how and why the technique is being used ('I have used words such as X and Y to show Z' / 'The colours indicate X' / 'The fact that she always answers with counter-questions reveals how…'). For example, you might want to draw attention to the naivety of Romeo and so you decide to write a new dialogue between Romeo and his father. You could convey your reading of the character through his boastful language and aggressive behaviour, the father's reactions, revealing stage directions, etc.

  List the means. You may also comment on them, especially if you are familiar with the literary work.

> See the Written assignments on pages 152 to 154 for the creative part.

Based on your observations, how convincing do you find the rationale and why? What mark would you award it?

Exercise 2

Study two more sample rationales based on Waugh's short story on the following pages, and answer these questions:

- Which one do you prefer and why? Which do you think will score better in assessment and why?

- How well is the literary work introduced? Does the author of the assignment convince you of his/her knowledge and understanding of Waugh's short story?

- How well is the focus of the assignment stated? How well is the aspect justified?

- What reasons are stated for the choice of text type?

- Based on reading the rationale, what details or features do you expect to see in the creative piece?

Rationale A

"Mr. Loveday little outing" by Evelyn Waugh talks about a young woman's visit to her father that is found in the county asylum were she meets her father's private secretary and believes that Mr. Loveday is innocent and deserves to leave the asylum because she does not feel that he is a criminal, yet Mr. Loveday look innocent and kind. On the other hand, after Mr. Loveday took his freedom he got back to the county asylum for him murdering another woman on her bicycle.

In this written assignment, I am going to write a diary entry by Mr. Loveday after he came back to the asylum for the second time, to explore further more about his deep and inner feelings and emotions after committing his crime. The use of words and the register that I will be using in my written assignment will be semi-formal to formal as it is shown by Mr. Loveday's language used throughout the story.

(155 words)

Rationale B

This short story is basically about an extraordinary man called "Loveday". A young girl named Angela pays her father a visit at the asylum, in which she gets to know Loveday. His gentleness and kindness in the way he talks, leads to Angela seeing it unfair for Loveday to stay at the asylum, and so therefore, she does her best do let him out, and succeeds. Loveday's delight was to kill woman on bicycles, and freedom is the chance he took in doing so again, which makes him return back to the asylum for the same reason he was there before, unrepentant.

In this written assignment, I decided to write a letter from Loveday to Angela, in which he would be slightly apologizing for her about his misuse of the freedom she helped him gain, as he misused it in her point of view and not his. This could be realized from the short story as Loveday says "Now I shall be able to settle down again to my work here without any regrets". Furthermore he would be expressing his thoughts and feelings generally about his life, in addition to the joy he has of murdering woman on bicycles, and the reason of loving the habit.

The aim of this assignment is to see deeply through an extraordinary man; Loveday. As Loveday's thoughts are not clearly expressed in the story, in which he says, "I expect we all have our secret ambitions, and there is one thing I often wish I could do", in addition to, "But I do feel that if I had done it, just for one day, art afternoon even, then I would die quiet", therefore those thoughts would be more clearly expressed in the letter.

The aim will be achieved by the use of effective language by Loveday, as he in the story uses words effectively as in, "Well, miss, it sounds ungrateful, but I can't deny I should welcome a little outing, once, before I get too old to enjoy it", and so by that ideas would be clearly understood by Angela.

The language to be used by Loveday in the letter is semi-formal to formal language, with a strong and effective use of words. Despite that the language is effective; it would be left vague on purpose. Loveday appears to be sane in the letter while I am aware that this is not the case with Loveday.

(433 words)

The diary entry and the letter are included in the Annex on pages 152 to 154.

Exercise 3

Next, read the following creative part of a written assignment based on a short story called *A Family Supper* by Kazuo Ishiguro, and study the comments an English B examiner has made on the student's work.

23 Temasek Street West
Singapore 96783

Mr.Ishiguro
Author
JABberwocky Literary Agency, Inc.
24-16 Queens Plaza South, Suite 505
Long Island City, NY 11101-4620

8 October 2013

Dear Mr. Ishiguro,

Re: Question about the Family Supper

I am writing this letter to you since I would want to concern some points about the story 'Family Supper'. The point I would want to concern is about the ending for the story. The story has ended by the sentence, "We fell silent once more, waiting for Kikuko to bring the tea." This is a very confusing ending since it does not tell us if the family members have all died or the family members are still alive.

I had a great time reading your story and I do know how the father feels and thinks because I am also Japanese, my grandfather is strict about these things too. This story relates to my family well so it was really interesting to read. As mentioned earlier, I am really curious about how the story ended and what happened after they all ate the fish served by the father. I think that the father was testing his son if he still trusts the father and wanted to make his son guilty. I would think this way because in the passage we can tell that the father still loves their children by the phrase; "'If you wish to stay here, I mean here in this house, you would be very welcome. That is, if you don't mind living with an old man". This phrase shows that the father would still want to live with their children.

The **text type** is clearly identifiable as a formal letter, and a number of conventions are followed (sender and recipient and their address details; date; greeting; closing).

The focus of the assignment becomes clear in the early part of the text: this looks like a letter to the author (Ishiguro) of the short story. The message is communicated quite well although the language is neither sophisticated nor effective at times.

The writer of the letter explains his/her purpose of writing although there is some redundancy.

The task is connected to the literary work by a few details from the story and its ending. Please note that direct quotes are not required!

149

The reason I thought why the father was testing his son was because he gave the son a bowl full of Fugu and before serving him the dish, the father showed his son the battle ship he has made saying, "These little gunboats here could have been better glued, don't you think?". This shows that the father is not accurate and precise in other words, he did not cut and cook the fish well that is served in the dinner table but if the son trust him and believes in him, he would not hesitate and take one piece and would eat it. Also, I think that the father used Fugu as the dish because the mother died from fish poising; Fugu. This is the reason why I think that the father was testing his son.

Personal observations and interpretation of the literary work show understanding and appreciation of the literary work.

The Fugu that was given by the father was just to test his son if his son still believes in his father or not. The father was just trying to give his son another chance and wanted to live back together again with the whole family. In conclusion I think that the father did not want to kill his own family by his hand but wanted to test if the son still believes in him and also wanted to live back together as a family again.

Some repetition of the point. The development of ideas, as well as their organization, could be better.

This is only my own opinion and what I think that story ends but I would want to know what really happened after that so, could you kindly tell me what occurred after the father and son was waiting for Kikuko to bring tea?

I would be looking forward to your favorable reply. Thank you.

Your sincerely,

Kikuko Kamakura

With fiction there is usually no 'what really happened' – stories end the way the author intended and speculating about 'consequent' events hardly adds to appreciating the work. However, this particular story does have an ending which invites such speculation, but this point should be spelled out in the rationale!

With 554 words, the piece follows the guidelines, but its effectiveness is somewhat questionable.

Now fill in a chart like the one below.

What literary work is the assignment based on?	What is the focus of the assignment? (aspect, topic)

What text type is used and why do you think the student chose it?	How does the student show knowledge and understanding of the literary work in the creative piece? This refers to including details from the creative piece linked to certain aspects of the literary work.

Activity

Based on the examiner's comments and your observations, write a rationale on behalf of the student who wrote the letter to Mr. Ishiguro. Don't worry if you are not familiar with the story, as this exercise focuses on writing a rationale with good links to the creative piece rather than your in-depth knowledge of the literary work. In your rationale of 150–250 words remember the following:

- Introduce the short story.
- Explain how the creative piece is connected to the short story.
- Explain what you are attempting to say about the short story or how you will show your

knowledge and understanding. What points will you make?

- State the text type you have chosen to use in your creative piece and why it fits with your purpose.

When you have finished your rationale, assess it with the questions we used in the first exercise (pages 146 and 147). You can also compare it with the draft version that follows, written by the student whose letter you read. What do you think is missing and what does the student need to add to make the rationale better?

Rationale / 1st draft

I have decided to write this letter since I wanted to clarify some points from the story written by Mr. Ishiguro; 'A last supper'. I have written this in a formal letter using polite words to the author.

I have split the letter into a total of 7 parts asking the author some questions about the story and giving an idea of what will happen after the end of the story since it was a really unjustified ending. While doing this process of guessing the ending of the story, I have given the author some evidence to prove my points are clear. Moreover I have structured the layout so it is in chronological order given one point each in each paragraph. In the conclusion, I was asking what really happened in the ending and thanking him for reading the letter.

You should now be familiar with the requirements for an effective rationale. Revisit the plan for your own assignment, fill in a chart like the one that follows, and start writing your rationale.

What literary work is your assignment based on?	What is the focus of your assignment? (aspect, topic)	What text type will you use and why?
What do you want to say about the literary work? (theme)	How will you show knowledge and understanding of the literary work in your creative piece? (This refers to including details from the creative piece linked to certain aspects of the literary work. These links might be chosen already in the mapping phase of the assignment or they become clear during the writing process. Nevertheless, it is important to review the rationale accordingly.)	

Step 4: finalizing the assignment

You now have your rationale as a map and the notes (from active reading in Step 1) to help you write the creative part of your written assignment (500–600 words). Don't be afraid of trying different ideas as word processing makes it easy to edit your text. You will also find page 52 in Chapter 2 useful when redrafting your assignment.

When you have finished writing, revisit your rationale and check it against your creative piece. Finally, save and print out your assignment, exhale and celebrate your achievement.

Annex

Written assignment 1

Mr. Loveday's letter to Angela, based on a short story by Evelyn Waugh. See Rationale on page 146.

Monday, March 26th 2013

County home for mental defectives

Texas – America

Dear Young Lady Angela,

I would like to start off by greeting you. For, from all the people I have met throughout my long stay in this asylum, whether an insane mad inmate or just a simple regular visitor as yourself, you, my dear Angela, are the most worthy of this warm greeting.

I have come to notice that you share many common traits with my beloved sir, your dear father Lord Moping. You, my young lady share your father's kindness and good manners, all that in addition to the fact that you seem to enjoy writing and signing documents, just like my old humble sir. Who knows, you might as well end up in this asylum too! I bet your father will be very pleased to see you then, especially now that we need a hand in typing his reports. You see, we are still not done from the Danube case yet! Do not trouble yourself though, I assure you that the asylum is not that of terrible place to be in, on the contrary it really is a really safe place to be in after all.

I, however, have come to realize that you have not payed us a visit for a while now; since the time of my last release, if my memory still serve me well. That my young fair lady had troubled me deeply.

Nevertheless, I would like to show my supreme gratitude for the delightful favor you showered me with. You, my young lady Angela have relieved my old, aging heart. You helped me achieve my only ambition. I remember very well when you asked me earlier of what I would do if I ever got the chance to leave this asylum and go out. I believe that you now got your answer. Yes my young lady, that was and still remains " my secret ambition ", that was what I have always dreamt of doing before I get too old to enjoy It, the reason behind my existence . No words can reveal my gratitude for your hard work, if it was not for you and that remarkable work of yours, my heart would not have been so full of that quantity of joy and relief. I have now accomplished my only desire, my only source of eternal joy and glory, my only hobby. The way her strangled body fell of her bicycle can not get out of my head, and for that I thank you.

I know that my actions might not have pleased you, and for this exact reason I apologize; not out of guilt for what I have done, but rather out of respect for the trust you entrusted me with, and for the hard work you showed. You, unfortunately have to excuse me now for my sir is calling me, I still have many reports to type and distribute. I fear he is losing his patience and temper, he's got all muddled with his card index again.

Best regards,

Loveday

Word count: 555 words

Written assignment 2

A diary entry by Mr. Loveday, based on a short story by Evelyn Waugh. See Rationale A on page 148.

Wednesday 25/10/2013

Dear diary,

I am writing to express my feelings and other certain issues and confessions on this special day exactly, today is my birthday, yes 25/10/1964. I wish to find the right person to share my own feelings with, I always set in the asylum alone enjoy my time, yet as I mentioned before; no one to trust!

I always hear people criticizing me for no reason; at least they don't know my deep feelings and what I have went through, they always say "he had the opportunity to leave the asylum, and he returned back in less than 2 hours, he is sick!", well no, I am not sick, get yourself in my shoes then judge me, why do people always judge a book by it is cover? People are just lifeless.

When I was three years old and when I was with my mom driving back home from my kindergarten in our brand new car, a nice lady was on her bicycle I saw her, I was surprised, I waved to her she also did that, and after that she went on our track on the street, we were about to hit her, my mom turned into the left side of the street in order not to avoid her, but suddenly a huge and very fast truck was on our way and hit us, as soon as I opened my eyes, I found myself in the county hospital, my dad was next to me, holding my hands, and crying so hard, he looked to me and said "I love you son", I asked him "what's wrong dad?" Until the doctor came and explained everything to me, yes it was the hardest thing I ever went through in my life. That's all what I remember.

I went through a very hard childhood, my stepmother used to scream, beat, and tease me; if I made something bad, she gets her bicycle and laugh and reminds me of my poor mother, she acts like an angel in front of my dad that always was my hero. I entered the asylum because of my stepmother that I killed while she was on her bicycle. On that particular day and while her cousin was at our home I heard her talking with her cousin about me and the way she treats me then both of them came to my room and started to beat me like an animal, after she her cousin left I could not take it anymore until I followed her and killed her while she was on her bicycle. On the other hand, as soon as I left the asylum my only aim was to kill me stepmothers' cousin that also was so mean to me, I saw here next to the county grocery, also on her bicycle and killed her, yes its fate.

Through all these years, I finally lived in dignity and did what I truly want to do through more than 20 years. My message to people is never judge until you know the background of that person, and the reasons behind him committing such crimes.

Word Count: 521 words

Written assignment 3

Mr. Loveday's letter to Angela, based on a short story by Evelyn
Waugh. See Rationale B on page 148.

5 Hill St.

Glasgow

March 26, 2002

Dear Lady Angela,

Undoubtedly, I know that you regret putting some effort helping me get out of the asylum and have the chance to feel the essence of freedom, which totally opposes my feelings towards what I have done. However, I apologize for what has happened, but you were the first in thirty five years to slightly see through me as a man with ambitions; ones that are treacherous and detrimental only in people's point of view.

I didn't misuse the freedom you gave me, but instead I have fulfilled a promise that I have been promising myself for years. It may be considered very short to complete, but it brings up the deep feeling of consummation, which for now will last forever and dwell.

It all started thirty five years ago when I was young, I had also slayed a woman riding a bicycle without any specific reason to do so. Afterwards, I had given up myself immediately to the asylum, not because I felt guilty, but instead I tried to prevent myself from redoing that again, and so I had stayed here for many years. But I believe that those years I spent here were a perfect chance to look through myself and figure out the reason. As soon as I did, I promised myself to do it again, and thanks to you, I did. I figured out that killing women on bicycles just makes me happy! It made me happy once, and now it did twice.

It's quite challenging to explain exactly how it feels because it comes from the inside, more than it does when murdering physically, and I know that you and many other people may find it very difficult to understand as it is just as difficult to express how appealing and enjoyable it feels to me. Maybe if you try it sometime, you will understand what I mean.

I have lived here for many years, and I have seen people dream and look forward for many things they wish could happen. In fact, I myself was one of them, but it takes a really strong will in order to achieve what we want. I am going to live here now for the rest of my life unregretful about anything I have done, happy, satisfied, and not waiting for anything to come about. I didn't break the promise to myself, and I have waited many years until I ensured it happened today.

Nevertheless, out of everything I have been through, I learned the most important thing one could learn; patience. I don't think I would wait for this day to come if I didn't know that it was going to make me happy. Do not rush, for God's secret is patience. Everything that is meant to be will come at the designated time.

Yours truly,

loveday

479 words

The written assignment – SL

The written assignment at SL is an essential component that aims at developing intertextual receptive and productive skills. The task should reflect your understanding of the subject matter or topic, ability to use information from different texts and organize them in one task.

- The written assignment is based on one of the CORE topics studied:
  - ▶ Global issues
  - ▶ Communication and media
  - ▶ Social relationships
- It is the independent work of the student.
- It is based on information collated from three or four different sources selected by the student under the teacher's guidance.
- It consists of a 300–400-word written task and a 150-200-word rationale.
- It should be completed in the final year of the course.

> 'Intertextual reading refers to the ability to read across different texts, one of which may be audio/audio-visual, that may be linked by a common theme.'
> **Language B guide**

" BUT IF YOU DON'T LEARN TO READ AND WRITE, HOW ARE YOU EVER GOING TO TEXT?"

Determining the topic

You should consider the topic of your written assignment very carefully. It is difficult to show understanding of the subject matter in only 300–400 words.

Thus, consider the following:

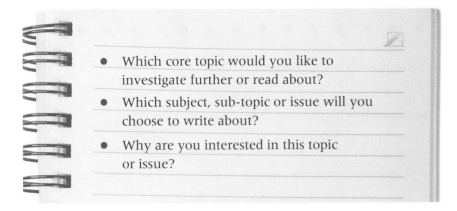

- Which core topic would you like to investigate further or read about?
- Which subject, sub-topic or issue will you choose to write about?
- Why are you interested in this topic or issue?

It is essential to choose something you are truly interested in. Are you interested in sports and would like to reflect on its effect in enhancing social relationships? Did you enjoy the renewable energy topic discussed in one of your English B lessons? Did you watch a documentary about disarmament and decided to further explore the effects of gun possession on society? **Jot down your ideas, consult with your teacher and explore the possible sources that can help you write the task.**

Choosing sources

Once you decide on the topic, start looking for different sources that can help you gather information and build on each to produce your task. During this process you might find yourself changing your specific topic or tweaking it. That is just fine as long as you know what you are aiming at. At this stage, it is helpful to answer the following questions:

> **Reminder:** The written assignment should be based on **three** or **four** sources chosen by the student in consultation with the teacher.

1.	What do you want to investigate/explore/ reflect upon?	Your narrowed down topic should appear here.
2.	Why are you writing about this issue?	AIM(s) should appear here.
3.	What are you writing?	TEXT TYPE (blog entry, feature article, letter to the editor, etc.)
4.	What is your communicative purpose?	Persuade? Inform? Complain? Propose? Argue?
5.	Which English-speaking country/culture will you be targeting?	Keep anglophone cultures in mind.
6.	To whom are you writing?	Think of your target audience.

While looking for your three or four sources, keep an eye on the table above. Although answers might be tentative at this stage, they will direct you to choose the appropriate sources that will enable you to meet the aim(s) set and reveal further understanding of the topic chosen.

Example

You want to investigate the topic of 'cartoons and movies promoting violence' under the core topic of Communication and Media. One aim could be to make a public appeal to ban such cartoons and movies by writing a newspaper article. In this case, you might be looking for sources that:

- provide statistics about violent incidents caused by watching such movies
- relate stories reported by parents or experts
- explain the laws that need to be implemented to make such a ban.

Practice

Complete the following table considering that the topic you have chosen is:

'Hollywood movies contribute to the increasing rates of teenage smokers and drinkers.'

Jot down all possible ideas that you can think of.

1.	What do you want to investigate?	
2.	Why are you writing about this issue?	
3.	What are you writing?	
4.	What is your communicative purpose?	
5.	Which English-speaking country/culture will you be targeting?	
6.	To whom are you writing? What kind of language do you use to address your audience?	

Start looking for sources that would meet your aim(s) and communicative purpose. These sources can be found anywhere: magazines, newspapers, books, blog entries, electronic material or in print.

How to use the sources

1. Read the three or four texts and note down the similarities and differences in the texts' approaches and ideas about the effects Hollywood movies have on teenagers.
2. Underline or highlight the points you would like to emphasize or further explore in your written assignment.
3. Remember that you need to gather information from each source **without copying.** Use your own words.
4. Re-visit the table above and make necessary amendments to points 1–6.

Example

A student has chosen to write a feature article on the topic of 'disarmament' with an aim to highlight the dangers of owning weaponry that result in increasing rates of violence and crime in Britain and the United States. The following excerpts are taken from two of the sources chosen to meet the aim set above.

Source 1

Though gun crime statistics are available for every one to see, many of us do not know how to use them. In fact, many people just gloss over the figures since they have no clue as to how to use them. The purpose of statistics, in general, is to make people informed of certain developments and gun crime statistics also have a similar purpose. We need to first look at the figures and then seek to understand the message conveyed by them. Gun crime statistics, also called gun death statistics or gun control facts, deal with the crimes resulting from the use of guns. They also cover information about gun ownership and both the possible and real consequences of allowing people to own guns without any control. Here are some highlights of gun crime statistics.

Gun crime statistics also show that the consequences of gun deaths have a wider reach in that even the economy of the country is affected. Estimates show that every year, the United States has been losing a whopping sum of USD 3.7 billion. This fact has been widely publicized by many gun control articles. But opponents of gun control do not seem to have woken up even to the danger to the economy which is bound to affect every one. Organizations like the NRA (National Rifles Association) that have been fighting gun control have been turning a blind eye to gun crime statistics. The NRA has made it clear that it will not accept any compromise.

http://guncontrolarticles.net/understanding-gun-crime-statistics/

Specific reference is made to the chosen anglophone society.

A point that can be used for rebuttal purposes.

Statistics of owning weaponry and the likelihood of them being more dangerous than safe will be integrated into the assignment to support the hypothesis that weaponry is in fact dangerous and that the disarmament movement has proved successful.

Source 2

Semiautomatic, handgun ban

Britain cracked down after gun enthusiast Michael Ryan massacred 16 people and wounded 13 others in 1987 in the rural English town of Hungerford. The slaughter led to a ban on semiautomatics like Ryan's Kalashnikov rifle.

In 1998, two years after suicide gunman Thomas Hamilton used four legally owned handguns to slay 16 children and a teacher at a kindergarten in Dunblane, Scotland, Britain extended the ban to handguns.

Today, under laws that make it illegal for private citizens to own anything larger than a .22-caliber and subject them to thorough background checks, Hamilton would have a

difficult time obtaining the guns he used in Dunblane: two .357-caliber Smith & Wesson revolvers and a pair of 9-mm Browning pistols. "I feel very safe," said Marion Collins, a college lecturer in Edinburgh. "Virginia Tech happened because guns are so accessible in America. I don't understand why they continue to allow this situation."

Britain has one of the world's lowest gun homicide rates — 0.04 slayings per 100,000 people, according to the Geneva-based Small Arms Survey for 2004. That puts Britain on par with Japan, where the rate is 0.03 per 100,000.

http://www.nbcnews.com/id/18334494/ns/us_news-crime_and_courts/t/some-nations-toughened-laws-after-shootings/#.UbJCV5wmxdg

Supporting anglophone society.

Supporting point

Laws supporting gun control are in fact being implemented, and have once again proven to be successful. The examples of positive effects of disarmament laws support the aim set and will be integrated into the article.

Developing the rationale

The 150–200-word rationale should:
• include a brief summary or description of the sources used
• introduce the topic and task
• state aim(s) clearly
• explain how aim(s) has/have been achieved
• mention which text type has been chosen and why
• clarify who your audience is and why.

> Explaining how aims have been achieved includes talking about the choice of text type, audience, register and style, in addition to how sources were used.

Both the rationale and the task are interlinked. Without a clear rationale, teachers and examiners will not be able to understand what your aim is or what you are doing. It is essential that you draft your rationale (just like you did in Chapter 4) and then re-visit it after the task has been completed.

The table you have already sketched and re-visited (pages 156 and 157) will be of benefit now since most of the required details are listed. All you need to do is re-visit the following:

1.	**WHY** am I writing about this issue?	Aim(s)
2.	**WHAT** am I writing?	Text type
3.	To **WHOM** am I writing?	Audience
4.	**WHY** have I chosen this text type and audience?	How will your choice help you achieve your aim(s)
5.	**HOW** will my aim(s) be achieved?	Link to both sources read and task

Aims and how to achieve them

You should state your aims clearly and link them to the topic investigated, chosen sources read and the 300–400-word task produced. Read the following aim. Does it tell you what the student plans to explore in his or her written assignment?

> "I want to write a feature article about renewable energy because I am interested in this field."

A clear aim tells the reader what he or she will be reading about. While a personal aim is commended, it does not clarify the position or angle you will be exploring in your written assignment, unlike what the following example manages to do:

"The blog entry produced aims to further explore the inner feelings and thoughts of a drug addict, which will shed light on the horrendous effects of substance abuse on American teenagers."

Start by drafting your aims and how you are going to achieve them.

AIM	HOW TO ACHIEVE AIM(S) WHY	
Raise awareness about the dangers of owning weaponry	**Link to sources** Source 1 reveals statistics of owning weaponry and the likelihood of them being more dangerous than safe.	**Link to task** I have embedded these statistics into the interview made with the gun expert to support the necessity of disarmament.

159

Text types

A good choice of text type helps you achieve the aim of the written assignment. A diary entry would be more suitable to explore the inner feelings of an abused child than a letter written to his/her teacher, for example.

You may choose one of the following text types for your written assignment:
- article
- blog/diary entry
- brochure/pamphlet/leaflet/advertisement/flyer
- interview
- speech
- news report
- official report
- review
- set of instructions or guidelines
- written correspondence
- any other text type approved by your teacher.

Audience

Deciding who your audience is will determine:
- your tone
- the level of formality used in the assignment
- the language used.

Sample rationale 1

For this following written assignment I have decided to focus on the global issue of disarmament. The reason for choosing this specific topic is because of all the recent shooting events besides grabbing my attention and getting me to wonder what it feels like to be in the shoes of shootings victims.

Topic specified

This is not an aim but rather a reason why the student is interested in this topic. This shows the student has carefully considered the topic investigated and knows what the aim is.

Owning weaponry – whether legally or not – has impacted society more negatively than positively in my perspective. Shootings are becoming more common nowadays, and almost anybody can get their hand on firearms.

The student clearly introduces the topic under discussion.

My aim in this written assignment is to provide facts, statistics and stories of shootings to help raise awareness and put an end/limit to owning firearms in hopes of decreasing the number of innocent deaths.

The aim is stated despite the redundancies and repetitions.

I have sued the statiscs of owning weaponry given in the first source to support my hypothesis which states that weaponry is in fact dangerous and that the disarmament movement has proved successful. The second source is a feature article that shows that laws supporting gun-control are in fact being implemented and have once again proven to be successful. I have sued the examples on positive effects of disarmament laws as well as pros and cons to such phenomenon to achieve my aim. The third source is an actual story of victims going through both a shooting and a bombing. Their emotions, events and post-traumatic events have been used as a major example to support my assignment.

Feature articles offer an opinion about current incidents or simply present a personal or serious perspective, and that is what I'm hoping to achieve through the feature article. An interview will be carried out with a victim of a shooting. All answers by the victim will be related to an actual interview carried out by an actual victim to ensure authenticity.

The audience targeted will obviously be the general public as they can all be involved with the current issue, but extra focus on those who own firearms will be implemented. The audience targeted needs to be aware of the possible negative effects of weaponry. Therefore, a feature article with a shooting victim in my opinion will prove to be most efficient in getting my hypothesis through and raising awareness regarding the matter. Not to mention that people actually sympathise with victims when they hear their stories, in other words, they leave more impact on the reader; all in a serious tone and register.

This paragraph explains how aims have been achieved by linking each source to the task and how each source has been used to achieve the aim. However, it lacks specific brief summaries of the sources. It is advisable that focus remains on HOW sources helped achieve the aim rather than describing what the source is.

There is clear awareness of the purpose of feature articles and why this text type has been chosen.

This could be rephrased to avoid redundancies. Also, further explanation on how this interview would help the student achieve the aim could be added.

A clear audience is targeted. However, how will the extra focus on firearms owners be made?

Sample rationale 2

In this written assignment, I will be writing about bullying and child abuse and particularly about the different side effects of both bullying and violence on children and people's own behavior. I will be writing a newspaper article and it will be a motivational and an informative article to people who experienced bullying and child abuse, and to express furthermore their feelings and to have glimpses about their own and different experiences that they lived through their life time.

The audience in my written assignment will be parents, teachers, and rehab centers, as all have the authority to decrease both child abuse and bullying and also can deal with different situations that anyone could pass through in home or even at school and to have different ways of teaching and training to provide the best essential life needs such as security, love, and belonging.

The use of words and the register will vary from semi formal to formal as it is a newspaper article, on the other hand, the tone will also be moderate.

Topic is confusing. Which aspect will be tackled: bullying or child abuse in general?

Text type and audience are mentioned but no reasons for this choice are given. Confusing.

Is this the aim? Why?

No specific summary of each source is mentioned.

Different from the audience mentioned above. How will the article target all those groups?

This needs to be re-phrased.

Practice

Read the following two rationales and comment on the strengths and weaknesses of each. What are the recommendations you would give for each student?

Rationale A

The media grabs our minds and latches it on its manipulative ideas. Body image has secretly been taking over society. Anorexia has become a threat nowadays, in which a person starves him or herself to get the body image that the media has created. To begin with, in my written assignment I have written an article which clarifies how the media promotes Anorexia through advertisements, magazines and TV shows. As mentioned in the song lyrics "Dear Diary"; "I have come to believe all of the things I'm seeing on magazines and TV shows , of every perfect being" and "all the girls with perfect bodies", which subconsciously plays with teenagers mind and manipulates it, as shown "advertising influences is quick, cumulative and for the most part its subconscious".

In addition, this assignment explores the symptoms of anorexia due to the pressure that the media puts on young women; such as "refusal to eat", "have an intense fear of gaining weight or becoming fat" and "using diet pills do decrease appetite". The role of media targeting women is also clarified in the written assignment as "girls tend to internalize pressure". Furthermore, I have chosen an article published in a teen fashion magazine as it interests most teenage girls. The audience of my written assignment are the girls that are showing symptoms of anorexia due to the media's interpretation of ideal beauty. Moreover, the article is written in a semi- formal register.

Rationale B

I decided to tackle one of the important issues that are facing our society nowadays which is drugs. This topic is the impact of drugs on a person's society and surroundings.

In my written assignment, I chose to write a public blog about a girl who has a brother who is addicted to drugs and this girl is trying to seek help in an indirect way.

My aim in this written assignment is to further explore the effect that the drugs make on family and society, furthermore to deduce the effect the drug makes on the drug abuser.

Based on three resources that I searched, they helped me to gather information about my topic. The first resource is an article that talks about the effect that the drug makes to family members and the physical and emotional abuse it causes.

The second resource is a song called "Novacane" which tackles the feelings that the drug abuser feels when using a certain drug.

Moreover, the third resource is a blog written by a business manager who is a drug abuser. What most people think is that a drug abuser is not educated and comes from a poor environment this is why this blog grabbed my attention as it shows that he is a drug abuser but he comes from a good well educated family.

The writing process

Now that you have drafted your rationale, knowing what your aim is, whom you want to address and which text type is best for the task, you are ready to start writing the 300–400-word assignment. While doing so, keep an eye on the table/sketch you drafted earlier (on page 159).

- Start writing your assignment. **Keep an eye on your rationale** and make sure you include all the features you mentioned in the rationale.
- Use the information you have gathered from the three or four sources and present it in a way that reflects your understanding of the core topic **without copying**.
- Study the **conventions/features of the text type** you have chosen (see Chapter 2 for suggestions). Organize your ideas in a way that suits the text type chosen.
- **Do not** focus on creativity and text type conventions at the expense of content or ideas.
- Use **language** appropriate to the text type and purpose.
- **Compare your assignment and the rationale**. Does the assignment cover the ideas mentioned in the rationale and achieve your aim(s)? Make amendments where necessary.
- Put your assignment aside and **re-visit it after a couple of days**. Evaluate its effectiveness with fresh eyes.
- **Re-visit the rationale** and make necessary amendments.
- **Check the assessment criteria**. Proofread, make any last minute adjustments.
- Do not exceed the **400-word limit**.

Sample

Here is a completed rationale and assignment, followed by some comments.

Rationale

The effects of divorce on children vary between physical and psychological as it affects their behaviors and skills. In most societies it has always been thought that the effects of divorce are harsher on the parent's, while children suffering where always neglected.

My written assignment however focuses more on the affects of divorce on children as this written assignment aims to show further exploration on the affects of divorce on children and their feelings towards it. This aim will be achieved by writing a letter from the girl (that wrote the blog entry in my second source) to her father explaining her devastation on her parent's divorce and the affects it had on her.

Although I am aware that as a divorce sufferer she might not have the strength to directly address her father, but the fact of her publicizing her feelings towards this divorce in her blog entry, makes it plausible to assume that she has the courage to address her father directly. And for that I believe that this text type is appropriate as she will be given the chance to finally speak up for herself causing the register of this letter to be semi-formal to informal with an sarcastic, angry tone similar to that in the blog.

Word count: 210

Topic is specified.

Aim is mentioned but there are some redundancies.

Text type is mentioned. Letter writer and recipient are mentioned. However, further explanation is required. How is this linked to sources? Why has the girl been chosen to write to her father? What's more, there is no specific summary of each source and how it was used.

We get to know here what the student is generally trying to do, but the links made to sources and task are weak.

Clear reason why the letter is chosen. Why semi-formal to her father? Explain. Clarify and give examples why and how the letter will be 'sarcastic and angry'?

Task

To my Father,

Writing this letter has been very hard to me especially that I have not seen you since we last met at court where you and mum got your divorce. When I first started writing it I was afraid from the thought of you viewing this letter as a friendly, normal daughter to dad letter, but then again I was always afraid of seeing the home I lived my entire life in, diminishing along with all those nice childhood memories in front of me eyes. You did not stop at divorcing her and replacing her with another women, but rather continued saying "I should never have married that woman" only then did I recognize that my entire life in addition to my entire childhood was basically nothing but a lie, nothing but a mistake to you.

And for some reason you even stopped asking about us or even answering our calls. Just in case you were wondering -if at all- of how me and George are doing, then listen to this; George was recently sent to rehab. As an adult George was never given the chance to grieve or to express his feelings towards this tragedy, George resorted to drugs as cigarettes were not enough to relief him.

Background details are provided, all pertinent to the core topic chosen. Tone is appropriate as per the rationale. Many language mistakes in even basic structures, but these do not obscure meaning in general.

Consequences of divorce and its effects on children/teens are clearly presented here. The problem is that no clarifications and links to the sources were made in the rationale.

As for me, I had to break up with my boyfriend as the fear of losing a beloved one was too much for me to handle. That's not just it, for I know that the worst is still yet to come. As adults you did not consider even telling us of your decision at first, as adults we were not even asked on our opinion for this equally concerning decision and finally as adults we were not even given the chance to express our devastation and grief towards this decision. But now after I was forced to face all that I believe that age was never an excuse, after all problems saw no age.

Losing the key to your safety door along with losing the concern and care you were used to receive from your parents would still affect you in all your life stages. This is the message I wish to pass to you from this message.

Good bye,

Kasey Edwards.

Word count: 369

Relevant and organized with appropriate tone used. Continues with effects of divorce and expresses innermost feelings and thoughts.

Letter ends abruptly.

Comments

Criterion	Comments
Rationale and task	Effects of divorce on children are mentioned. However, there is nothing in the rationale that explains how the information has been gathered. Rationale is a bit confusing. Aim and text type are mentioned, but there is a reference to one source only. No clarifications are given about how aims are to be achieved. Tone and register are generally appropriate. The student does refer to a 'sarcastic' and 'angry' tone in the rationale, but fails to explain how and why. Register seems a bit formal at times, but this is justifiable.
Organization and development	Student organizes ideas and develops them in an effective way generally speaking.
Language	Student uses a good range of vocabulary and grammar generally effectively. However, in many cases there are very basic errors that flaw the structure of the letter.

The art of effective communication

The internal assessment (individual oral plus interactive oral) is an integral part of the Language B course. This component assesses your receptive, productive and interactive skills in English and allows you to reflect on the anglophone cultures studied. This chapter tackles the individual oral and aims to familiarize you with how to explore the photograph chosen by the teacher effectively, link it to its option and title, organize your ideas, map the presentation and handle the discussion part.

"It's in case I need a laugh track."

Remember

The individual oral is based on a photograph with a caption linked to one of the OPTIONS studied:

- Cultural diversity
- Customs and traditions
- Health
- Science and technology
- Leisure

1. It is conducted in the second year of the programme.

2. It is recorded.

3. **SL students** choose ONE photograph from the TWO unseen ones shown by the teacher. Each photograph has a title or caption and is linked to a different option.

4. **HL students** are shown ONE photograph with a caption linked to one option.

5. Specific knowledge is NOT assessed, but what you have studied about certain options will be an asset to use.

6. You have 15 minutes to prepare your presentation.

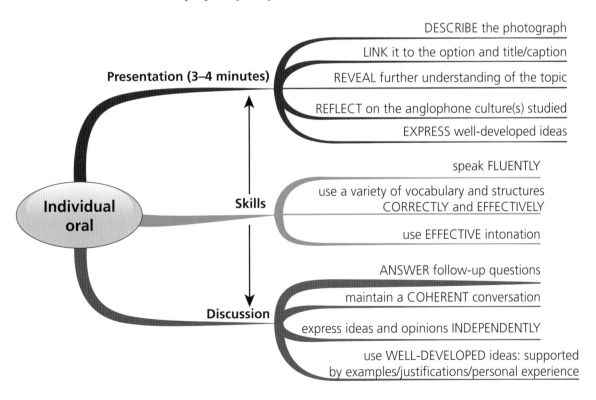

Presentation (3–4 minutes)
- DESCRIBE the photograph
- LINK it to the option and title/caption
- REVEAL further understanding of the topic
- REFLECT on the anglophone culture(s) studied
- EXPRESS well-developed ideas

Skills
- speak FLUENTLY
- use a variety of vocabulary and structures CORRECTLY and EFFECTIVELY
- use EFFECTIVE intonation

Discussion
- ANSWER follow-up questions
- maintain a COHERENT conversation
- express ideas and opinions INDEPENDENTLY
- use WELL-DEVELOPED ideas: supported by examples/justifications/personal experience

Individual oral

Reading the photograph

The photograph you receive at HL or SL will be accompanied with a caption or title that should quickly and directly guide you to the option or topic you should discuss. Both the graphic text of the photo and the caption should be used as the springboard for your presentation.

What do you do when you first receive the photo and caption?

1. Which option is indicated in the caption?
2. Describe what you see in a sentence or two and link it to the option.
3. Re-read the caption. Underline or circle key words.
4. What is the topic tackled?
5. Think of English-speaking cultures. What does the photograph tell you about them?
6. What is your stance or viewpoint on the issue suggested by the photograph?

> Note that both the photograph and the caption should enable you to narrow down your focus and plan your presentation.
>
> The six steps here should take no more than 3–4 minutes to complete during the 15-minute preparation time.

Example

Based on the photograph and caption below, follow the six steps suggested above.

Technology in the 21st century: a means of social communication or isolation?

1.	Which option is indicated in the caption?	Science and technology
2.	Describe what you see in a sentence or two and link it to the option.	I see a group of young people sitting in one room, each is busy with his/her mobile phone. Although they are together, they seem isolated; they are either chatting, sending messages or probably checking updates.
3.	Re-read the caption. Underline/circle key words.	technology social communication or isolation
4.	What is the topic tackled?	Effect of technology on social communication
5.	Think of English-speaking cultures. What does the photograph tell you about them?	Draw examples from what you have read or studied. Express opinions and provide examples.
6.	What is your stance/viewpoint?	– I agree that technology isolates people… – I believe technology facilitates social communication… – Technology isolates people BUT it also unites them socially…

Activity

Apply the same steps above to the following photograph and caption.

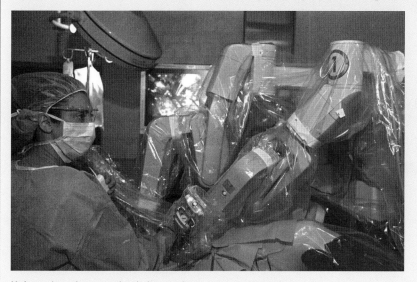

Using robots in surgeries is becoming an asset these days.

Tip: Captions might present two sides of the argument or only one. Even if you adopt the one-sided stance, it is always helpful to use the counter viewpoint in your presentation and refute it as this lends strength to your argument.

1.	Which option is indicated in the caption?	
2.	Describe what you see in a sentence or two and link it to the option.	
3.	Re-read the caption. Underline/circle key words.	
4.	What is the topic tackled?	
5.	Think of English-speaking cultures. What does the photograph tell you about them?	
6.	What is your stance/viewpoint?	

Is there more than one way to read a photograph?

Your reading of a photograph might differ from the teacher's or another student's. This is expected and accepted as long as you create coherent links to the OPTION and CAPTION and remain within the topic under discussion. Remember that this component assesses receptive, productive and interactive skills; therefore, your opinions and ideas are valid as long as they are relevant, well developed and justified. What determines your 'reading' is not only the photograph itself but also the caption or title provided.

Types of reading a photograph

- **Dominant/preferred reading:** When you agree with the caption given.
- **Oppositional reading:** When you oppose the caption provided.
- **Negotiated reading:** When you accept some parts of the caption but also have your own viewpoints.

How might your interpretation or reading of the photograph below differ based on each caption provided?

1. Cloning diminishes the sense of individuality and identity. (Agree with the caption)

2. We are still different. (Oppose the caption)

3. Identical copies with different personalities. (Agree with some parts of the caption but also have your own viewpoints)

> In your individual oral, you might agree with, oppose, or negotiate the photograph's reading. What is important is that you remain within the topic or option handled and justify ideas and opinions well.

Activity

Can you come up with three different readings for the photo below?

We all look alike in school uniform

Preferred reading	
Oppositional reading	
Negotiated reading	

Mapping the presentation

You need to plan/map your presentation just like you plan your writing and organize your ideas in a coherent manner. Use the information and tips given in Chapter 2 to construct an argument and present ideas clearly. Start with the 'thesis statement' (stance/viewpoint) you drafted in the six-step stage, then list the main ideas you have to support this statement and provide examples or justifications to support each one. Always keep English-speaking cultures in mind and remain within the boundaries of the option and topic discussed.

Always remember that a good presentation = a well-mapped presentation.

"What I'm going to tell you about my summer vacation may shock you...."

Remember to:

1. keep an eye on **photo, caption and option (P+C+O)**

2. address both sides of the argument and refute counter opinions if you adopt a one-sided approach.

Step 1

Thesis statement/viewpoint
Main idea 1
Example/evidence/justification
Main idea 2
Example/evidence/justification
Main idea 3
Example/evidence/justification

Step 2

First, draft your conclusion then go back to write a brief introduction. You may express your own opinion in either of those.

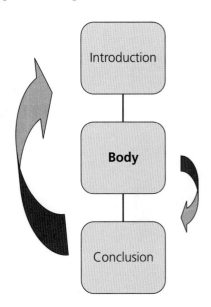

Based on the photograph and caption on page 171, two different arguments or approaches can be developed as follows:

Is a school uniform necessary?

A) Approach: Agree

State thesis: Uniform is necessary.

Supporting point 1: School uniform prevents students from wearing inappropriate clothes or forming cliques.

Supporting point 2: Some parents cannot afford to buy different types of fashionable clothes.

Supporting point 3: School uniform creates a sense of self identity and discipline in the school.

Finish: State conclusion or restate thesis.

B) Approach: Disagree

State thesis: Uniform is not necessary.

Supporting point 1: School uniform limits students' freedom and self-expression.

Supporting point 2: Students can still form cliques with or without a school uniform.

Supporting point 3: Wearing an undesirable uniform might reflect negatively on academic performance.

Finish: State conclusion or restate thesis.

Is your presentation problem-driven or thesis-driven?

A thesis-driven presentation starts with a main idea and proves it with supporting points and evidence.

A problem-driven text starts with a question. It proves the answer stage by stage and it ends with a conclusion.

See Chapter 2 (page 49) for more information on this approach.

- Use **discourse markers** (firstly, in addition, however, therefore, what's more, although, etc.) to glue ideas together.
- Do not restrict your presentation to facts only. Include opinions and supporting details.

Activity

1. Add explanations and examples to support each of the main ideas listed above in both approaches.

2. Refer to the table you completed from page 169 and apply Steps 1 and 2 to map a presentation about using robots in surgeries.

Getting ready

Reading the photograph and preparing/mapping your presentation should take place as effectively as possible during the 15-minute preparation time. You need to practise constantly to avoid nerves affecting your performance on the day of your exam.

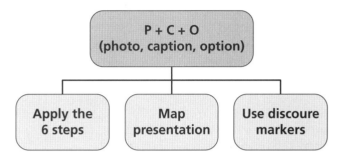

1. You are allowed to take brief working notes into the interview room for reference. These can be approximately 10 short points.

2. Do not attempt to memorise parts of your presentation. Be authentic and spontaneous.

3. Your presentation should reflect understanding of the topic and option under discussion as well as reflection on the anglophone cultures studied. You have been exploring this option/topic for two years, and now it is time to deploy all that you have learned effectively as this will strengthen your presentation. Still, ONLY receptive, productive and interactive skills are assessed, NOT what was covered in the classroom.

Activity

Based on the photograph and caption below, take 15 minutes to map a good presentation using all the steps outlined on pages 171 and 172.

Healthy food: a conscious decision or a life sentence?

Presentation time

Here you will be able to present all that you have prepared in the 15 minutes. You need to express ideas and opinions clearly and coherently while using correct, varied and expressive language.

Your presentation:

- should last 3–4 minutes
- has to be related to the option to which the photograph and caption refer
- needs to reveal understanding of the option and topic as well as the English-speaking culture handled
- should be spontaneous.

You:

- may take brief notes with you and use them as reference
- must reveal a good command of language while speaking
- do not have to fret if you forget something; you can start the sentence again from the beginning
- need to make sure you neither speak too fast nor too slow, but at a natural tempo.

> Remember the following points:
>
> - P+C+O – start your presentation with this.
> - Briefly describe the photograph and relate it to the caption and the option.
> - Introduction – state the thesis statement. You may include your opinion here.
> - Main ideas and examples/ justifications/evidence – use cohesive devices to link ideas and paragraphs together. Address both sides of an issue. Refute counter arguments. Focus on English-speaking cultures.
> - Conclusion – restate main idea. You may restate your opinion here and refer back to P+C+O.

Activity

Based on the photo and caption below:

- prepare a well-mapped presentation in 15 minutes
- present it in 3–4 minutes in class.

A desire for bonding or a fashion statement?

Language is assessed under Criterion A: Receptive skills. Here are some points to help you.

1. **Vary** the vocabulary and structures you use. Avoid repetition and redundancy.
2. Produce **accurate** and **effective** language.
   - **Accurate:** grammatically correct/well-expressed
   - **Effective:** conveys the desired meaning/purpose/result in context

- ▶ **Example 1:** 'I <u>have studied</u> English for twelve years.' (A grammatically accurate production of the present perfect. However, if, in context, you are still studying English, then '<u>have been studying</u>' is more effective to use.)

- ▶ **Example 2:** 'The theory was tested by a group of scientists.' (An accurate production of the passive voice. However, passive here would be ineffective if your focal discussion point is the 'scientists' not the 'theory'.)

3. Use words and structures **effectively**.

4. Use **idiomatic phrases and expressions**.

- ● **Idiomatic expressions:** phrases/structures that are natural to native speakers of English. For example:
  'Give someone the sack'
  'Drop someone a line'

5. Speak **fluently** (neither too fast nor too slow).

- ● **Fluently** means speaking smoothly and with ease. It does not mean you are expected to be a native speaker.

6. Vary your **intonation** patterns and pronounce words clearly.

- ● Intonation means the rise and fall of your voice while you are speaking, and how clearly single words are pronounced.

Discussion time

In this part your teacher will ask you follow-up questions that will allow you to express ideas and opinions freely and independently. You should reveal further understanding of the topic discussed and reflect on the English-speaking cultures studied. You may also need to refute counter opinions and defend your own opinion. This part lasts between **5 and 6 minutes**. You need to:

- ● listen to each question carefully

- ● provide relevant answers

- ● provide full responses – do not answer with only 'yes' or 'no' even if the question requires that

- ● be active and express well-developed ideas (response + explanation + example)

- ● avoid repeating ideas

- ● use a good command of language.

"Jimmy! Will you stop texting on your mobile phone. We are trying to discuss how technology has changed society!"

What if?

You do not understand a question?	Ask the teacher to repeat or re-phrase.
You stutter while speaking?	This is normal; we all do that. Just make sure you are mostly fluent.
The teacher asks a knowledge-based question that you cannot answer?	Be subtle. Answers like, 'Well, I do not smoke myself, but based on what I read, I assume that …' are suitable.
You make a grammatical mistake?	You can correct yourself.
You forget what you want to say?	Improvise, start the answer all over again or express your opinion.
The question requires examples or evidence that you do not know?	You may use your own personal experience to support the idea.
The teacher offers a strong counter opinion?	That is expected, so do not panic. Support your own viewpoint, argue the counter idea and refute it, using examples or explanations. Be respectful and sensitive.

> 'The aim of argument, or of discussion, should not be victory, but progress.'
> **Joseph Joubert**

Putting it together

Further exam practice – Paper 1

Standard level

Text A

Green-Fingered Mauritian Farmers Go Green

By Kritan and Beeharry's side are thousands of watermelon seedlings that he has grown in small pots without the use of chemical fertilisers. As the farmer prepares his half-
5 hectare piece of land in Soreze, near Mauritius' capital Port-Louis, to plant the two-week-old seedlings, he takes a minute to admire his achievement. "Look at these, they look solid and better grown — it's the compost," he says.

10 It has been about a month now since the government teamed up with a private compost-manufacturer to offer farmers here a 30-percent subsidy for compost made from domestic waste and an increasing number are
15 realising the benefits of going green.

"This has not been available for decades because animal husbandry has declined here — we had no choice but to use chemicals, and this has damaged our soil."

20 The Compost Subsidy Scheme offered by the government since Feb. 1 means that farmers now pay 50 dollars less per tonne for the compost they buy from Solid Waste Recycling Ltd, a private enterprise that
25 produces compost from domestic waste.

Roopesh Beekharry, manager at the Small Farmers Welfare Fund, which administers the subsidy, says 525 of the country's 12,000 farmers have utilised the discount since the
30 scheme's official launch earlier this month. "And the number is growing everyday," the fund manager told IPS.

The benefits of going organic are nothing new to Manoj Vaghjee, president of Resources
35 and Nature Foundation, a non-governmental organisation promoting sustainable agriculture on the island. For the last five years, he has been training farmers in biological agriculture and the use of organic compost.

40 He says that plants grow stronger, resist insects and pests, and farmers obtain a better yield when they use organic compost. "Our trainees have cultivated 30 to 40 percent more ladyfingers, maize, tapioca, calabash and
45 brinjals with compost than with chemicals per harvest," Vaghjee told IPS.

What's more, compost helps develop better roots and prevents soil erosion, according to agricultural engineer Eric Mangar from the
50 Movement for Self-Sufficiency, an NGO for agricultural development. "Chemical fertilisers affect the soil, reduce the plant's resistance to diseases and pests," he told IPS. "They pollute the rivers and lakes and underground
55 reservoirs and also affect the quality of the vegetables."

Back at Beeharry's melon farm, the green grower looks at his latest transition holistically. "When we care for the environment, we care
60 for natural resources that are made up of land, water and air. This not only helps us to get a better production, but it also gives us our daily food, now and in the future."

Nasseem Ackbarally, *IPS News,* **2013**

Text B

An interview with an Ed.D. student

Sarah Na Li is Assistant English Panel Head at a university-affiliated primary and secondary school in Hong Kong, China. She is currently studying online for a Doctor of Education
5 (Ed.D.) from the University of Liverpool.

[-X-]

The reputation of the university as one of the top researching universities in the UK and its support for online study attracted me.

You could have chosen to study for a PhD. Why
10 *does a professional doctorate suit you better?*

Studying for a professional doctorate fits with my professional and academic interests. As a constructivist learner, I enjoy putting what I learn into practice. I'm a lifelong learner,
15 motivated by the desire to make a difference in my workplace.

[-9-]

I have a better and more in-depth knowledge about learners and the organisational context in which learning takes place. I have a greater
20 understanding of the ideas and policies being put forth in my organisation and a greater ability to suggest evaluations and measures to maintain or improve the status quo. The content matter is highly relevant to my
25 current role in my workplace. I am already finding that people are starting to pay more attention to me and are taking my opinions more seriously.

[-10-]

I am thoroughly enjoying the collaborative
30 learning environment in the virtual classroom. Interactions with my fellow students are thought provoking and engaging. Our tutors are all professional facilitators who are doing an excellent job in guiding us through this
35 doctoral journey.

I enjoy the asynchronous learning environment as it allows me to work and study at the same time. However, it has been challenging to balance my study with
40 my fulltime job. What helps is the friendly and encouraging learning atmosphere in the classroom.

[-11-]

I stay connected. With my laptop, mobile and iPad all connected to the Internet, I can study
45 wherever and whenever I want. Usually I'll do my reading when I am commuting to and from work. I then either make mental notes or jot down notes on my iPad throughout the day. Strong family support is essential.

[-12-]

50 I hope to move up the administrative ladder in my organisation upon graduation. I expect that people will take my opinion more seriously – as mentioned, this is already starting to happen – and that the Ed.D. will be
55 a valuable qualification for future endeavours.

I would recommend the University of Liverpool...

... because of its research reputation and its thorough support for online students.

University of Liverpool, 2013

Text C
The problem with political correctness

Mom was wrong when she taught me that "sticks and stones may break my bones, but names will never hurt me". Names *do* hurt … names can shame, ridicule, and humiliate. Some pertain to race or gender; others refer to weight, facial features, or a particular part of one's anatomy. Names that refer to social class or what part of the country you're from
5 can be hurtful, as can names that involve age, religion, or physical ability. Even slang names for certain occupations can be hurtful. Certainly, no one likes to be called a name that is disrespectful, unkind, or downright mean. But there is another category of name-calling that is also hurtful and destructive: names such as "racist," "sexist," "homophobe" and the like. Yet many throw these labels around at the drop of a hat, without understanding what the labels
10 actually mean, not to mention the damage done by accusing someone of racism, sexism, etc. The accusation alone- even without merit – can be enough to besmirch a reputation, kill a career, and/or be used to invalidate a lifetime of good work.

Let's consider the definition of *racism*: "a belief that race is the primary determinant of human traits and capacities and that racial difference produce an inherent superiority of a
15 particular race". How about the definition of *sexism*: "prejudice or discrimination based on sex; especially: discrimination against women". I wonder, do the TV talking heads understand the true definition of the labels they hurl at public figures: "racist," "sexist" or worse, based on nothing more than a comment taken out of context, someone's clumsy attempt at humor, or a photo or image that's the artistic expression of a creative person?

20 My point is that the political correctness movement has gone way too far. While the original intent of political correctness may have been good (to encourage tact and sensitivity to others' feelings around issues of gender, race, religion, sexual orientation, physical abilities, and such), the *effect* of political correctness has been to make everyone avoid these topics altogether, thereby hindering our ability to get comfortable in living and working with those
25 who are different from us. It's gone so far that political correctness has become a bigger problem than the problem it was intended to [-X-]! These days everyone is so [-24-] of being called "sexist" or "racist" or some other career-killing label, that we all tiptoe carefully around [-25-] issues, and avoid them altogether if we [-26-] can.

But the question is: How are we ever going to be able to live and work together more
30 [-27-] if we can't talk about our feelings, fears, aspirations, anxieties, assumptions, hopes, worries, dreams, and concerns? How can we ever build [-28-] with those who are different from us? If we must constantly self-censor any conversation pertaining to race, gender, religion, sexual orientation, or physical ability, then we are doomed to perpetuate the very barriers we say we want to overcome.

BJ Gallagher, 2013

Text D

The story behind the legend of Sweeney Todd

In the unlikely event you're unfamiliar with the Sweeney Todd story, the plot can be summarised succinctly. Todd, a Fleet Street barber, surreptitiously murders his clients

5 and their corpses are profitably made into delicious meat pies by his obliging neighbor, Mrs Lovett. 'We'll serve anyone… to anyone' as the lyric artfully puts it.

Todd is, of course, a Victorian serial killer,

10 though his exploits predate that very modern label. He is, moreover, probably one of London's most enduring villains. In recent years, Sondheim's portrayal of Todd has done much to keep his name alive. An unlikely

15 Broadway hit in 1979, blending elements of comedy and horror, it introduced the character to the United States, garnered legions of fans and ultimately made a relatively obscure piece of London folklore world famous. Yet,

20 in the UK, we have always enjoyed the antics of this particular monster in film, television and theatre. But where does the tale of the butchering barber originate? It has long been assumed that Todd's fictional exploits were

25 based on a true story. Many people are still convinced that Todd's crimes were as real as those of Jack the Ripper. The facts, however, are somewhat different.

Todd's main legacy to modern culture was a

30 story called 'The String of Pearls' published in a weekly magazine during the winter of 1846/47, written by an anonymous author.

Set in 1785, it features as principal villain a certain Sweeney Todd and includes all the plot

35 elements that have been used by Sondheim and others ever since. There is the barber's shop, from which a remarkable number of customers never return, an ill-used apprentice boy and the enterprising Mrs Lovett,

40 whose pies are finally discovered to contain something rather more exotic than mince.

It seems much more likely that the story originated in urban myth. Even today, most of us have heard scare stories of various bits

45 of anatomy appearing in fast food. Imagine, then, how it must have been in mid-Victorian London, when food was frequently coloured and doctored to make it more saleable and few legal restrictions were in place. Indeed, in the

50 1840s and 1850s, many Londoners feared – with good reason – that their sausages and pies were being filled with cheap horsemeat; it didn't require much imagination to take that scam one stage further.

Lee Jackson, Timeout.com

SL Paper 1 question and answer booklet

Text A – Green-Fingered Mauritian Farmers Go Green

Answer the following questions.

1. What is special about the way Kretan and Beehary grow
    watermelons?

    ....

2. How long have the watermelon seedlings been in small pots?

    ....

3. Where is 'here' in 'to offer farmers here' (line 12)?

    ....

4. What is the compost produced by Solid Waste Recycling Ltd.
    made from?

    ....

5. Give two benefits for using organic compost as mentioned
    between lines 33 and 63.   *[2 marks]*

    a. ....

    b. ....

**Match the first part of the sentence with the appropriate
ending on the right. Write the appropriate letter in the boxes
provided.**

Example: More than 500 farmers   [D]   A. negatively affect the soil to which it is added.

6. Chemical fertilisers   [   ]   B. have yet to make use of the discount on compost.

7. Water reservoirs   [   ]   C. help farmers make more money.

8. Caring for the environment   [   ]   D. *made use of the discount on compost.*
    schemes

                                                 E. are polluted when organic compost is used.

                                                 F. help in producing food for years to come.

                                                 G. are polluted when chemical fertilisers are used.

                                                 H. hardly affect the soil to which it is added.

Text B – An interview with an Ed.D. student

Match the questions with the answers in the text. Write the appropriate letter in the boxes provided.

Example: [-X-] [H]

9. [-9-] [ ]

10. [-10-] [ ]

11. [-11-] [ ]

12. [-12-] [ ]

A. What is your experience of the Ed.D. programme so far?

B. How have you academically benefited from the programme?

C. How did you find this programme?

D. How do you fit online study into your life?

E. What are your expectations upon graduating?

F. How relevant is the Ed.D. programme to your current work?

G. How difficult is studying online?

H. *Why have you chosen the University of Liverpool?*

I. What do you think of virtual collaboration?

J. Will you be taken more seriously when you graduate?

Answer the following questions.

13. What does Sarah do for a living?

....

14. According to Sarah, why is an Ed.D. better than a PhD.?

....

15. Which word between lines 20 and 25 is closest in meaning to 'uphold'?

....

16. As mentioned between lines 36 and 42, what has Sarah found difficult about online learning?

....

17. Which word between lines 50 and 58 is closest in meaning to 'full'?

....

Text C – The problem with political correctness

18. From statements A to J, select the four that are true according to text C. Write the appropriate letters in the boxes provided   **[4 marks]**

Example:

| B |

A. TV presenters are careful when they accuse someone of racism.

B. *All types of name calling can be cruel.*

C. Accusations cause damage even if they are not true.

D. Political correctness facilitates our dealing with others nowadays.

E. TV presenters indiscriminately throw accusations at people.

F. Political correctness was originally used to protect people's feelings.

G. Invalid accusations do not hurt.

H. Political correctness makes it difficult for us to deal with others nowadays.

I. Political correctness is used with tactless people.

J. Some types of name calling can be harmless.

[questions continued on next page]

Find the word in the right-hand column that could meaningfully replace one of the words on the left.

Example: shame (line 2) `D`   **A.** honour

19. ridicule (line 2) ☐   **B.** affect

20. pertain (line 3) ☐   **C.** exclude

21. involve (line 5) ☐   **D.** *embarrass*

22. besmirch (line 11) ☐   **E.** discredit

23. invalidate (line 12) ☐   **F.** include

G. mock

H. sully

I. concern

J. praise

Which words go in the gaps between lines 26 and 31? Choose the words from the list and write them in the spaces below.

address   afraid   casual   certainly   clearly   comfortably
correctness   diversity   ignore   independence   possibly   trust

Example [-X-] .... *address*...

24. ....

25. ....

26. ....

27. ....

28. ....

Text D – The story behind the legend of Sweeney Todd

The sentences below are either true or false. Tick [✓] the correct response then justify it with a relevant brief quotation from the text. Both a tick [✓] and a quotation are required for one mark.

	True	False
Example: The author believes everyone is familiar with the legend of Sweeney Todd.	✓	

Justification: 'In the unlikely event you're unfamiliar with the Sweeney Todd story'.

	True	False
29. The plot of the story of Sweeney Todd cannot be summarized.		

Justification: ....

29. The plot of the story of Sweeney Todd cannot be summarized.

Justification: ....

30. Sweeney Todd was a serial killer before the term was invented.

Justification: ....

31. The British people mostly like the theatrical adaptation of the story of Sweeney Todd.

Justification: ....

32. The story of Sweeney Todd is based on the true story of a killer.

Justification: ....

33. People believe that Todd's crimes were as true as Jack the Ripper's.

Justification: ....

Complete the following table by indicating to whom or to what the word(s) underlined refer(s).

In the phrase ...	the word(s) ...	refer(s) to ...
Example: ... and their corpses are... (line 5)	'it'	...........Todd's clients...........
34. ... to keep his name alive... *(line 14)*	'his'	....
35. ... it features as principal villain ... *(line 33)*	'it'	....
36. ... from which a remarkable number ... *(line 37)*	'which'	....
37. ... to take that scam ... *(lines 53–54)*	'that scam'	....

Choose the correct answer from A, B, C, or D. Write the letter in the box provided.

38. 'surreptitiously' (line 4) is closest in meaning to:
   A. clearly.
   B. secretly.
   C. openly.
   D. violently.

39. The corpses of the victims are:
   A. made into meat pies.
   B. buried in Todd's barbershop.
   C. disposed of by the apprentice.
   D. never discovered.

40. Todd is seen as:
   A. one of London's unknown villains.
   B. one of London's infamous villains.
   C. an insufferable villain.
   D. an atrocious villain worldwide.

41. In the 19th century, British people:
   A. found horsemeat in their food.
   B. put restrictions in place to control the quality of food.
   C. worried about the quality of meat put in their food.
   D. doctored food to make it less appealing.

Further exam practice – Paper 1

Higher level

Text A

Eco-friendly transportation

This is the story of a modern man and his car-sharing membership. George Dizvolitsis lives in a condo with his wife. Both work downtown, take public transit, and walk during the summer. But their epic journeys to visit family in the suburbs or trek to get groceries were wearing them down. They tried to be as completely car-free as possible and yet they still
5   couldn't pull it off. They struggled with a solution and then discovered a car-share program in the parking lot of their building and signed up.

Saving money with car-sharing

Before we met George, we expected a sandal-wearing, granola-eating renegade. Instead, he was the perfect picture of an everyday dude, gym bag over one shoulder and a baseball cap on his head.
10   The green benefits were nice, he explained, but the real motivation was dollars and sense. They saved $300 to $400 a month on fuel, parking and insurance. Plus, the share-cars were always available and easy to take out. We had an epiphany on the parking spot: Had the green movement got the guilt pitch wrong all these decades? Give people cost-effective and convenient alternatives to driving a car and they will take them.

Eco-friendly transportation alternatives

15   In George's case, the decision to car-share came down **[-X-]**. But surely there are other reasons to ditch and drive? Driving is one of the single biggest polluting acts a person can make. Yet, three quarters of us **[-6-]** even when we could easily use another form of transportation. We get it, the True North, Strong and Free, with its inclement weather and massive size, feels like it was built for a car. But maybe we can start by cutting back on our
20   car usage?

7 tips for eco-friendly transportation

1. **[-7-]**, catching on in Ottawa and other cities, where children walk together in groups with parental supervision.

2. Check out car-sharing companies available in your town or city.

3. Bike-sharing options are popular at several universities across Canada, while the Bixi
25   bike-sharing program is rolling in Toronto, Montreal and Vancouver.

4. **[-8-]**, invest in an e-bike or scooter for quick, inter-city trips.

5. Challenge yourself by leaving the car at home for a week. By week's end, you'll appreciate your wheels and pinpoint places where you can use **[-9-]**.

6. Rural Canadians can scout out local bus and charter companies to get across back-country
30   roads.

7. **[-10-]**, plan ahead and carpool with neighbours or nearby families.

Excerpted from the book *Living Me to We: The Guide for Socially Conscious Canadians*, **2012, by Craig Kielburger and Marc Kielburger**

Text B

Educated women hold the key to ending poverty

In Koraro in Ethiopia, a dozen or so young women gathered at the primary school to describe their progress as the first girls from their village at the secondary school
5 in the next valley. With beaming eyes, soft voices and determination, each described how she would soon return to the village as a teacher, or plumber, or electrician, helping to create new jobs and bring
10 new prosperity.

An hour earlier, their fathers had nearly burst with pride as they described the reality of these young women's education. If it takes a village to raise a child, it is
15 also true that one child can inspire a whole village.

Koraro is a Millennium Village that powerfully demonstrates how an impoverished rural community, through
20 its own efforts and just a little help from the outside, can lift itself out of grinding poverty. The community's future now rests with the coming generation of skilled young women who will teach in the new
25 schools, create new jobs and improve the local harvests.

Sustainable development is a cumulative process. The first young women graduating from school are already inspiring the
30 12-year-old girls who will soon follow in their footsteps. They will marry later, have fewer and healthier children, and send their own children to school.

Koraro is powerful evidence of how
35 women can hold the key to development in some of the world's poorest countries – in education, enterprise, micro-finance and healthcare. Investing in women pays dividends throughout the entire
40 community. So how can we put women at the heart of our vision for international development?

First, the UK needs to meet our moral commitment to increase spending on aid to
45 0.7 per cent gross national income. But this investment has to go hand-in-hand with greater transparency, ensuring the money reaches the people who need it most.

Second, with women making up a
50 significant majority of the world's poorest people, we need targeted action to support women the world over. Take maternal mortality, for example: 350,000 women die during childbirth every year, a figure that
55 has barely fallen in the past two decades in many regions.

Third, because a joined-up international approach is essential, we need to ensure that action on women and development
60 is on the agenda at key global meetings. The British government will work closely with countries such as Canada and the US, which have already said that tackling maternal and child mortality should be an
65 urgent global priority as part of achieving the Millennium Development Goals.

The Big Society is about bringing together the global community as much as it is about building stronger local
70 communities. We will not stand by while eradicable disease and poverty continues to blight our world – and will make sure the money and the policies are in place to make a lasting difference.

The Independent, 2010

Text C

Rebel Without a Cause

"You're tearing me apart! You say one thing, he says another, and everybody changes back again."

James Dean shouts these words in an anguished howl that seems to owe more to acting class than to his character, the rebellious and causeless Jim Stark in *Rebel without a Cause*. Because he died in a car crash a month before the movie opened in 1955, the performance took on an eerie kind of fame: it was the posthumous complaint of an actor widely expected to have a long and famous career.

The film has not aged well, and Dean's performance seems more like marked-down Brando than the birth of an important talent. But *Rebel without a Cause* was enormously influential at the time, a milestone in the creation of a new idea about young people. Marlon Brando as a surly motorcycle gang leader in *The Wild One* (1953), James Dean in 1955, and the emergence of Elvis Presley in 1956: these three role models decisively altered the way young men could be seen in popular culture.

"What can you do when you have to be a man?" Jim Stark asks his father, the emasculated Frank Stark (Jim Backus). But his father doesn't know, and in one grotesque scene, wears a frilly apron over his business suit while cleaning up spilled food. Jim comes from a household ruled by his overbearing mother (Ann Doran) and her mother (Virginia Brissac). Early in the film, he regards his father and tells a juvenile officer: "If he had guts to knock Mom cold once, then maybe she'd be happy, and she'd stop picking on him."

The movie is based on a 1944 book of the same name by Robert Lindner, and reflected concern about "juvenile delinquency", a term then much in use; its more immediate inspiration may have been the now-forgotten 1943 book *A Generation of Vipers*, by Philip Wylie, which coined the term "Momism" and blamed an ascendant female dominance for much of what was wrong with modern America. "She eats him alive, and he takes it," Jim Stark tells the cop about his father.

Like Hamlet's disgust at his mother's betrayal of his father, Jim's feelings mask a deeper malaise, a feeling that life is a pointless choice between being and not being. In France at the time, that was called existentialism, but in Jim's Los Angeles, rebels were not so articulate.

In addition, the dialogue often seems to be making plot points that the director, Nicholas Ray, and the writer, Irving Shulman, may not have fully intended. Or perhaps they did, and guessed that some of the film's implications would not be fully recognized by 1955 audiences. Seen today, *Rebel without a Cause* plays like a Todd Solondz movie, in which characters with bizarre problems perform a charade of normal behavior.

Because of the way weirdness seems to bubble just beneath the surface of the melodramatic plot, because of the oddness of Dean's mannered acting and Mineo's narcissistic self-pity, because of the cluelessness of the hero's father, because of all of these apparent flaws, *Rebel without a Cause* has a greater interest than if it had been tidier and more sensible. You can sense an energy trying to break through emotions unexamined but urgent.

Like its hero, *Rebel without a Cause* desperately wants to say something and doesn't know what it is. If it did know, it would lose its fascination. More perhaps than it realized, it is a subversive document of its time.

Roger Ebert, 2005

Text D
The Oval Portrait

THE CHATEAU into which my valet had ventured to make forcible entrance, rather than permit me, in my desperately wounded condition, to pass a night in the open air, was one of those piles of commingled gloom and grandeur which have so long frowned among the Appennines, not less in fact than in the fancy of Mrs. Radcliffe. To all appearance
5   it had been temporarily and very lately abandoned. We established ourselves in one of the smallest and least sumptuously furnished apartments. It lay in a remote turret of the building. Its decorations were rich, yet tattered and antique. Its walls were hung with tapestry and bedecked with manifold and multiform armorial trophies, together with an unusually great number of very spirited modern paintings in frames of rich golden
10   arabesque. In these paintings, which depended from the walls not only in their main surfaces, but in very many nooks which the bizarre architecture of the chateau rendered necessary – in these paintings my incipient delirium, perhaps, had caused me to take deep interest; so that I bade Pedro to close the heavy shutters of the room – since it was already night – to light the tongues of a tall candelabrum which stood by the head of my bed – and
15   to throw open far and wide the fringed curtains of black velvet which enveloped the bed itself. I wished all this done that I might resign myself, if not to sleep, at least alternately to the contemplation of these pictures, and the perusal of a small volume which had been found upon the pillow, and which purported to criticise and describe them.

Long – long I read – and devoutly, devotedly I gazed. Rapidly and gloriously the hours
20   flew by and the deep midnight came. The position of the candelabrum displeased me, and outreaching my hand with difficulty, rather than disturb my slumbering valet, I placed it so as to throw its rays more fully upon the book.

But the action produced an effect altogether unanticipated. The rays of the numerous candles (for there were many) now fell within a niche of the room which had hitherto
25   been thrown into deep shade by one of the bed-posts. I thus saw in vivid light a picture all unnoticed before. It was the portrait of a young girl just ripening into womanhood. I glanced at the painting hurriedly, and then closed my eyes. Why I did this was not at first apparent even to my own perception. But while my lids remained thus shut, I ran over in my mind my reason for so shutting them. It was an impulsive movement to gain
30   time for thought- to make sure that my vision had not deceived me – to calm and subdue my fancy for a more sober and more certain gaze. In a very few moments I again looked fixedly at the painting.

That I now saw aright I could not and would not doubt; for the first flashing of the candles upon that canvas had seemed to dissipate the dreamy stupor which was stealing
35   over my senses, and to startle me at once into waking life.

The portrait, I have already said, was that of a young girl. It was a mere head and shoulders, done in what is technically termed a vignette manner; much in the style of the favorite heads of Sully. The arms, the bosom, and even the ends of the radiant hair melted imperceptibly into the vague yet deep shadow which formed the back-ground of
40   the whole. The frame was oval, richly gilded and filigreed in Moresque. As a thing of art nothing could be more admirable than the painting itself. But it could have been neither the execution of the work, nor the immortal beauty of the countenance, which had so suddenly and so vehemently moved me. Least of all, could it have been that my fancy, shaken from its half slumber, had mistaken the head for that of a living person.

Edgar Alan Poe, *The Oval Portrait,* **1850**

Text E

South Africa: Social Media 'Breaking Barriers' in South Africa

Social networking in South Africa has crossed the age barrier, the urban-rural divide, and even the relationship gap, according to new research findings from technology
5 market researchers World Wide Worx and information analysts Fuseware.

The South African Social Media Landscape 2012 study, released recently by World Wide Worx and Fuseware, shows that the fastest
10 growing age group among Facebook users in South Africa is the over-60s.

[-X-]

From August 2011 to August 2012, the number of over-60s on Facebook in South Africa grew by 44%, compared to less than
15 30% for those aged 30–60, less than 20% for those aged 19–30, and less than 10% for teenagers, the study found.

"This is a reflection of Facebook going mainstream in South Africa," World Wide
20 Worx managing director Arthur Goldstuck said in a statement. "The younger segments are still far from saturation, but we're not seeing the same heady pace of growth among the youth as before."

[-52-]

25 Both Facebook and Twitter have traversed the South African urban-rural divide, according to the study. The proportion of urban adults using Facebook is a little less than double rural users – but rural users are now at the level
30 where urban users were 18 months ago.

Twitter's urban penetration is a little more than double its rural penetration, but the rural proportion has also caught up to where the urban proportion was 18 months ago.

[-53-]

35 At the end of August, 5.33-million South Africans were using Facebook on the Web; 2.43-million were on Twitter and 9.35-million on Mxit. However, because Facebook does not measure mobile-only usage among those
40 who have registered via their cellphones, the full extent of its penetration is significantly understated: primary research by World Wide Worx shows that 6.8-million South Africans access Facebook on their phones.

45 South African Twitter use measured in the study indicates that its user base had grown to 2.2 million by the end of June, or 100,000 new users a month since August last year.

Fuseware data, collected directly from Twitter
50 through an API (application programme interface), shows that the number reached 2.4 million at the end of August, exactly matching the growth rate measured by World Wide Worx, and validating the earlier data.

[-54-]

55 Another of the study's findings is that the number of single users of social networks in South Africa has grown faster than any other relationship group, by almost 25%, to reach 957:000. The number of married and
60 engaged users has each grown by 16%, while the category of those "in a relationship" has increased by 9%.

"Clearly, Facebook is filling a relationship gap in the lives of many South Africans,"
65 said Goldstuck. "But social networks are also so much more; we see them playing the roles of communication, information and entertainment networks."

Allafrica.com, 2012

HL Paper 1 question and answer booklet

Text A – Eco-friendly transportation

Answer the following questions.

1. Why were Mr and Mrs Dizvolitsis tired of visiting family or going to the grocery store?

   ....

2. Which phrase between lines 1 and 6 shows that Mr and Mrs Dizvolitsis were forced to use a car at times?

   ....

3. How did the authors assume George would be?

   ....

4. What was George's main reason for joining the car-share programme?

   ....

5. Which word between lines 7 and 14 is closest in meaning to 'sudden realization'?

   ....

Some phrases have been removed from the text between lines 15 and 31. Which phrases go in the gaps? Write the appropriate letter in the boxes provided.

Example	E	**A.** try the walking school bus revolution
6. [-6-]	☐	**B.** to being green
7. [-7-]	☐	**C.** although you are late
8. [-8-]	☐	**D.** alternate forms of transportation
9. [-9-]	☐	**E.** *to money and convenience*
10. [-10-]	☐	**F.** avoid the walking school bus revolution
		G. for the fast and fashionable
		H. similar forms of transportation
		I. guiltily admit to getting behind the wheel
		J. if everything works
		K. happily admit to avoiding driving
		L. when all else fails

Text B – Educated women hold the key to ending poverty

11. **From statements A to L, select the five that are true according to text B. Write the appropriate letters in the boxes provided.** [5 marks]

Example:

A. *The Ethiopian girls were the first in their village to attend secondary school.*

B. The girls' fathers were delighted by their daughters' achievement.

C. Women should be relieved from their role in improving their villages.

D. Koraro's economic situation is improving.

E. Sustainable development rests in the hands of women.

F. The UK should solely increase its aid to disadvantaged countries.

G. The girls' fathers insisted they all played a role in their daughters' success.

H. In many regions, the percentage of maternal mortality has dropped drastically.

I. The UK should take serious steps to improve the livelihood of women in disadvantaged countries.

J. The Ethiopian girls were plumbers, teachers and electricians in their village.

K. Poverty in Koraro is an unsolvable problem.

L. In many regions, the percentage of maternal mortality has dropped slightly.

Answer the following questions.

12. As mentioned between lines 1 and 26, how can poor communities improve their economic situation?

....

13. Which sentence between lines 27 and 42 shows that the education of women positively affects the whole community?

....

14. With what should increasing British aid to poorer communities be accompanied?

....

193

Choose the correct answer from A, B, C, or D. Write the letter in the box provided.

15. The writer believes that providing aid to poorer communities is

    A. a collective responsibility.

    B. necessary for the UK.

    C. required to educate women.

    D. a UK priority.

16. The writer believes that building stronger local communities is

    A. more important than uniting the global community.

    B. required but voluntary.

    C. as important as uniting the global community.

    D. hardly going to make a difference.

Text C—Rebel Without a Cause

The sentences below are either true or false. Tick [✓] the correct response then justify it with a relevant brief quotation from the text. Both a tick [✓] and a quotation are required for one mark.

Example: James Dean tragically died before the debut of *Rebel Without a Cause*.

Justification: 'died in a car crash a month before the movie opened'.

	True	False
	✓	

17. Dean's performance in *Rebel without a Cause* marked the birth of a great actor.

	True	False

   Justification: ....

18. Presley, Dean and Brando hardly affected the perception of young men in pop culture.

   Justification: ....

19. Robert Lindner's book is titled *Rebel without a Cause*.

   Justification: ....

20. *A Generation of Vipers* attributed the problems in modern America to female emancipation.

   Justification: ....

21. Jim's abhorrence of his mother is more profound than that of Hamlet.

   Justification: ....

22. Jim represents existentialist ideas.

   Justification: ....

Based on the information that appears between lines 59 and 86 in the text, which words go in the gaps in the text below? Choose the words from the list below and write them in the spaces provided.

The **[-X-]** and director of *Rebel without a Cause* **[-23-]** that the film may not be understood by the 1950s' audience. The characters in the film are best described as **[-24-]** human beings with strange problems. The film is best described as **[-25-]** and full of **[-26-]** flaws; however, the film's inability to communicate the message lurking behind it adds to its **[-27-]**.

anticipated	appeal	irrational	knew	non-existent	obscurity
ostensible	producer	sensible	typical	unusual	*writer*

Example: [-X-] .... *writer*..

23. ....

24. ....

25. ....

26. ....

27. ....

Text D – The Oval Portrait

Find the word in the right-hand column that could meaningfully replace one of the words on the left.

Example: ventured (line 1) | D | **A.** separated

28. commingled (line 3) | | **B.** uninhabited

29. abandoned (line 5) | | **C.** decorated

30. remote (line 6) | | **D.** *dared*

31. tattered (line 7) | | **E.** nearby

32. bedecked (line 8) | | **F.** messy

G. restricted

H. uninhibited

I. mixed

J. worn

K. stripped

L. secluded

Choose the correct answer from A, B, C, or D. Write the letter in the box provided.

33. The narrator was interested in the paintings because he was
    A. sleepy.
    B. feverish.
    C. riveted.
    D. bored.

34. Once settled in the room, the narrator
    A. lights the candles next to the bed.
    B. sleeps in the black curtained bed.
    C. examines the chateau's grounds and surroundings.
    D. examines a book that describes the paintings on the walls.

35. Around midnight, the narrator
    E. changes the position of the candelabrum.
    F. wakes Pedro to adjust the candelabrum.
    G. changes his position so that more light falls on the book.
    H. busies himself with studying the paintings intently.

36. The painting of the young woman was not initially noticed by the narrator because it was
    A. placed at the far end of the room.
    B. hidden behind the bed.
    C. placed where candlelight could not reach it.
    D. not deemed important by the narrator.

37. The painting of the young woman was
    A. a portrait.
    B. a full-length one.
    C. frameless.
    D. insipid.

38. The narrator was shaken because he
    A. thought the woman in the painting was a living person.
    B. saw an extremely beautiful woman in the painting.
    C. saw the most beautiful piece of art.
    D. recognised the work of a renowned artist.

Complete the following table by indicating to whom or to what the word(s) underlined refer(s).

In the phrase ...	the word(s) ...	refer(s) to ...
Example: ... To all appearance it had... (line 4)	'it'	..........the chateau..........
39. ... I placed it... *(line 21)*	'it'	....
40. ... But the action produced ... *(line 23)*	'the action'	....
41. ... did this was not ... *(line 27)*	'this'	....
42. ... for so shutting them ... *(line 29)*	'them'	....
43. ... fixedly at the painting ... *(line 32)*	'the painting'	....
44. ... shaken from its ... *(line 44)*	'its'	....

Text E – South Africa: Social Media 'Breaking Barriers' in South Africa

Answer the following questions.

45. Give two findings of the research done on social networking in South Africa. *[2 marks]*

    a. ....

    b. ....

46. What do the results of the study on Facebook signify?

    ....

47. Which word between lines 18 and 24 is closest in meaning to 'capacity'?

    ....

48. Which word between lines 25 and 30 is closest in meaning to 'gap'?

    ....

49. Why are the results regarding the full extent of Facebook infiltration of South African society considered unreliable?

    ....

50. What do the research results regarding single users of social networks show?

    ....

51. Give two relationship categories that the study included. *[2 marks]*

    a. ....

    b. ....

Match the headings with the paragraphs in the text. Write the appropriate letter in the boxes provided.

Example: [-X-]	`C`	A. Crossing the urban-rural divide
52. [-52-]	☐	B. Fuseware versus World Wide Worx data
53. [-53-]	☐	C. *'Reflection of Facebook going mainstream'*
54. [-54-]	☐	D. Social status on social networks
		E. Bridging the urban-rural divide
		F. Facebook, Twitter numbers
		G. Single users on the increase
		H. Facebook in the lead

Further exam practice – Paper 2

Standard level

Complete one of the following tasks. Write 250 to 400 words.

1. **Cultural Diversity**

   You are a new student who has just moved to an international school in an English-speaking country to take the IB Diploma. Write a diary entry describing your first days at your new school.

2. **Customs and traditions**

   Fashions are constantly changing. Write a blog entry to describe one of the latest trends in clothes, music or social media.

3. **Health**

   You are taking part in a class debate on the motion 'Sport is essential to health and happiness'. Write the text of the debate's opening speech in which you support this motion.

4. **Leisure**

   Recently you went to a music concert or a theatre production, or watched a sporting event at your school. Write a review of the event to be published in your school magazine.

5. **Science and technology**

   Your school has launched a campaign to encourage the community to cut down on carbon emissions. Write a letter to parents suggesting ways in which they could find alternatives to using cars and other motor vehicles.

Further exam practice – Paper 2

Higher level

SECTION A

Complete one of the following tasks. Write 250 to 400 words.

1. **Cultural Diversity**

   You are a student who moved to an international school in an English-speaking country to take the IB Diploma. Write an article to be published in your school magazine on the differences between your experience of education in your previous school and your present one.

2. **Customs and traditions**

   Last holiday you were invited by a local family in an English-speaking country to participate in the celebration of a major festival, ceremony or sporting event. You decide to post your experiences in a blog. Write the blog entry.

3. **Health**

   Stress is a real problem for IB Diploma students. You have been asked to write a set of guidelines for students about to take their IB exams. You may wish to write about the causes and possible solutions.

4. **Leisure**

   A well-known sports star is visiting your school, and you have been asked to interview him or her about their career and their future. Write the text of this interview to be published in your school magazine.

5. Science and technology

Have new technologies had a negative effect on the way in which friends communicate with each other? Write a speech to your school council **either** defending **or** opposing this idea.

SECTION B

Based on the following stimulus, give a personal response and justify it. Choose any text type that you have studied in class. Write 150 to 250 words.

"Give a man a fish; you have fed him for today. Teach a man to fish; and you have fed him for a lifetime."

Traditional proverb

Markschemes
Standard level Paper 1

Text A – Green-Fingered Mauritian Farmers Go Green

1. grown (in small pots) without the use of chemical fertilisers
2. two weeks
3. Soreze / near Mauritius' capital Port-Louis
4. domestic waste
5. Any two from: plants grow stronger / plants resist insects and pests / farmers obtain a better yield.
6. A
7. G
8. F   **[9 marks]**

Text B – An interview with an Ed.D. student

9. F
10. A
11. D
12. E
13. Assistant English Panel Head (at a university-affiliated primary and secondary school in Hong Kong, China)
14. It fits with my professional and academic interests / She enjoys putting what she learns into practice / She's a lifelong learner, motivated by the desire to make a difference in her workplace.
15. maintain
16. balancing her study with her full-time job
17. thorough   **[9 marks]**

Text C – The problem with political correctness

18. C, E, F, H (in any order)
19. G
20. I
21. F
22. H
23. E
24. afraid
25. diversity
26. possibly
27. comfortably
28. trust   **[14 marks]**

Text D – The story behind the legend of Sweeney Todd

29. False— the plot can be summarized succinctly
30. True— his exploits predate that very modern label
31. False— in the UK, we have always enjoyed the antics of this particular monster in film, television and theatre
32. False— It has long been assumed that Todd's fictional exploits were based on a true story
33. True— Todd's crimes were as real as those of Jack the Ripper
34. Sweeney Todd
35. 'The String of Pearls'
36. the barber's shop
37. filling sausages and pies with horsemeat
38. B
39. A
40. B
41. C   **[13 marks]**

Higher level Paper 1

Text A – Eco-friendly transportation

1. They were trying to avoid using their car as much as possible / 'They tried to be as completely car-free as possible'
2. (yet they still) couldn't pull it off
3. a sandal-wearing, granola-eating renegade
4. money and sense / saved $300 to $400 a month on fuel, parking and insurance AND the share-cars were always available and easy to take out
5. epiphany
6. I
7. A
8. G
9. D
10. L   **[10 marks]**

Text B – Educated women hold the key to ending poverty

11. B, D, E, I, L (in any order)
12. by educating (women) / internal efforts and just a little help from the outside
13. Investing in women pays dividends throughout the entire community
14. (greater) transparency
15. A
16. C   **[10 marks]**

Text C – Rebel Without a Cause

17. False—Dean's performance seems more like marked-down Brando than the birth of an important talent
18. False—these three role models decisively altered the way young men could be seen in popular culture
19. True—The movie is based on a 1944 book of the same name by Robert Lindner
20. False—blamed an ascendant female dominance for much of what was wrong with modern America
21. True—Like Hamlet's disgust at his mother's betrayal of his father, Jim's feelings mask a deeper malaise
22. True—was called existentialism, but in Jim's Los Angeles, rebels were not so articulate
23. anticipated
24. typical
25. irrational
26. ostensible
27. appeal   **[11 marks]**

Text D – The Oval Portrait

28. I
29. B
30. L
31. J
32. C
33. B
34. D
35. A
36. C
37. A
38. A
39. the candelabrum
40. changing the position of the candelabrum
41. closing his eyes
42. (the narrator's) eyes
43. the portrait of a young girl just ripening into womanhood
44. the narrator's fancy   **[17 marks]**

Text E – South Africa: Social Media 'Breaking Barriers' in South Africa

45. Any two from: crossed the age barrier / crossed the urban-rural divide / crossed the relationship gap
46. Facebook going mainstream in South Africa
47. saturation
48. divide
49. mobile-only usage among those who have registered via their cellphones was not measured
50. grew faster than any other relationship group
51. Any two from: single / married / engaged / in a relationship
52. A
53. F
54. G